The Art of Home Canning

The Art of Home Canning

Economy in the kitchen/ Canning fruits and vegetables

By
Angelo Sorzio

Adapted by
Helen Feingold

Leon Amiel · Publisher
New York   Paris

Color Plates

Vegetables, 16A
Vegetables, 16B
Fruit, 16C
Fruit, 16D
Caramelized apple marmalade
    Apricot chutney, 32A
Apricots in sugar syrup
    Apricots in alcohol
    Apricot marmalade
    Apricots in Marsala syrup, 32B
Cherries in red wine
    Cherry marmalade
    Cherries in liquor, 32C
Wild cherry jelly
    Candied wild cherries in rum
    Wild cherry jam, 32D

Lemon curd
    Lemon flip, 48A
Melon in syrup
    Melon jam, 48B
Mint sauce
    Mint marmalade, 48C
Orange syrup
    Orange wedges in alcohol
    Orange jelly
    Orange marmalade, 48D

Pineapple in syrup
    Pineapple jam, 64A
Rhubarb jam
    Rhubarb in syrup, 64B
Rose jam, 64C

Strawberry jam, 64D
Red tomato marmalade in liquor
    Green tomato marmalade, 80A
Coffee marmalade
    Milk marmalade, 80B
Green beans with tomatoes
    Plain canned green beans, 80C
Canned beans
    Beans all'uccelletto, 80D
Capers in salt
    Basil in salt, 96A
Corn-on-the-cob in brine, 96B
Artichokes in oil
    Eggplant in oil, 96C
Dried mint, 96D

Plain canned peas
    Plain canned celery
    Plain canned asparagus, 112A
Piquant onions
    Onions, Venetian style
    Bittersweet onions, 112B
Bell peppers, Apulia style
    Peppers in oil, 112C
Pepper relish, 112D

Peeled whole tomatoes
    Tomato sauce, 128A
Pickled cucumbers
    Beets in vinegar
    Pickled bell peppers
    Pickled cauliflower, 128B
Italian antipasto, 128C
Devil's sauce
    Catsup, 128D

Copyright 1976
by Leon Amiel · Publisher
All Rights Reserved
Library of Congress Catalog Card No. 76-263
ISBN 0-8148-0653-8
Manufactured in the United States of America

Contents

Food preserving:
 Some general rules, 7

Fruits

Apple marmalade, 18
Apple compote, 18
Candied apples, 19
Dried apples, 20
Apple chutney, 20
Applesauce, 21
Caramelized apple marmalade, 21
Apple marmalade
 with chocolate, 22
Apricot marmalade, 22
Apricots in marsala syrup, 23
Apricots preserved in alcohol, 23
Apricots in sugar syrup, 24
Apricot nectar, 24
Banana marmalade, 25
Banana liqueur, 25
Bilberries (or whortleberries) in
 syrup, 26
Bilberry and currant syrup, 26
Bilberries in maraschino, 27
Bilberry jam, 27
Blackberries in syrup, 28
Wild blackberry jam, 28
Blackberry jelly, 29
Wild blackberry syrup, 29
Cherry marmalade, 30
Cornelian cherry marmalade, 30
Cherry jam with honey, 31
Sugared (or crystallized)
 cherries, 31
Dried cherries, 32
Cherries in vinegar, 32
Bittersweet cherries
 "dolce garbo," 33
Cherries in red wine, 33
Cherry nectar, 34
Cherries in syrup, 34
Cherries in liquor, 35
Wild cherries in rum, 35
Wild cherry jam, 36
Wild cherry jelly, 36
Candied wild cherries in rum, 37
Wild cherry syrup, 37
Chestnut or marron glaces, 38

Chestnut preserves in brandy, 39
Chestnut marmalade with rum, 39
Chestnut balls in rum, 40
Chestnuts in syrup, 40
Plain currant jelly, 41
Rose compote of currants, 41
Bittersweet currant sauce, 42
Currants in grappa, 42
Elderberry jam, 43
Elderberry syrup, 43
Fig compote, 44
Convent figs, 44
Dried figs in liquor, 45
Fig and brandy preserves, 45
Grape jam, 46
Grapes in syrup, 46
Grapes in alcohol (or in liquor), 47
Sultana grapes in grappa, 47
Grape juice, 48
Plain grape juice, 48
Grapefruit jelly, 49
Grapefruit wedges in syrup, 49
Bitter lemon jam, 50
Lemon curd, 50
Lemon flip, 51
Lemon syrup, 51
Lemons in oil, 52
Grated citrus rind, 52
Flavored sugar cubes, 53
Melon jam, 53
Melon preserve, 54
Melon in syrup, 54
Melons alla certosina, 55
Mint marmalade, 55
Mint sauce, 56
Mint jelly, 56
Orange sections in syrup, 57
Orange jelly, 57
Orange marmalade, 58
Orange and lemon marmalade, 58
Orange wedges in alcohol, 59
Orange sauce, 59
Candied orange rind, 60
Orange juice, 60
Orange syrup, 61
Peach marmalade, 61
Candied peaches, 62
Peaches in syrup, 63
Peaches in alcohol, 63

Peaches in vinegar, 64
Pear jam, 64
San Martino pear jam, 65
Pears in compote, 65
Pears in red wine, 66
Marinated pears, 66
Pears in chocolate, 67
Pears "limara", 67
Persimmon jelly, 68
Persimmon marmalade, 68
Pineapple jam, 69
Bittersweet pineapple jam, 69
Pineapple in kirsch, 70
Pineapple in syrup, 70
Prickly pear marmalade, 71
Prickly pear compote, 71
Plum jam, 72
Black plum marmalade, 72
Plum jelly, 73
Brandied plums, 73
Prunes in syrup, 74
Bittersweet prunes, 74
Quince delight, 75
Quince delight in brandy, 75
Raspberry jam, 76
Raspberry jelly, 76
Raspberries in syrup, 77
Raspberry syrup, 77
Rhubarb jam, 78
Rhubarb marmalade, 78
Rhubarb in syrup, 79
Rhubarb wine, 79
Rose jam, 80
Rose jelly, 80
Strawberry jam, 81
Strawberries in syrup, 81
Strawberry custard, 82
Strawberry juice, 82
Tangerine jelly, 83
Tangerine wedges in syrup, 83
Candied violets, 84
Violet syrup, 84

Miscellaneous preserves

Red "summer" jam, 85
"Black Forest" jelly, 85
Cooked wine, 86

Grandpa's preserve, 86
Fruit cup, 87
Milanese mustard, 87
Red tomato marmalade in liquor, 88
Green tomato marmalade, 88
Coffee marmalade, 89
Milk marmalade, 89
Old-fashioned jam, 90
Indian marmalade, 90
Chinese jam, 91
Wine jelly, 91

Vegetables

Plain artichokes, 92
Artichokes Italian style, 92
Pickled artichokes, 93
Artichokes in oil, 93
Plain asparagus, 94
Asparagus in vinegar, 94
Basil leaves in oil, 95
Basil leaves in salt, 95
Beans Roman style, 96
Beans all'uccelletto, 96
Beans in oil, 97
Canned beans, 97
Plain canned green beans, 98
Green beans, home style, 98
Pickled green beans, 99
Green beans with tomatoes, 99
Sweet-sour green beans, 100
Marinated beets, 100
Beets in vinegar, 101
Braised cabbage, 101
Plain savoy cabbage, 102
Pickled savoy cabbage, 102
Sauerkraut, 103
Capers in salt, 103
Capers in vinegar, 104
Plain carrots, 104
Pickled carrots, 105
Pickled cauliflower, 105
Plain celery, 106
Sweet celery relish, 106
Pickled celery, 107
Celery in oil, 107
Corn preserved for vegetable courses, 108
Corn on the cob in brine, 108
Pickled baby ears of corn, 109
Cucumbers in oil, 109
Cucumbers in brine, 110
Pickled cucumbers, 110

Plain eggplant, 111
Pickled eggplant, 111
Eggplant cubes, 112
Eggplant a la chanterelle, 112
Dried eggplant, 113
Eggplant in brine, 113
Eggplant in oil, 114
Grape leaves in oil, 114
Salted grape leaves, 115
Plain leeks, 115
Leeks, Indian style, 116
Preserved lettuce, 116
Marinated lettuce, 117
Mint syrup, 117
Dried mint, 118
Piquant button mushrooms in oil, 118
Button mushrooms in salt, 119
Cultivated mushrooms, hunter style, 119
Cultivated mushrooms pickled, 120
Plain chanterelles, 120
Chanterelles in oil, 121
Marinated boletus, 121
Dried boletus, 122
Boletus Piedmont style, 122
Green olive compote, 123
Olives in brine, 123
Olives in "vandalusa" sauce, 124
Olives in oil, Andalusian style, 124
Onions, Venetian style, 125
Bittersweet onions, 125
Onions, Far Eastern style, 126
Piquant onions, 126
Onions in oil, 127
Pickled onions, 127
Parsley in oil, 128
Dried parsley, 128
Plain peas, 129
Gourmet peas, 129
Stuffed bell peppers, 130
Red bell peppers, Apulia style, 130
Pickled bell peppers, 131
Peppers in brine, 131
Peppers in oil, 132
Pepper relish, 132
Dried chili peppers, 133
Chili peppers in syrup, 133
Pepper sauce, 134
Candied pumpkin, 134
Plain salsify, 135
Salsify, Piedmont style, 135
Plain spinach, 136
Spinach, Piedmont style, 136

Squash in brine, 137
Plain tarragon, 137
Tarragon in vinegar, 138
Whole tomatoes for sauce, 138
Dried tomatoes, 139
Peeled whole tomatoes, 139
Tomato sauce, 140
Tomato puree, 140
Tomato concentrate, 141
Tomato sauce with herbs, 141
Plain tomato juice, 142
Plain truffles, 142
Liver and truffles, 143
Truffle sauce, 144
Marinated zucchini, 144
Marinated zucchini, Rumanian style, 145
Garlic herb vinegar, 145
Tarragon vinegar, 146
Aromatic vinegar, 146
Rosewater vinegar, 147
Raspberry flavored vinegar, 147

Miscellaneous preserves

Salted vegetables for minestrone, 148
Minestrone, 148
Garden medley, 149
Vegetable macedoine, 149
Italian antipasto, 150
Marinade for fried fish, 150
Ketchup, 151
Italian mustard, 151
Dried herb mixtures, 152
Curry sauce, 153
Devil's sauce, 153
Bagnet-ross sauce, 154
Springtime sauce, 154
Garlic in oil, 155
Eggplant rolls, 155
Stuffed grape (vine) leaves, Venetian style, 156
Chicken in gelatin, 156
Preserved loin of pork, 157
Duck, Friuli style, 157
Quail in oil, 158
Chicken and vegetables alla certosina, 158
Marinated eel, 159
Sardines in oil, 159

Conversion Table, 160

Food preserving: Some general rules

Fruits and vegetables may be preserved in many ways: (1) in syrup or brine; (2) cooked with sugar into jams, jellies, preserves, butters, or conserves; (3) pickled, salted, dried, or preserved in oil; and (4) cooked into juices or sauces. Whatever the method used, certain general rules must be carefully followed to get the best results and to prevent spoilage. (Note: In this book, yields will not be mentioned in the recipes, since they may vary noticeably according to the individual size of and the amount of waste for each fruit and vegetable.)

Choosing and gathering vegetables and fruits

All vegetables and fruits for canning should be in perfect condition. If you grow your own vegetables and fruits, pick them just as they have fully ripened (unless otherwise indicated in a particular recipe); choose only the best-looking specimens and, preferably, select produce which has not been sprayed with insecticides. Also be sure that the plants have not been recently treated with manure or other fertilizers. Vegetables and fruits for canning or preserving by any method should be picked at the height of their growing season, both for reasons of greater abundance and better choice and also because fully ripened vegetables and fruits generally are better-tasting than those from the earliest picking.

If the food to be canned is bought at the market, obviously you cannot be sure it has not been sprayed or treated with chemical fertilizers. For that reason, all vegetables and fruits purchased should be washed much more carefully than if they had come from your own garden. Whenever possible, home-grown produce should be canned on the same day it is picked; if it is purchased instead, it should be canned as soon as possible after being brought home.

Preparing vegetables

Blanching of vegetables to be canned in brine or water should be done in copper, Pyrex, stainless steel, enamelware, or aluminum pots or kettles. When cooking, use ladles, spoons, spatulas, scrapers, and other kitchen utensils made of wood or of heat-resistant rubber or plastic.

Peel the vegetables if necessary, and cut them into pieces as directed in the recipe. Tomatoes, for example, should be peeled by dipping them first in boiling water for 30 seconds; then dip them quickly into cold water, drain, and peel; finally, remove their cores and prepare as directed by the particular recipe.

To preserve the natural coloring of vegetables during cooking, plunge them into rapidly boiling water, push down on them with a wooden spoon or spatula, and cook as quickly as possible—without covering the pot. Be sure not to oversalt the water, because too much salt will toughen fresh vegetables. Also, in general, it is best to avoid common table salt; use coarse kitchen salt or koshering salt instead.

Observe very carefully the cooking time for all vegetables as given in the recipes. Excessive boiling will cause the vegetables to break apart and become mushy. Overcooked vegetables will look unappetizing, will have poor consistency, and will very likely be tasteless.

In preparing mixed vegetables *jardini*ère or other combinations, cook each vegetable to be canned separately, because each of them calls for a different cooking time.

Preparing fruits

Remove the hulls, stems, cores, seeds, or pits from the fruit. Then peel as thinly as possible, and cut into pieces as directed by the recipe. Peaches and plums can be peeled easily, if desired, by submerging them whole in boiling water for 30 seconds; then transfer them to cold water, drain, and peel. Peeled fruits that discolor on exposure to air should be dropped into a "holding" solution of water and a common kitchen acid such as lemon juice, vinegar, or ascorbic acid (1 tablespoon per quart of water). Wash delicate fruit and berries in a deep pan already filled with cold water, for rapidly running water can bruise them.

Selection and care of equipment

Vegetables can be preserved as sauces, pickled, plain, dried, or in oil, vinegar, or brine. You will need more or less similar kitchen equipment for each of these various processes. Basic food-preserving equipment should include:

Bottle capper and caps
Pressure canner or water bath apparatus, with jar rack
Canning jars of various sizes with two-piece screw-seal

lids (or clamp lids or one-piece screw caps with rubber rings)
Jar clamp or long tongs for manipulating hot jars
Small wooden boxes for dried herbs
Chopping board
Colander for rinsing and draining
Food mill
Stainless steel grater
Several large odorless plastic or enamelware bowls
Several large glass or ceramic mixing bowls
Kettle for cooking vegetables (*see below*)
Several large saucepans (*see below*)
Knives of various sizes and grades
Wooden spoons
Ladles, scrapers (heat-resistant, nonmetallic)
Measuring cup
Kitchen scale
Sieves, food strainers
Flat skimmer
Kitchen towels

Most items in this list are inexpensive housewares that are usually found in any well-equipped kitchen.

Untinned copper pots are by far the best for cooking vegetables for canning—but should *not* be used for pickling. Use enamelware, aluminum, or stainless steel pots for this latter method. Aluminum saucepans or kettles should be used only if they are heavy-gauge. Stainless steel pots are acceptable substitutes for copper ones, but they should have copper or heavy aluminum bottoms to ensure uniform heating. For stirring vegetables while cooking, the best tools are wooden spoons and spatulas. Sieves and the perforated plates of food mills should be made of stainless steel or rustproof galvanized iron.

Jars or other containers in which foods are to be preserved may be of any desired size, but for ordinary canning it is best to use many small or moderate-sized containers rather than a few large ones, so that their contents will be consumed quickly once they are opened. Jars meant for home canning may be bought in various stores—complete with zinc, glass-disk, or all-glass lids and separate rubber sealing rings, or fitted with two-piece metal screw caps having rubber sealing rims inside the lid to ensure airtight storage.

Since the separate rubber rings for sealing purposes must be kept fresh and pliable without losing their characteristic shape, it is best to store them flat, one on top of another, in plastic containers in a cool, dry place. (Hanging them on a hook can distort them.) When you are ready to use the rubber rings, rinse them well in cold water, then soak them for a few minutes in a quart of warm water containing 2 tablespoons of baking soda. Give them a final rinse in cold running water. If rubber sealing rings are cracked and dry from storage, discard them and replace them with new, pliable rings.

In canning, cleanliness is absolutely essential. Remember that the jar *must* be a sterile environment. Just a little carelessness on your part can permit subsequent growth of molds or other harmful microorganisms in the jars. Therefore, sterilization of the jars must be perfect. Just before using, jars and sealing items should be completely submerged and boiled in water for 15 minutes, then removed with tongs, turned upside down on a rack, and left there to drip-dry. *Don't* use a dish towel, either for drying the jars or as an absorbent surface underneath. Kitchen towels used in canning should never be washed in detergents. If they have come in contact with detergents, rinse them very well in cold running water. This same caveat holds true for sieves and food mills.

Filling the jars

Prepare vegetables to be preserved as directed in the recipe, and pour them into the sterilized jars—filling the jars to ¾ inch from the top for non-acid vegetables and fruits, and to ½ inch from the top for tomatoes and acid fruits (*see list below*). Cover the contents of the jar with liquid as specified in the recipe. After you have worked out all air bubbles, close the jars according to directions given for the particular type of closure used. Jars sealed with two-piece metal lids having rubber inner rims should be screwed as tightly as possible. Jars with zinc or glass lids and separate rubber ring seals should be screwed tightly but then turned backward one-quarter turn. Jars with clamp lids should have the lid set in place, but with the side clamp left loose (i.e., turned upward). Next, arrange the filled jars in a water bath or pressure canner, and proceed as directed in the recipe.

Acid vegetables and fruits can be preserved in containers sterilized by simple boiling in water bath. Non-acid vegetables and fruits, meats, fish, and poultry must be pressure-sterilized at high temperatures in a pressure canner.

General types of vegetables and fruits

Acid: Tomatoes, berries, rhubarb
Non-acid: All other vegetables and fruits except the abovementioned

Vegetables not recommended for home canning

Baked beans
Cabbage (except for sauerkraut)

Cauliflower (but can be pickled & preserved in oil)
Celery (but can be pickled & preserved in oil)
Cucumber (but can be pickled & preserved in oil)
Eggplant (but can be pickled & preserved in oil)
Lettuce
Onions (but can be pickled & preserved in oil)
Parsnips
Turnips
Vegetable mixtures (in general)

Water bath

Water bath canning involves boiling the hermetically sealed jars in a water bath for the exact amount of time specified by each recipe. Although you can buy a special water bath sterilizer, ordinary kitchen equipment can also be satisfactorily adapted for this purpose if you wish. Such everyday substitutes for the special apparatus are any fairly deep and broad saucepans and kettles—that is, vessels at least 4 inches higher than the jars to be sterilized, since the boiling water must cover them to a depth at least 1 or 2 inches above their tops. It is also a good idea to use a rather wide-mouthed pot or kettle, to allow sterilization of several containers at once. If your water bath sterilizer is large enough to cover several stove burners, so much the better, because by using as many burners as possible simultaneously you can bring to a boil faster the sizeable quantity of water required.

Place a metal rack on the bottom of the sterilizer pot or kettle to keep the jars from knocking against the bottom as they are being boiled. Keep the jars separated from the sides of the pot and also from each other, to prevent breakage. A good general rule for beginning the sterilizing is: jars containing hot foods should be set in a warm or hot water bath; those containing cold foods should be set in a cold water bath, which is then brought quickly to a boil. Only when the water has come to a full, rolling boil has the timing for the sterilization process started. If the water in the bath begins to boil off to an inadequate level before sterilization is completed, add more *boiling* water so that the sterilizing is not interrupted and the jars remain entirely submerged in boiling water. Finish timing the moment that boiling stops (with a tolerance range of 5 minutes).

Remove the hot jars with tongs and place them on a board or towel. Before storing the jars, check that sterilization has been thoroughly complete and effective. Jars with a two-piece metal-disk lid are adequately sealed and sterilized if, when the outer metal rim is loosened, the top disk of the lid remains firmly in place. Jars with separate rubber sealing rings and with zinc or glass-disk tops should be hand-screwed as tightly as possible. For jars with a clamp lid and separate rubber ring, the wire clamp at the side should be turned down tightly against the neck of the jar.

After processing and cooling, test the jars to make sure they are tightly sealed and leakproof by turning them upside down. If this shows that the seal is not perfect, then the sterilizing procedure must be repeated, after first checking to see that the rubber seal is in good condition and that the cover fits the jar perfectly. (Note: Canning at high altitudes requires extending the boiling time in the water bath. For every 1,000 feet above sea level, add 1 minute to the required time if under 20 minutes; for over 20 minutes, add 2 minutes for each 1,000 feet of altitude.) When properly sterilized, the jars should be labeled and dated, and then stored in a cool, dark, dry place.

Pressure canner

This method, which ensures a much wider margin of safety in preventing botulism, is of particular use for canning meats, fish, poultry, and non-acid fruits and vegetables. A pressure canner, which should be of 16- to 20-quart capacity, is a large, heavy kettle that is usually fitted with a jar rack having handles for easily removing

Chart for processing vegetables

Vegetable	Boiling time at 10 lb. pressure	Boiling time in water bath
Artichokes	25 min.	
Asparagus	40	
Beans, lima	55	
Beans, wax or green	40	
Beets	45	
Carrots	45	
Corn, kernel	75	
Mushrooms	40	
Peas	45	
Sauerkraut	10	
Sweet potatoes	1 hr. 55 min.	
Tomatoes	—	45 min.

(*Note:* Add 1 teaspoon of salt for each quart of vegetable.)

the jars from hot water. It has an airtight cover with a safety valve, vent, and pressure gauge.

Arrange the filled jars in the rack and lower it into the pressure canner. Fill the canner with boiling water until the water level is about 3 inches deep, and then set it over high heat. Carefully lock its cover in place. Keep the burner on high heat until steam has been escaping from the vent for at least 10 minutes, thereby making sure the canner is filled with steam. Next, close the steam vent, and watch the gauge until the pressure reading is 10 lb. Now lower the heat slightly, and keep adjusting it to hold the pressure constant at 10 lb. (or other amount of pressure as required by the recipe). Process the food for the length of time indicated by the recipe. The timing starts as soon as the necessary pressure is reached. When the required time has elapsed, turn the heat off and allow the canner to cool until the pressure gauge registers "0" (zero). Two minutes later, remove the cover from the canner. While doing this, tilt the cover away from you, so that live steam does not hit your face. Remove the jars with tongs and place them on a board or towel to cool gradually, away from drafts. While the jars are still hot, tighten their seals as much as possible. After cooling, test for airtightness.

Preserving food in sugar, vinegar, or oil

Fruits preserved in sugar as in jams, jellies, preserves, conserves, and butters and vegetables preserved in vinegar, salt, or oil as in pickles, relishes, chutneys, catsups, and mincemeat do not need sterilization in a water bath or pressure canner. They need only be packed in sterilized jars while they are still boiling hot. Sauces and juices must be processed as directed in the recipe.

Syrup used in canning fruit

Consistency	Sugar, cups	Water, cups	Yield, cups
Thin	1	2	2½
Medium	1½	2	2¾
Heavy	2⅓	2	3¼

Add sugar to water in a saucepan. Boil the mixture for 5 minutes or until clear. Use the syrup hot. Fruits may also be canned in water and, if so, are processed for the

Altitude chart

The processing times given in this book are for foods canned at altitudes less than 1,000 feet above sea level, when using the water bath canner. When using the steam-pressure canner, the pressure given is for altitudes less than 2,000 feet above sea level. If you live in an area of a higher altitude, it is necessary to make the following adjustment in time or pressure.

WATER BATH CANNER

Increase processing time if the time called for is:

Altitude	20 Minutes or Less	More than 20 Minutes
1,000 feet	1 minute	2 minutes
2,000 feet	2 minutes	4 minutes
3,000 feet	3 minutes	6 minutes
4,000 feet	4 minutes	8 minutes
5,000 feet	5 minutes	10 minutes
6,000 feet	6 minutes	12 minutes
7,000 feet	7 minutes	14 minutes
8,000 feet	8 minutes	16 minutes
9,000 feet	9 minutes	18 minutes
10,000 feet	10 minutes	20 minutes

STEAM-PRESSURE CANNER

Altitude	Process at pressure of:
2,000– 3,000 feet	11½ pounds
3,000– 4,000 feet	12 pounds
4,000– 5,000 feet	12½ pounds
5,000– 6,000 feet	13 pounds
6,000– 7,000 feet	13½ pounds
7,000– 8,000 feet	14 pounds
8,000– 9,000 feet	14½ pounds
9,000–10,000 feet	15 pounds

Chart for processing fruits

Fruit	Type of sugar syrup	Boiling time at 10 lb. pressure	Boiling time in water bath
Apples	Thin	10 min.	20 min.
Applesauce	—	8	10
Apricots	Heavy	10	25
Berries, firm (except strawberries)	Heavy	8	15
Cherries	Heavy	10	15
Cranberries	Heavy	—	3
Peaches	Thin or medium	10	20
Pears	Thin or medium	10	20
Pineapples	Medium	10	20
Plums	Thin or medium	10	25
Rhubarb	Heavy	5	10
Raspberries (& other soft berries)	Thin	8	10
Strawberries	Heavy	5	15

same length of time as fruit in syrup. Honey can be used to replace *one-half* of the sugar; corn syrup can be used to replace *one-third* of the sugar.

Paraffin

After jams, jellies, or conserves are placed into sterilized jars, while they are still hot, they should be covered with a ⅛ inch thick layer of melted paraffin. To melt paraffin, grate paraffin coarsely into a saucepan and stir over low heat until clear and melted.

Miscellaneous tips

If you are preserving vegetables for the first time and want to avoid disappointing results and unnecessary expense, try canning only small quantities at your first attempt. Gradually, as you become more experienced, you will be able to vary your selections, quantities, and methods.

Before storing the jars, check to make sure that sterilization has been thorough and effective, by turning the jars upside down for a time and watching out for leaking liquids. Then, during the first week of storage, check the jars often to be sure there are no telltale signs of spoilage, such as bubbles or clouding. If you notice the beginnings of any such warning signs, open the jar and use its contents immediately—but first boil the contents for 15 minutes, stirring constantly. If, by the time you first notice any such unfavorable signs, the food already has a distinct odor of fermentation, you must discard it unhesitatingly.

Once the jars have been stored, avoid moving them about as much as possible before using, since any change in storage location may mean a significant change in temperature or humidity, which could affect the rubber seal. The best storage place is a good dry cellar.

To open glass jars with clamp lids, lift up the metal clamp at the side and pull the rubber sealing ring toward you. If a jar does not open easily, run hot water over the lid and then pull the rubber seal again. Other covers may be unscrewed, depending on the type of jar and closure. Preferably, the screw-type lids should be used only once. Used or long-stored rubber rings must be discarded when they appear dry and cracked or are squeezed out of shape.

Once a jar of home-preserved food has been opened, try to use it as quickly as possible. If you do not finish it at one sitting, it must be refrigerated till you are ready to serve the remainder.

Be sure to label all jars. Ideally, the label should show the following data: (1) contents; (2) date of canning; (3) quantity, by volume or weight; (4) date when food can be used, if not immediately. It is also a good idea to leave some space on the label for any notes you might wish to add after sampling the contents of the jar. Such observations might be useful when the next canning season comes around.

Conditions which might occur in home canned food, the causes and remedies

CONDITION (Product usable unless spoilage is indicated)	CAUSE	PREVENTION
Foods darken in top of jar.	1. Liquid did not cover food product. 2. Food not processed long enough to destroy enzymes. 3. Manner of packing and processing did not produce a high vacuum. 4. Air was sealed in the jars either because head space was too large or air bubbles were not removed.	1. Cover food product with liquid before capping jar. 2. Process each food by recommended method and for recommended length of time. 3. Pack and process as recommended. 4. Use amount of head space as recommended. Remove air bubbles by running rubber bottle scraper between food and jar.
Fruits darken after they have been removed from jar.	Fruits have not been processed long enough to destroy enzymes.	Process each fruit by recommended method and for recommended length of time. Time is counted when water reaches a full boil in the canner.
Corn is brown.	1. Corn was too mature for canning. 2. Liquid did not cover corn. 3. Jars were processed at too high a temperature. 4. Variety of corn used.	1. Use freshly picked corn which has plump, shiny kernels filled with milk. 2. Cover corn with liquid before capping jar. 3. Keep pressure in canner at recommended pounds; gauge may be faulty and should be checked. 4. Use different variety next time.
Pink, red, blue or purple color in canned apples, pears, peaches and quinces.	A natural chemical change which occurs in cooking the fruit.	None.
Green vegetables lose their bright green color.	Heat breaks down chlorophyll, the green coloring matter in plants.	None.

12

Conditions which might occur in home canned food, the causes and remedies—*Continued*

Green vegetables turn brown.	1. Vegetables were overcooked.	1. Time precooking and processing exactly.
	2. Vegetables were too mature for canning.	2. Asparagus tips should be tight and the entire green portion tender. Pods of green beans should be crisp and meaty and the beans tiny. Peas, lima beans and all other beans and peas which are shelled should be green.
Some foods become black, brown or gray.	Natural chemical substances (tannins, sulfur compounds and acids) in food react with minerals in water or with metal utensils used in preparing food.	Use soft water. Avoid using copper, iron or chipped enameled ware, also utensils from which tinplate has worn.
Crystals in grape products. (see jelly contains glass-like particles)	Tartaric acid which is naturally found in grapes.	In juice, carefully ladle into clean hot jars, cap and reprocess original length of time.
Yellow crystals on canned green vegetables.	Glucoside, natural and harmless substance, in vegetables.	None.
White crystals on canned spinach.	Calcium and oxalic acid in spinach combine to form harmless calcium oxalate.	None.
White sediment in bottom of jars of vegetables. May denote spoilage.	1. Starch from the food. 2. Minerals in water used. 3. Bacterial spoilage... liquid is usually murky, food soft. (DO NOT USE.)	1. None. 2. Use soft water. 3. Process each food by recommended method and for recommended length of time.
Fruit floats in jar.	Fruit is lighter than the syrup.	Use firm, ripe fruit. Heat fruit before packing it. Use a light to medium syrup. Pack fruit as closely as possible without crushing it.
Cloudy liquids. May denote spoilage	1. Spoilage. (DO NOT USE.) 2. Minerals in water. 3. Starch in vegetable. 4. Fillers in table salt.	1. Process each food by recommended method and for recommended length of time. 2. Use soft water. 3. None. 4. None, except by using a pure refined salt.

Continued

Conditions which might occur in home canned food, the causes and remedies—*Continued*

Loss of liquid during processing. (Food may darken, but will not spoil. Do not open jars to replace liquid.)	1. Food not heated before packing. 2. Food packed too tightly. 3. Air bubbles not removed before capping the jar. 4. Pressure canner not operated correctly. 5. Jars not covered with water in water bath canner. 6. Starchy foods absorbed liquid.	1. Heat food before packing. 2. Pack food more loosely. 3. Remove air bubbles by running rubber bottle scraper between food and jar. 4. Pressure should not be allowed to fluctuate during processing time. Allow pressure to drop to zero naturally; wait 2 minutes before opening lid. 5. Jars should be covered 1 inch with water in canner throughout the processing period. 6. None.
Jar seals, then comes open. Spoilage evident. (DO NOT USE.)	1. Food spoilage from under-processing. 2. Disintegration of particles of food left on the sealing surface. 3. Hairlike crack in the jar.	1. Process each food by recommended method and for recommended length of time. 2. Wipe sealing surface and threads of jar with clean, damp cloth before capping. 3. Check jars; discard ones unsuitable for canning.
Jar of food fails to seal. (Correct cause and reprocess the full time or use the food immediately.)	Many factors could be involved, such as failure to follow instructions for using jar and cap, or a bit of food may have been forced up between the jar and lid during processing.	Carefully follow methods and instructions for using jars and caps and for foods to be canned.
Zinc caps bulge. May denote spoilage.	1. Cap screwed too tight before processing. (Condition is evident as jar is removed from canner.) 2. Food spoils from under-processing. (Condition evident after jar has cooled and has been stored from a day to a few months.) DO NOT USE.	1. Screw cap tight, then loosen about ¼ inch before putting jar in canner. 2. Process each food by recommended method and for recommended length of time.
Black spots on underside of metal lid. (If jar has been sealed and then comes open, spoilage is evident. DO NOT USE.)	Natural compounds in some foods cause a brown or black deposit on the underside of the lid. This deposit is harmless and does not mean the food is unsafe to eat.	None.

Conditions which might occur in home canned food, the causes and remedies—*Continued*

Hollow pickles.	1. Faulty growth of cucumbers	1. None. In washing cucumbers, hollow cucumbers usually float. They may be used in relishes.
	2. Cucumbers were stale when pickling was begun.	2. Pickling process should be started within 24 hours of picking cucumbers.
Soft or slippery pickles. Spoilage evident. (DO NOT USE.)	1. Brine or vinegar used was too weak.	1. Use pure refined salt. Use vinegar of 4–6% acidity. Use a recipe developed for modern day use.
	2. Pickles were not kept covered with liquid.	2. Pickles should be covered with liquid at all times during the brining process and when in the jar.
	3. Scum was not kept removed from top of brine.	3. Scum should be removed daily during the brining process.
	4. Pickles were not heated long enough to destroy spoilage microorganisms.	4. Process each food by recommended method and for recommended length of time.
	5. Jars were not sealed airtight while boiling hot.	5. Each jar should be filled boiling hot and capped immediately before filling next jar. Pickles should be kept boiling hot throughout packing process.
Darkened and discolored pickles.	1. Minerals present in hard water used in making the pickles.	1. Use soft water.
	2. Brass, iron, copper or zinc utensils were used in making the pickles.	2. Use enameled ware, glass, aluminum, stainless steel or stoneware utensils.
	3. Ground spices used.	3. Use whole spices.
	4. Whole spices left in jars of pickles.	4. Whole cloves, stick cinnamon and other whole spices should be used only to flavor the pickling liquid; they should not be packed in the jars.
Shriveled pickles.	Too much salt, sugar or vinegar was added to the cucumbers at one time.	Start with a weaker solution of brine, sugar or vinegar and gradually add the full amount called for in recipe. Use recipe developed for modern day use.

Continued

Conditions which might occur in home canned food, the causes and remedies—*Continued*

White sediment in bottom of jars of firm pickles. (If pickles are soft, spoilage is evident. DO NOT USE.)	Harmless yeasts have grown on the surface and then settled.	None. The presence of a small amount of the white sediment is normal.
Jelly is cloudy.	1. Fruit used was too green. 2. Fruit may have been cooked too long before straining. 3. Juice may have been squeezed from fruit. 4. Jelly poured into jars too slowly. 5. Jelly mixture was allowed to stand before it was poured into the jars.	1. Fruit should be firm-ripe. 2. Fruit should be cooked only until it is tender. 3. To obtain the clearest jelly possible, let juice drip through cotton flannel bag. 4. Next time work more quickly. 5. Immediately upon reaching jellying point, pour into jars and seal.
Jelly contains glass-like particles.	1. Too much sugar was used. 2. The mixture may have been cooked too little. 3. The mixture may have been cooked too slowly or too long. 4. Undissolved sugar, which was sticking to the pan, washed into jelly as it was poured. 5. If jelly is grape, the crystals may be tartaric acid, the natural substance in grapes from which cream of tartar is made.	1. Use a recipe developed for modern day use. 2. Too short a cooking period results in the sugar not dissolving completely and not mixing thoroughly with the fruit juice. 3. Long, slow cooking results in too much evaporation of the water content of the fruit. 4. Ladle juice into jars instead of pouring it. Or, carefully wipe side of pan free of sugar crystals with a damp cloth before filling jars. 5. Allow juice to stand in refrigerator for several days; then strain it through two thicknesses of damp cheesecloth before preparing jelly. Use canned juice; if sediment is in bottom of jar, carefully pour juice off so not to disturb sediment.
Jelly is low in fruit flavor.	1. Fruit used had little flavor. 2. Jelly stored too long. 3. Storage area too warm.	1. Use full-flavored fruit; tree ripened is the best. 2. Jelly should not be stored over a year. 3. Storage area should be cool, dark and dry.
Bubbles are in jelly. May denote spoilage.	1. If bubbles are moving, jelly is spoiling; usually the airtight seal has been broken. (DO NOT USE.)	1. Use vacuum sealing. Be sure to test for seal before storing jars.

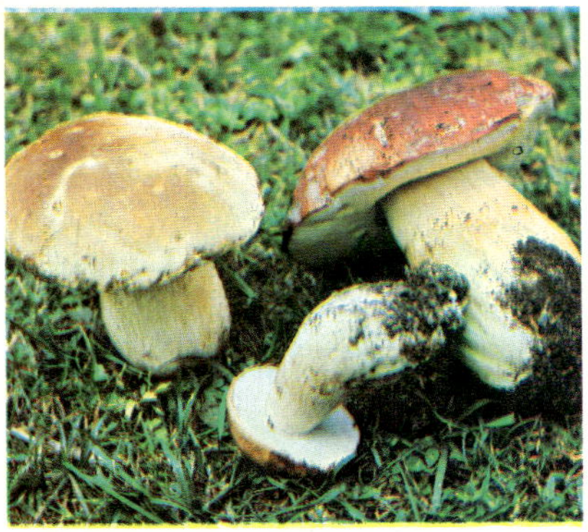
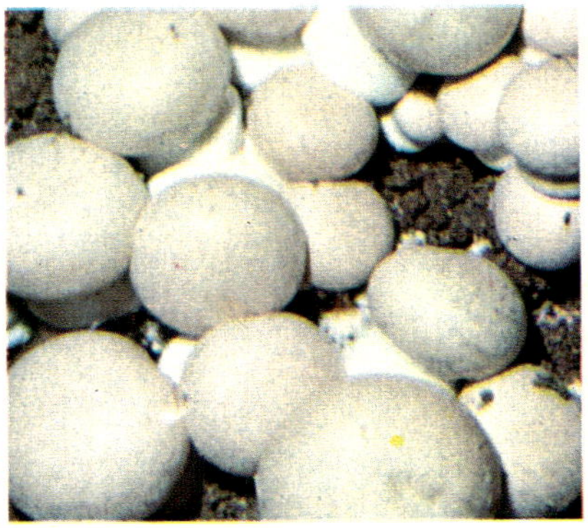
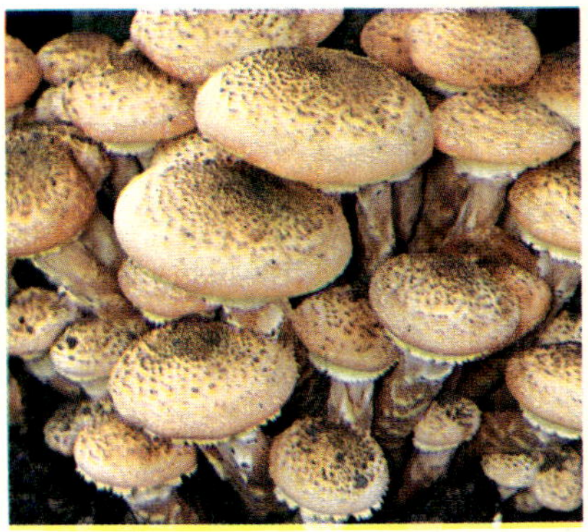
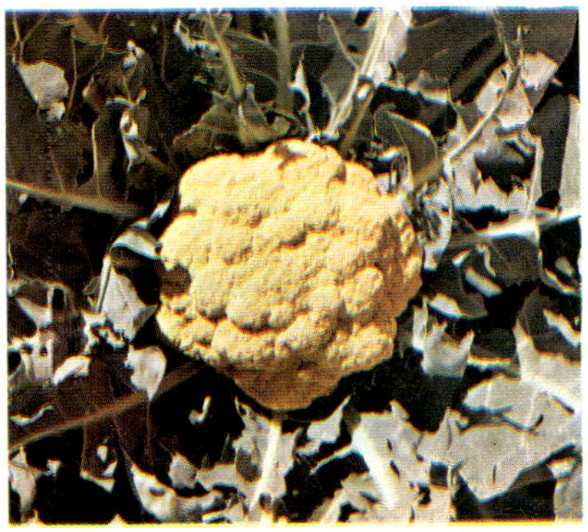
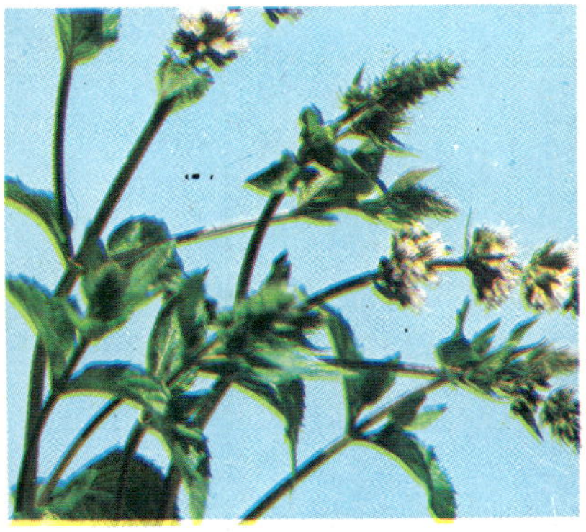
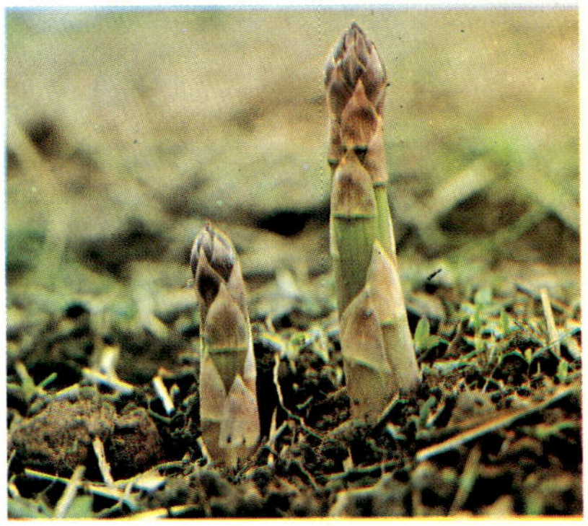
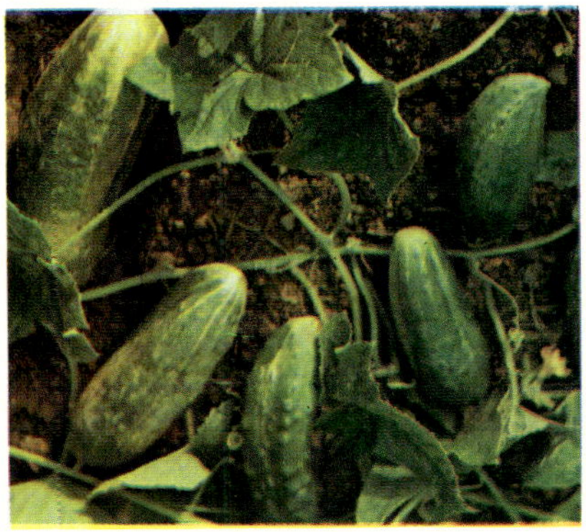
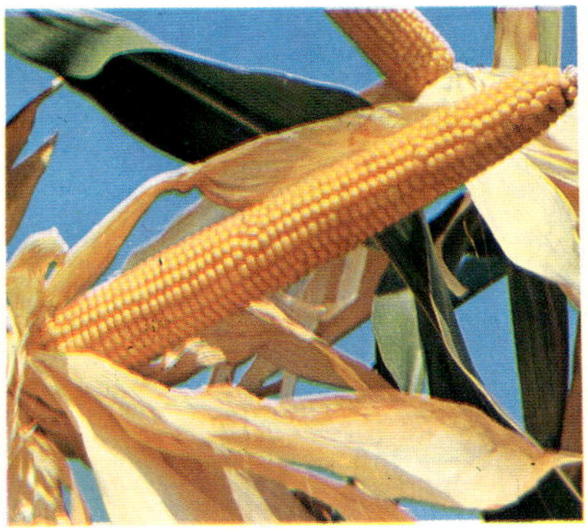
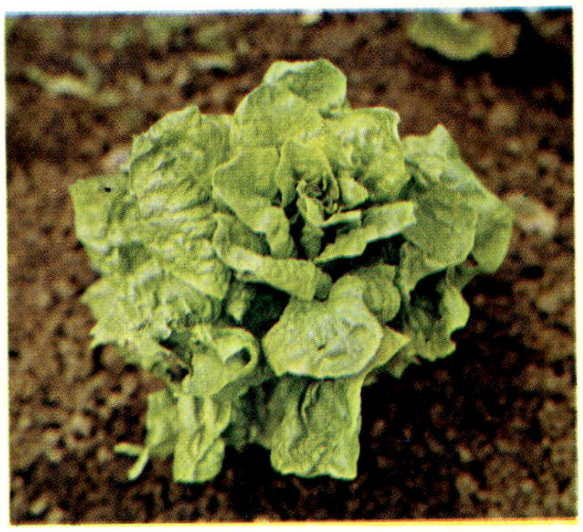
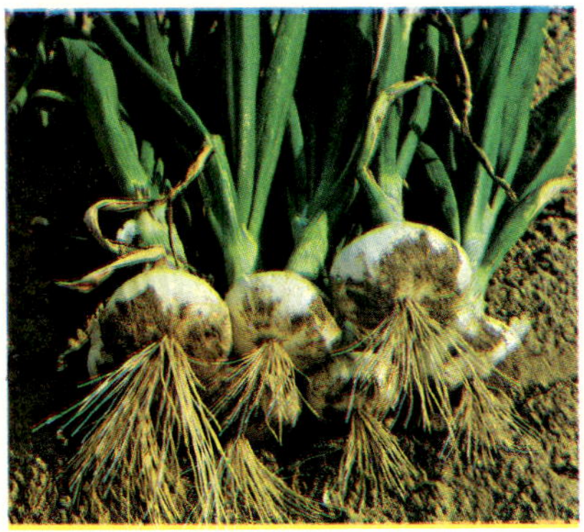
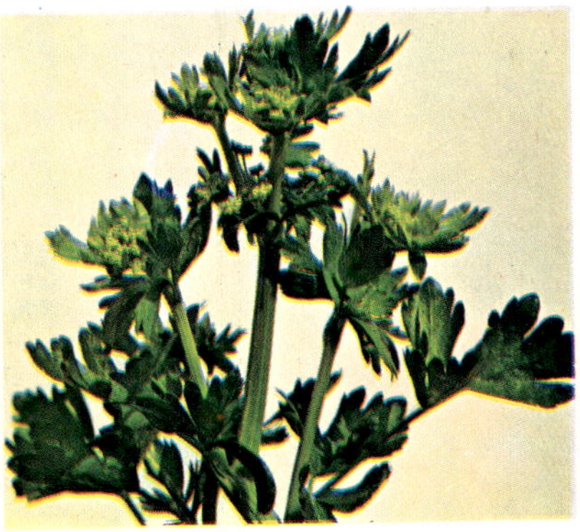
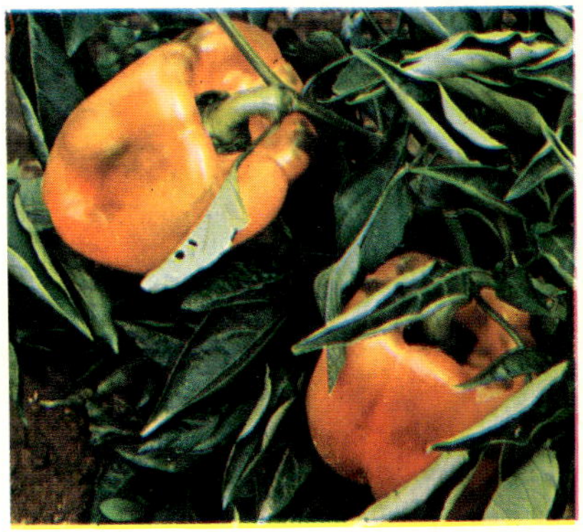

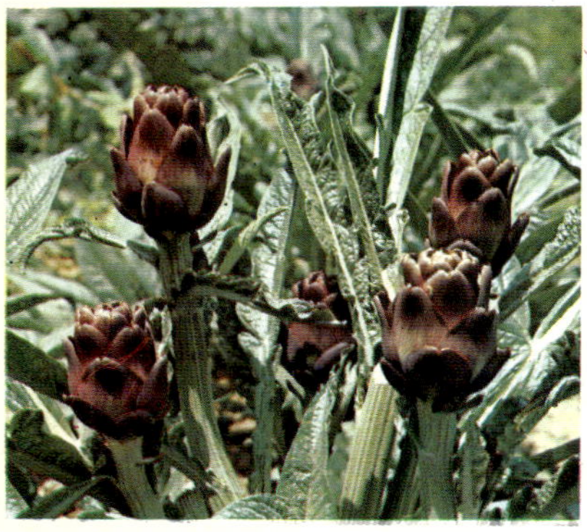
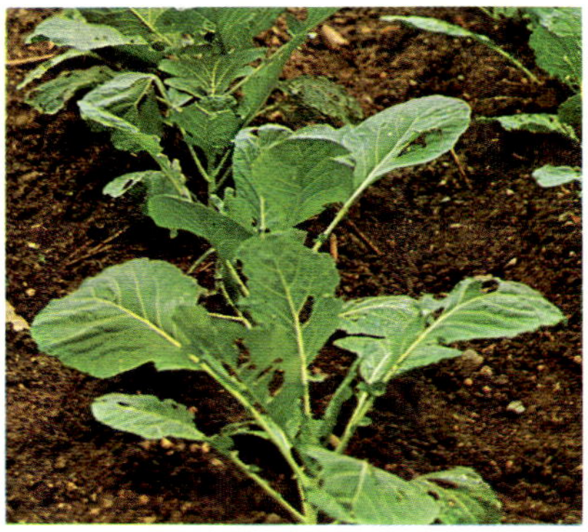
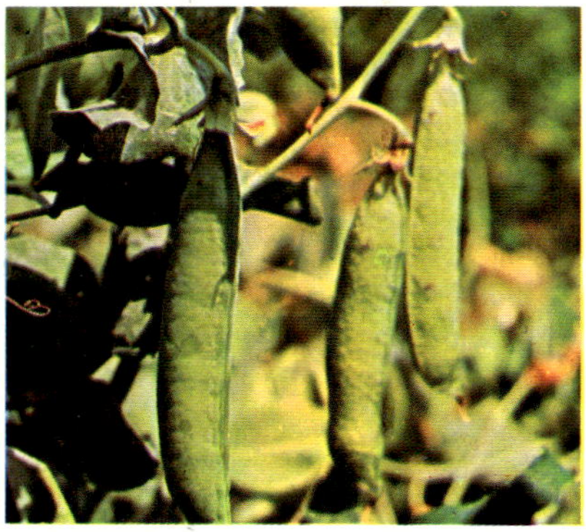
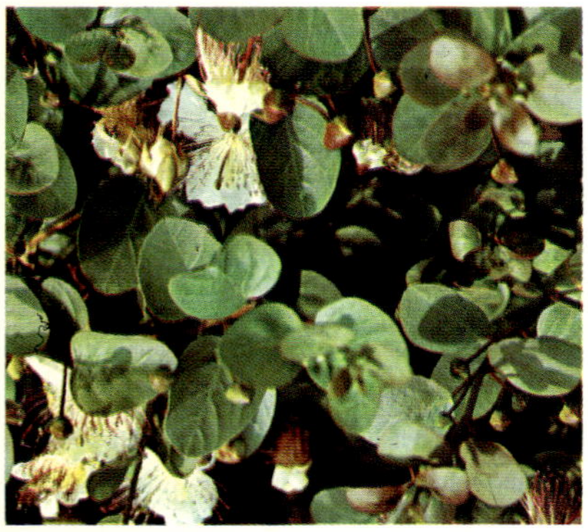
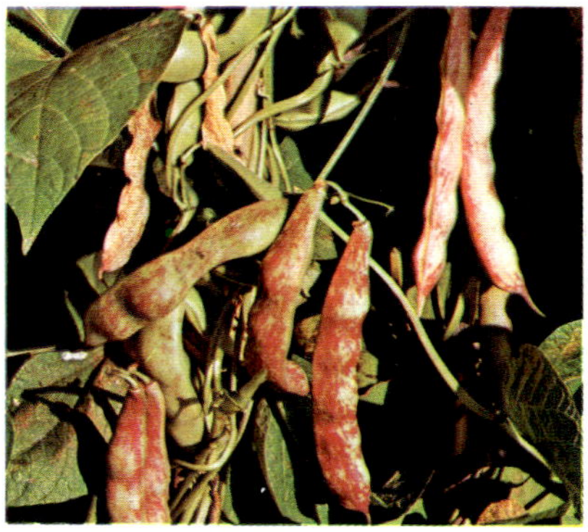
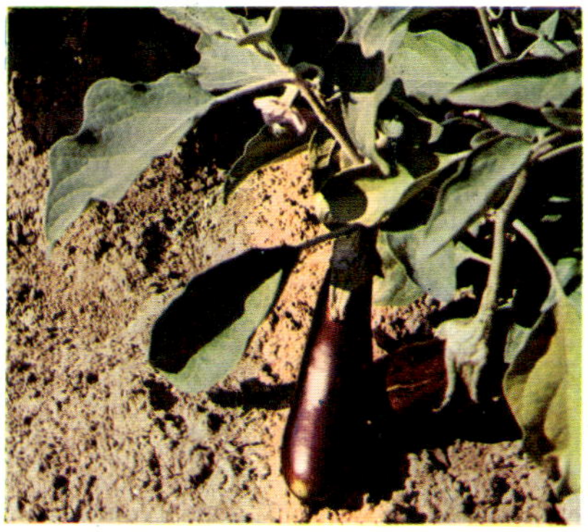
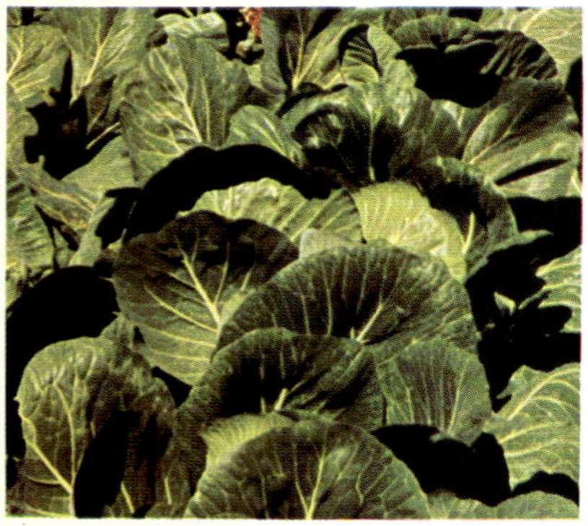
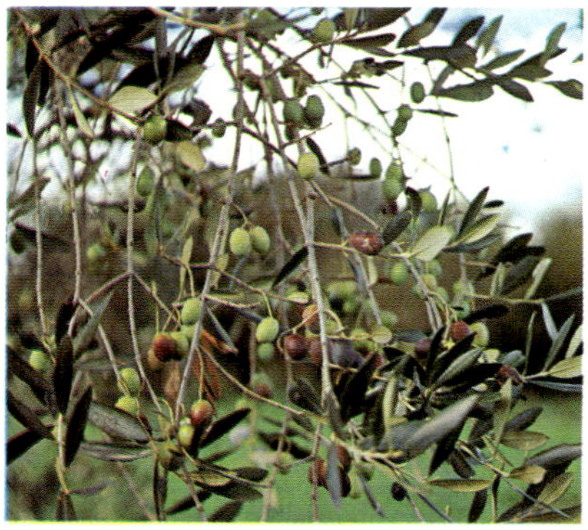
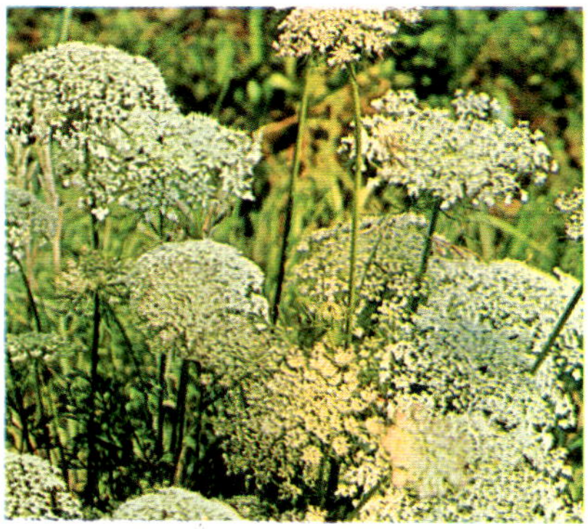
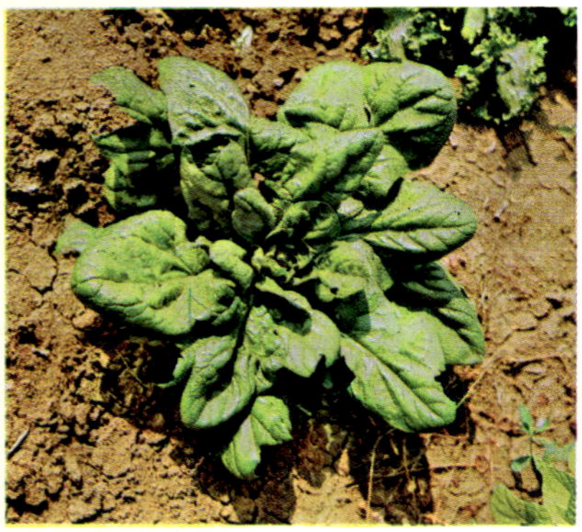
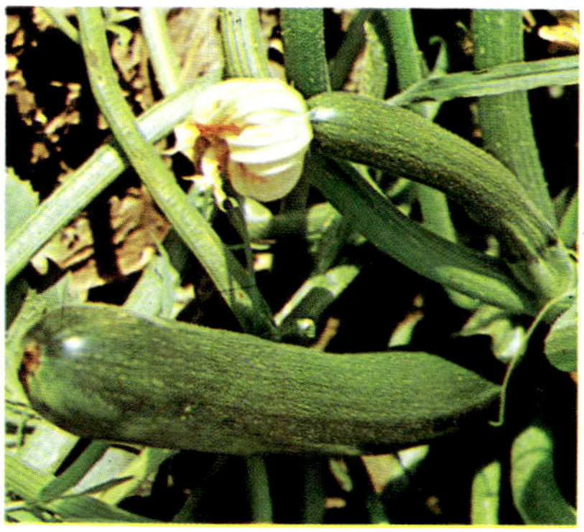
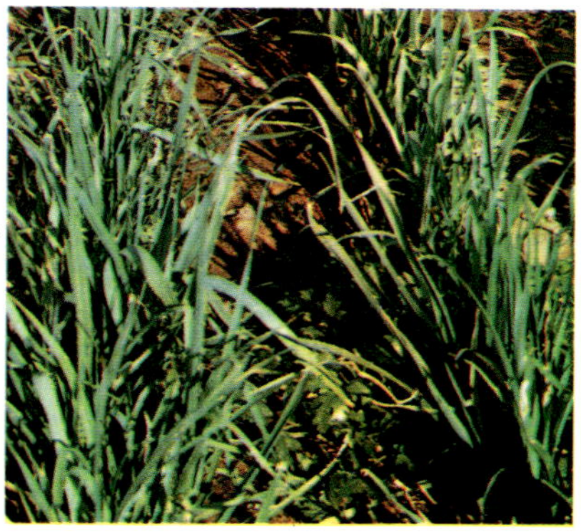

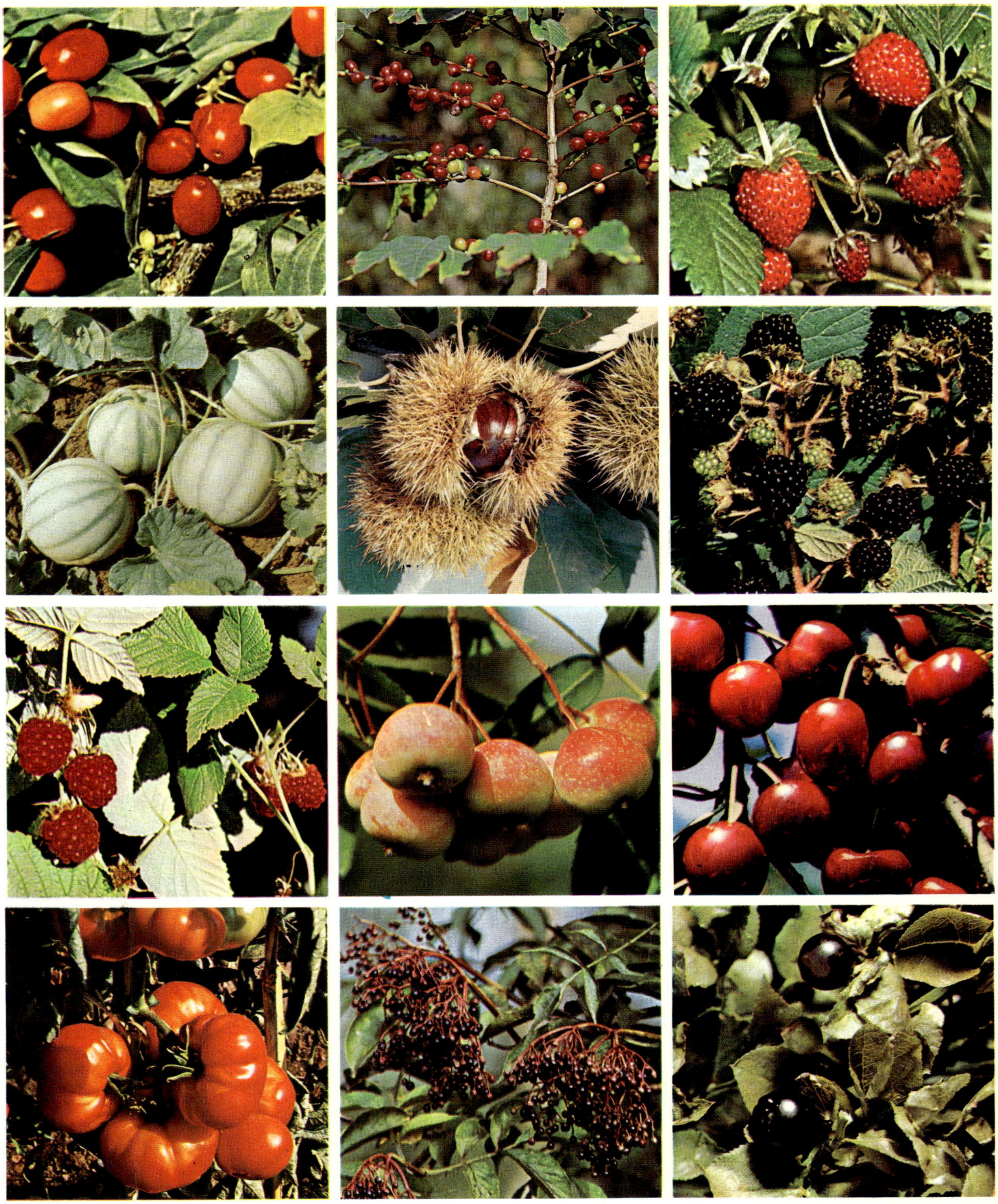

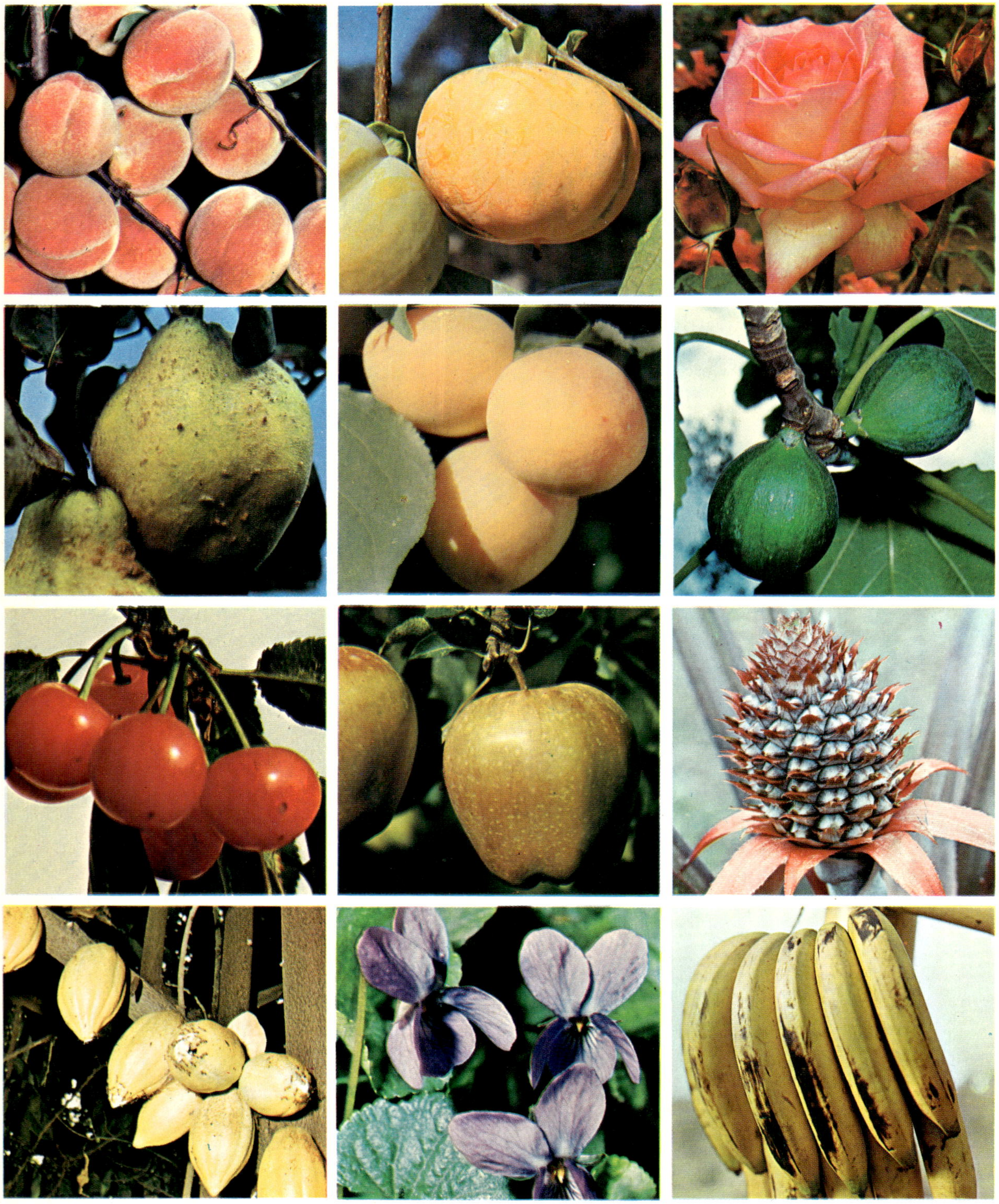

Conditions which might occur in home canned food, the causes and remedies—*Continued*

	2. If bubbles are standing still, utensil from which jelly was poured was not held close to top of jar or jelly was poured slowly and air was trapped in the hot jelly.	2. Hold utensil close to top of jar and pour into jar quickly.
Jelly "weeps."	1. Syneresis or "weeping" usually occurs in quick-setting jellies and is due to the quantity of acid and the quality of pectin in the fruit.	1. None.
	2. Storage conditions were not ideal.	2. Store in a cool, dark, dry place.
Jelly is too soft.	1. Proportions of sugar and juice not correct.	1. Use a recipe developed for modern day use.
	2. Too large a batch made at one time.	2. Use not more than 4 to 6 cups of juice in each batch of jelly. Never increase the recipe supplied by the manufacturer of pectin.
Jelly is tough or stiff.	1. Too much pectin in fruit.	1. Use fruit which is riper. If adding pectin, don't add as much.
	2. Jelly was overcooked.	2. Process each food by recommended method and for recommended length of time.
	3. Too little sugar, so mixture had to be cooked too long to reach jellying stage.	3. When pectin is not added, ¾ cup sugar to 1 cup juice is the right amount for most fruits. When measuring, use graduated dry measuring cups; level off sugar with straight edge of a knife.
Jelly ferments. Spoilage evident. (DO NOT USE.)	Yeasts grow on jelly when seal is not airtight (usually noticeable on jars sealed with paraffin) causing the jelly to break through paraffin and to weep.	Use vacuum sealing next time. Test for seal before storing jelly.
Jelly molds. May denote spoilage; if growth of mold is heavy, DO NOT USE.	Jar was not sealed properly, allowing mold to grow on surface of jelly.	Use vacuum sealing next time. Test for seal before storing jelly.

Fruits

Apple marmalade

Ingredients:
5½ pounds cooking apples
Grated rind and juice of 1 lemon
3 pounds (6 cups) sugar

Preparation:
Peel, core and slice apples. If apples are hard, dice them into one-half inch cubes. Put them in a bowl and sprinkle them with lemon juice to prevent darkening. Pour apples into a large stainless steel pot and add sugar. Bring to a boil and cook slowly, stirring and skimming foam and at the same time crushing apples with a wooden spoon. When they have reached the consistency of a thickish puree, spoon while hot into sterilized jars. If apples are of a particularly hard variety, they should be cut quite small so that they will cook more quickly. If desired, stir grated lemon rind into apple marmalade while cooking to add more flavor.

Apple compote

Warmed, the apples are eaten as a dessert.

Ingredients:
9 pounds firm-fleshed apples
Grated rind and juice of 2 lemons
1 pound 12 ounces (3½ cups) sugar
6 cups water

Preparation:
Peel apples and quarter them. Remove cores. Drop them immediately into cold water to cover to which has been added juice of one of the lemons. Heat a large pot with four quarts water and remaining lemon juice until it boils. Place some of the apples in a colander. Dip into boiling water and boil for two to three minutes. Drain and spread them on a clean, dry cloth to dry. Cook apples in several batches. After all the apples have been cooked and dried, place them in sterilized jars.

Boil sugar, six cups water and lemon rind for three to five minutes. Pour hot syrup over apples in jars. It is not necessary for the apples to be covered with syrup; the level need not reach to more than two fingers below top of apples.

Seal and sterilize jars in a boiling water bath (see page 9) for ten to fifteen minutes. Store in a cool, dark, dry place.

Candied apples

Ingredients:
2 pounds rennet or crab apples (or another variety that is firm-fleshed) of small size
3 pounds (6 cups) sugar
2 cups water, about
Juice of 1 lemon

Preparation:
Rub apples with a dry cloth, leaving the stem. Puncture skin in about fifteen places with a toothpick. In a pot large enough to hold the apples, bring two and two-third cups of the sugar and one and three-quarter cups of the water to a boil. Let syrup boil for two minutes. Remove from heat and while syrup is still hot, add apples, making sure that they are not crowded. Stir in lemon juice. Cover pot and let stand for a day. The next day uncover pot and bring to a boil. Just before syrup begins to boil, remove apples and set them aside to dry. Boil syrup without apples for five minutes. Remove from heat and add apples again. Cover pot and let stand another day. The next day repeat operation, and continue in this manner for three or four times, until syrup with apples is quite thick and slightly darker than honey. Make sure that apples do not boil at any time for more than one or two minutes. In the meantime, apples should have become smaller and wrinkled. Now prepare another syrup with two and two-third cups sugar and one-third cup water and boil for two minutes. Remove apples from first syrup, let drain and put them in new syrup, which should be hot and very thick. Let stand for a day, covered. The next day heat new syrup until it steams, remove apples and boil syrup for about ten minutes. While syrup is still hot, place apples in it, turning them gently. Cover and let stand for a day. The next day heat syrup until it steams. Remove apples and place them on a rack to drain and dry. Roll apples gently in remaining two-third cup sugar and place in a single layer on wax paper. Let dry for two days in a dry, airy place.

When apples are perfectly candied and dry put them in tins lined with wax paper, cover tightly and store in a cool, dark, dry place.

Dried apples

Warmed, the apples are eaten as a dessert.

Ingredients:
Sound, ripe apples

Preparation:
Peel and core apples whole. Cut horizontally into slices about a half-inch thick. Place slices in a single layer on a shallow baking pan. Dry them in a warm oven with door slightly open, about 150° F. on an electric range or pilot light in gas range, making sure they do not cook. After eight hours in the oven, expose apple slices to the sun to finish drying, turning slices two or three times a day for a few days. When drying is completed, apples should still be tender and pliable. Remember to bring apples into house each evening.

Store apples in clean, wooden boxes lined with sulphured paper (to prevent darkening) or wax paper.

To use dried apples, soak them overnight in warm water so they will reabsorb liquid lost during drying process. During soaking make sure that slices are completely under water; if necessary, weigh them down. Cook apples in same water in which they were soaked until they are plump and tender.

Apple chutney

Chutney is a basic condiment in Indian cooking. Today it can be found ready-made in many food stores. It is well worth making at home even though its exotic flavor may seem strange to American tastes. It is generally served with cold meats.

Ingredients:
2 pounds not too ripe apples
½ cup best white vinegar
2 chili peppers
2 tablespoons powdered mustard
1 small onion, chopped
1 celery stalk, chopped
12 ounces (1½ cups) sugar
1 cup sultana grapes
1 pinch ginger
1 clove garlic, chopped
¼ teaspoon coriander seeds

Preparation:
Peel, core and slice apples. Put them in a pot with vinegar, chili peppers and mustard. Cook at a slow boil until apples are tender. Press apples through a sieve or food mill. Replace apples in pot and add onion, celery and remaining ingredients. Boil for ten minutes over a low heat stirring constantly. Remove from heat and let stand for one day. The next day stir and reheat to a boil. Boil for five minutes over very low heat, stirring constantly to prevent sticking. The chutney should be very thick. Pour hot into sterilized jars and seal. Store in a cool, dark, dry place.

Applesauce

Applesauce is a good accompaniment to pork, game and the like.

Ingredients:
2 pounds apples
Rind of 1 lemon, in large pieces
Juice of 1 lemon
5 whole cloves
¼ teaspoon ground cinnamon
½ cup dry white wine
1 cup sugar
1 pinch dry mustard
1 pinch ground pepper
1 pinch salt

Preparation:
Peel and slice apples, putting them in a *non-aluminum* pot with lemon rind, lemon juice, cloves, cinnamon and white wine. Bring to a boil and cook until apples are tender and no longer watery. Press apples through a sieve or food mill. Replace puree in pot. Stir in sugar, dry mustard, pepper and salt. Reheat to a boil. Stir constantly until a thickish puree. Pour it hot into sterilized small jars. Seal and store in a cool, dark, dry place.

Caramelized apple marmalade

Ingredients:
5 pounds apples
Juice of 1 lemon
2 pounds (4 cups) sugar
¼ cup water
½ cup brandy

Preparation:
Peel, core and slice apples. Toss with lemon juice to prevent darkening. In a pot that absolutely must *not* be aluminum, mix one and one-half cups sugar and water and bring to a slow boil. Cook until sugar turns golden brown (close attention must be paid at this point for it takes but a moment too much to burn it). Remove from heat and add apples. Do this carefully as hot caramel syrup can cause a violent jet of steam to be released. Stir apples in immediately to stop cooking of sugar. Stir in remaining sugar. Replace on heat and bring to a slow boil, stirring apples frequently. When apples are tender, press them through a sieve. Replace in pot. If puree is already very thick, bring it to a boil for one to two minutes, but if puree is somewhat watery, boil it slowly until it thickens, stirring constantly to prevent sticking. Stir in brandy and while hot pour into sterilized jars. Seal and store in a cool, dark, dry place.

Apple marmalade with chocolate

In addition to being an excellent breakfast spread, this marmalade can be used as a filling for tarts or to garnish desserts.

Ingredients:
Juice of 1 lemon
Grated rind of ½ lemon
2 pounds peeled, cored and sliced rennet or other hard cooking apples
1 pound, 6 ounces (2¾ cups) sugar
1½ ounces (6 tablespoons) unsweetened cocoa
1 piece vanilla bean, 1 inch long

Preparation:
Put lemon juice and lemon rind into a *non-aluminum* pot. Stir in apples, coating all pieces to prevent darkening. In a separate bowl, mix sugar and cocoa. Stir into apples while cold in order to avoid lumping of cocoa. Add vanilla bean. Heat while stirring constantly, and bring slowly to a boil. As soon as the boiling begins, lower heat and continue stirring with a wooden spoon. When apples are tender press them through a sieve or food mill. Return puree to same pot and bring to a slow boil again. Cook, stirring occasionally until marmalade is thick. Pour while hot into sterilized jars to about half an inch from top. Seal and store in a cool, dark, dry place.

Apricot marmalade

Ingredients:
8 pounds perfect, ripe apricots
4 pounds (8 cups) sugar
Grated rind and juice of 1 lemon

Preparation:
Wash, drain, and pit apricots. Cut half of them into small pieces; put the remainder through a food mill or sieve. Put the diced and sieved apricots in a saucepan (do *not* use aluminum), add lemon juice and grated lemon rind, and place over heat. Boil gently for several minutes, removing froth with a spoon. Stir in sugar, and let mixture come to a boil again. Boil slowly until marmalade thickens, stirring occasionally, for about 25 minutes. When marmalade seems thick enough, remove the pan from heat and pour its contents immediately into sterilized jars. Seal and store jars in cool, dry place.

Apricots in marsala syrup

Ingredients:
2¾ cups sugar
2 cups water
2 cups dry Marsala wine
Juice and rind of 1 lemon
1 pinch of ground cinnamon
2 whole cloves
6 pounds perfect, not overly ripe apricots

Preparation:
First boil sugar and water for a few minutes until sugar has dissolved. Remove this syrup from heat and add Marsala, lemon juice, several twists of lemon rind, cinnamon, and cloves. Let cool. Meanwhile, clean the apricots carefully or wash them quickly in cold water and place them in fresh air to dry. With a sharp knife, carefully open them half way or enough to remove pits. Close apricots and arrange them in sterilized jars. After jars have been filled and Marsala syrup has cooled, cover apricots to three-quarters of jar contents with this liquid, which must not be less than half an inch from the rim. Seal jars and sterilize them in a water bath (see page 9) for 10 minutes for half pints, 15 minutes for pints, and 20 minutes for 1½ pints and quarts.

Apricots preserved in alcohol

Ingredients:
1¾ cups sugar
2 cups water
1 twist of lemon rind
4 pounds not overly ripe appricots
2¼ cups 180-proof (90%) grain alcohol, about

Preparation:
In a large saucepan (do not use aluminum), bring water and sugar to a boil, adding lemon rind. After it begins to boil, add apricots, which have been washed and punctured in several places with a needle. Boil apricots gently for 5 minutes. Do not allow them to overcook, or they will become mushy. Remove apricots from the syrup and arrange them in sterilized jars. Let stand to cool. Strain residual liquid through cheesecloth, then measure and add an equal amount of alcohol. Mix well and pour into filled jars, covering apricots to within ½ inch of the top. Seal jars and store in a dry, cool place.

Apricots can be preserved in alcohol alone in the following manner: Pack raw, pitted apricots into sterilized jars, sprinkling each layer with sugar. Then pour in enough alcohol to cover. Seal and store jars in a dry, cool place.

Apricots in sugar syrup

Ingredients:
6 pounds perfect, not overly ripe apricots
1 pound (2 cups) sugar
1 quart water
1 twist of lemon rind

Preparation:
Wash apricots quickly in cold water; dry them with a clean cloth and let them stand in the sun for half an hour. Meanwhile, add sugar and lemon rind to water and boil the mixture for 2 to 3 minutes; then cool the syrup obtained. Halve the apricots, discarding pits, and arrange them in sterilized jars with their cut side down, arranging and gently pressing them so they will fill the jar as solidly as possible. When the syrup has cooled, pour it over apricots in jars to within one inch of the top layer of fruit. Seal and sterilize jars in a water bath (see page 9): 20 minutes for half pints, 25 minutes for pints, and 30 minutes for 1½ pints and quarts. For the first 10 days, check to make sure the jars have been perfectly sealed and sterilized. If syrup in any jars begins to cloud, use their contents immediately.

Apricot nectar

Ingredients:
1½ cups water
1½ pounds (3 cups) sugar
7 pounds ripe, perfect apricots
Juice of 2 lemons

Preparation:
In a saucepan boil water and sugar for two minutes, then let cool.

Carefully wash and pit apricots and force them through a sieve or food mill. You should have about 10 cups pulp. Stir in lemon juice and cold syrup. Pour nectar immediately into sterilized bottles to within ¾ of an inch from the stopper. These operations must be carried out as rapidly as possible in order to avoid any contamination of the nectar. Using a bottle capping tool, cap bottles and sterilize them for 15 to 20 minutes in a boiling water bath (see page 9). Let bottles cool in the same water. Store in a cool, dark place.

Banana marmalade

This is a highly nutritious but also highly perishable marmalade. It is, therefore, necessary to be exceedingly particular both in the choice of the fruit and its preparation.

Ingredients:
3½ cups sugar
½ cup water
2 pounds peeled bananas
Juice of 1 lemon

Preparation:
Boil sugar and water together for three to four minutes. Meanwhile, press bananas through a sieve, sprinkling banana pulp with lemon juice. Stir banana pulp into hot sugar syrup. (If you are making a very large quantity, puree the bananas little by little and add to hot syrup; this will keep pulp from darkening.) Boil over low heat stirring constantly to prevent sticking. As soon as marmalade has thickened to the right consistency, pour it hot into sterilized jars. Sprinkle surface of marmalade with sugar. Seal and sterilize jars in a boiling water bath (see page 9) for about ten minutes. Store in a cool, dry place.

Banana liqueur

Ingredients:
1 pound peeled bananas
1 pound (2 cups) sugar
1 cup Cointreau
3 whole cloves
1 pinch ground cinnamon
Grated rind of 1 lemon
2 cups grain alcohol

Preparation:
Cut bananas into half inch slices and arrange slices in layers in large sterilized glass jar, sprinkling a layer of sugar between each layer of bananas. Add Cointreau, close jar and let it stand in the sun for about ten days. Add cloves, cinnamon, lemon rind and alcohol and stir gently but thoroughly. Close jar and steep in cellar for about a month. Then pour through a fine strainer lined with a double thickness cheesecloth. Pour into sterilized bottles with an airtight closure. Store in a cool, dry place. Do not serve sooner than two to three months.

This recipe yields a rather sweet liqueur that is highly alcoholic. It is an excellent flavoring for fruit cups and ice cream.

Bilberries (or blueberries) in syrup

Ingredients:
5 pounds bilberries (or blueberries)
Rind of 1 lemon, in large pieces
1 quart water
1½ pounds (3 cups) sugar
Juice of 1 lemon

Preparation:
Place cleaned but not washed bilberries in sterilized jars, adding a piece of lemon rind to each jar. In a pot combine water and sugar and boil for three to four minutes. Stir in lemon juice. Pour hot syrup into jars, covering bilberries to a little more than three-quarters full. Seal jars and sterilize in a boiling water bath (see page 9) for twenty minutes. Store in a cool, dark, dry place.

Out of season they may be used in fruit cups, served over ice cream or to make fruit soup.

Bilberry and currant syrup

Ingredients:
2½ pounds each bilberries (or blueberries) and currants
4 pounds (8 cups) sugar
Rind of 1 lemon in large pieces
Juice of 1 lemon

Preparation:
Press bilberries and currants through a double thickness cheesecloth into a glass bowl. They should yield about four cups juice. Stir in sugar, lemon rind and juice. Let stand for two hours. Pour mixture into an untinned copper pot and boil for two minutes, stirring and skimming foam. Remove lemon rind. Pour syrup hot into sterilized bottles. Cap with a bottle capper and store in a cool, dark, dry place.

In the summer it is delicious for making cold beverages; in the winter it adds flavor to fruit cups.

Bilberries in maraschino

Ingredients:
2 pounds perfect bilberries (or blueberries)
2 pounds (4 cups) sugar
Rind of 1 lemon, in large pieces
Juice of 1 lemon
1 cup good maraschino liqueur, about

Preparation:
Clean but do not wash bilberries. In a bowl mix bilberries gently with sugar, using a wooden spoon. Pour berries and sugar into sterilized jars, adding a piece of lemon rind and some of the lemon juice to each jar. Seal jars and let stand for a day. The next day cover berries with maraschino. Seal jars and place in hot sun for two hours a day for a week, turning jars upside down occasionally to mix contents. Store in a cool, dark, dry place.

The berries may be served at the end of the meal as an aid to digestion, like cherries or wild cherries in alcohol. They may also be served as a dessert garnish or added to fruit cups.

Bilberry jam

Bilberry jam diluted with a bit of brandy makes an excellent sauce to serve with turkey, duck and other fowl.

Ingredients:
2 pounds wild bilberries (huckleberries or blueberries)
1 pound (2 cups) sugar
Grated rind and juice of 1 lemon

Preparation:
Wild bilberries are the most flavorful and therefore the best for making jam. Rinse berries in a colander with cold water. Drain. Put berries in a pottery bowl and pour over the sugar, lemon rind and juice. Mix gently and set aside, covered, for one day. The next day put them in a pot not made of aluminum and bring to a boil very slowly. Skim foam and stir frequently, for jam has a tendency to stick to the bottom of pot. When jam is thick and smooth, pour it hot into sterilized jars. Seal and store in a cool, dark, dry place.

Blackberries in syrup

Ingredients:
2 pounds ripe, perfect wild blackberries
Grated rind and juice of 1 lemon
1 pound (2 cups) sugar
1½ cups water

Preparation:
Clean berries but do not wash. Put berries in sterilized jars. Add some lemon rind and juice to each jar. Tap jars lightly on a dishcloth so berries are snug and jars well-filled. In a pot combine sugar and water and boil for three minutes. While still boiling pour syrup over blackberries to within three-quarters of the top of jar. Seal jars immediately and sterilize in a boiling water bath (see page 9) for ten minutes. Store in a cool, dark, dry place.

Wild blackberry jam

Ingredients:
5 pounds perfect, ripe blackberries
3 pounds (6 cups) sugar
½ cup water
Grated rind of 1 lemon
Juice of 2 lemons

Preparation:
Place blackberries in a colander and rinse quickly with cold water. Drain and dry berries on paper towels. In a pot combine sugar and water and bring to a boil. Lower heat and boil gently for two to three minutes. Pour berries into boiling syrup, stirring them in well and letting them come to a boil. Set pot aside for four hours. Stir in lemon rind. Bring to a boil and stir and skim foam. Boil slowly until thick. Stir in lemon juice and reheat to boiling. Pour while hot into sterilized jars. Seal and store in a cool, dark, dry place.

Blackberry jelly

Ingredients:
4 pounds perfect, ripe blackberries, but include a few that are still red
1 pound peeled, sliced apples
Grated rind of 1 lemon
Juice of 2 lemons
1 piece vanilla bean, 2 inches long
3½ pounds (7 cups) sugar

Preparation:
Put washed and drained berries in an untinned copper pot. Add apples, lemon rind and juice of one of the lemons. Bring to a boil over high heat, skimming foam and stirring constantly. Add vanilla. Let boil for eight to ten minutes, crushing the berries and apples into a pulp. Press hot mixture through double thickness cheesecloth, pressing pulp vigorously to extract all juice. Replace in pot and stir in sugar and remaining lemon juice. Bring to a boil slowly, stirring and skimming foam. Boil for about fifteen to twenty minutes, or until a drop on a cold plate becomes firm. Pour while hot into sterilized jars. Seal and store in a cool, dark, dry place.

Wild blackberry syrup

Ingredients:
3½ pounds wild blackberries
3½ pounds (7 cups) sugar
Grated rind and juice of 1 lemon

Preparation:
Press cleaned berries through a double thickness cheesecloth to extract juice. The yield should be about 1 quart juice. Pour juice into a glass or ceramic bowl and let stand for a day and a half, stirring occasionally. Pour juice into a pot and stir in sugar, grated lemon rind and juice. Boil for two minutes, skimming foam. Let cool. Pour into sterilized bottles and cap with a bottle capper. Store in a cool, dark, dry place.

Cherry marmalade

Ingredients:
11 pounds Bing (dark-sweet) cherries
7 pounds (14 cups) sugar
Several cherry leaves (optional)

Preparation:
Stem, wash and pit cherries. Pour cherries into a large pot (preferably of untinned copper) and stir in sugar. Bring to a boil, stirring constantly to prevent sticking. Boil gently and, if necessary, skim foam. Cook until desired consistency. Test for doneness by letting a drop of the mixture fall on a plate; if it becomes firm and jam-like on cooling, remove marmalade from heat and pour it hot into sterilized jars. Put a couple of cherry leaves in each jar. Seal immediately and store in a cool, dark, dry place.

Cornelian cherry marmalade

This marmalade or relish is served especially with boiled meats and roasted game birds.

Ingredients:
3 pounds perfectly ripe Cornelian (bright red, sour) cherries
2 cups dry white wine
Rind of ½ lemon, in large pieces
2 green apples, peeled, cored and sliced
12 ounces (1½ cups) sugar
½ cup honey
Juice of ½ lemon
1 pinch ground cinnamon

Preparation:
Remove stems and wash in cold water. Drain, do not pit, and put in a large pot. Add wine, lemon rind and apples. Bring to a boil gently, stirring occasionally and skimming foam. When cherries are soft, remove from heat and press them through a sieve or food mill. Pour puree, which will be quite liquid and should weigh about two pounds, back into pot. Stir in sugar, honey, lemon juice and cinnamon. Cook at a slow boil, stirring until marmalade has thickened to a consistency of a thickish puree (see CHERRY MARMALADE). Remove from heat and pour immediately into small sterilized jars. Seal and store in cool, dark, dry place.

Cherry jam with honey

Ingredients:
2 pounds ripe, perfect and pitted Bing (dark-sweet) cherries
1 pound 12 ounces (3¼ cups) honey
Rind of 1 lemon, in large pieces
Juice of ½ lemon

Preparation:
Wash and pit cherries. Place into a pot, preferably of untinned copper. Add honey and lemon rind. Bring slowly to a boil, stirring with a wooden spoon and skimming foam. Allow mixture to boil for about ten minutes until cherries thicken and look like any other jam. Remove from heat and stir in lemon juice. Remove lemon rind. Pour hot jam into sterilized jars, sealing them immediately. Store jam in a cool, dark, dry place.

Sugared (or crystallized) cherries

Sugared cherries are used to garnish cakes and other desserts.

Ingredients:
2 pounds sour cherries, not too ripe but in perfect condition
2 cups your favorite liquor (rum, brandy, grappa or vodka, etc.)
2 ounces gum arabic (sold in bakery or confectioners' supply houses)
6 tablespoons water
About 1 pound (2 cups) sugar

Preparation:
Remove pits from cherries carefully to avoid damage to the fruit. Use a cherry pitter. Cover cherries with whatever liquor you prefer and let stand for two days. Drain (save that liquor and use it in your drinks) and spread on paper towels and let dry.

Heat gum arabic and water over low heat until hot but not boiling. Place cherries in solution for a few minutes, stirring them to coat all cherries. Remove cherries, drain well. Place sugar in a large flat pan. While cherries are still warm, roll them in sugar and leave them there for two days. Move them about gently from time to time until they are well covered with sugar.

Keep them in wide-mouthed sterilized glass containers that are not too large. Seal. Use the cherries quickly as they will last only two to three months in a cool, dark, dry place.

Dried cherries

Ingredients:
Mature, perfect Bing (dark-sweet) cherries (preferably large ones)

Preparation:
Put cherries in colander large enough to hold fruit. Place in sink. Pour boiling water over cherries allowing them to drain well. Spread cherries out to dry on paper towels in a single layer. Arrange dry cherries on a screen or rack so that they are not touching one another and air can circulate around them. Put them in the sun during the hottest hours of the day, occasionally turning them until they have become perfectly dried. This will take a few days.

Store them in a covered tin in a cool, dark, dry place.

Before cooking dried cherries, wash to remove any dust and soak for three or four hours in cold water. Pour them with soaking water into a large pot and cook them until plump and tender.

If desired, grated rind of 1 lemon may be added and then cook.

Cherries in vinegar

Cherries in vinegar are served like olives as an hors d'oeuvre.

Ingredients:
7 pounds, firm, sour cherries
10 small cherry leaves
½ cup sugar
2 whole cloves
1 stick cinnamon
1 pinch ground ginger
2½ quarts white vinegar of best quality

Preparation:
Wash and dry cherries. Cut stem to within one sixteenth of an inch. Place cherries and leaves in a colander and dip them into boiling water for thirty seconds. Drain and spread out on a cloth to dry.

In a large pot, combine sugar, spices and vinegar. Heat only until sugar is dissolved. Do not boil. Cook and then strain.

Arrange cherries in sterilized jars, taking care not to leave empty spaces and to fill the jar as tightly as possible. Between the layers of cherries place cherry leaves. Cover cherries with vinegar. Seal jars and store in a cool, dark, dry place.

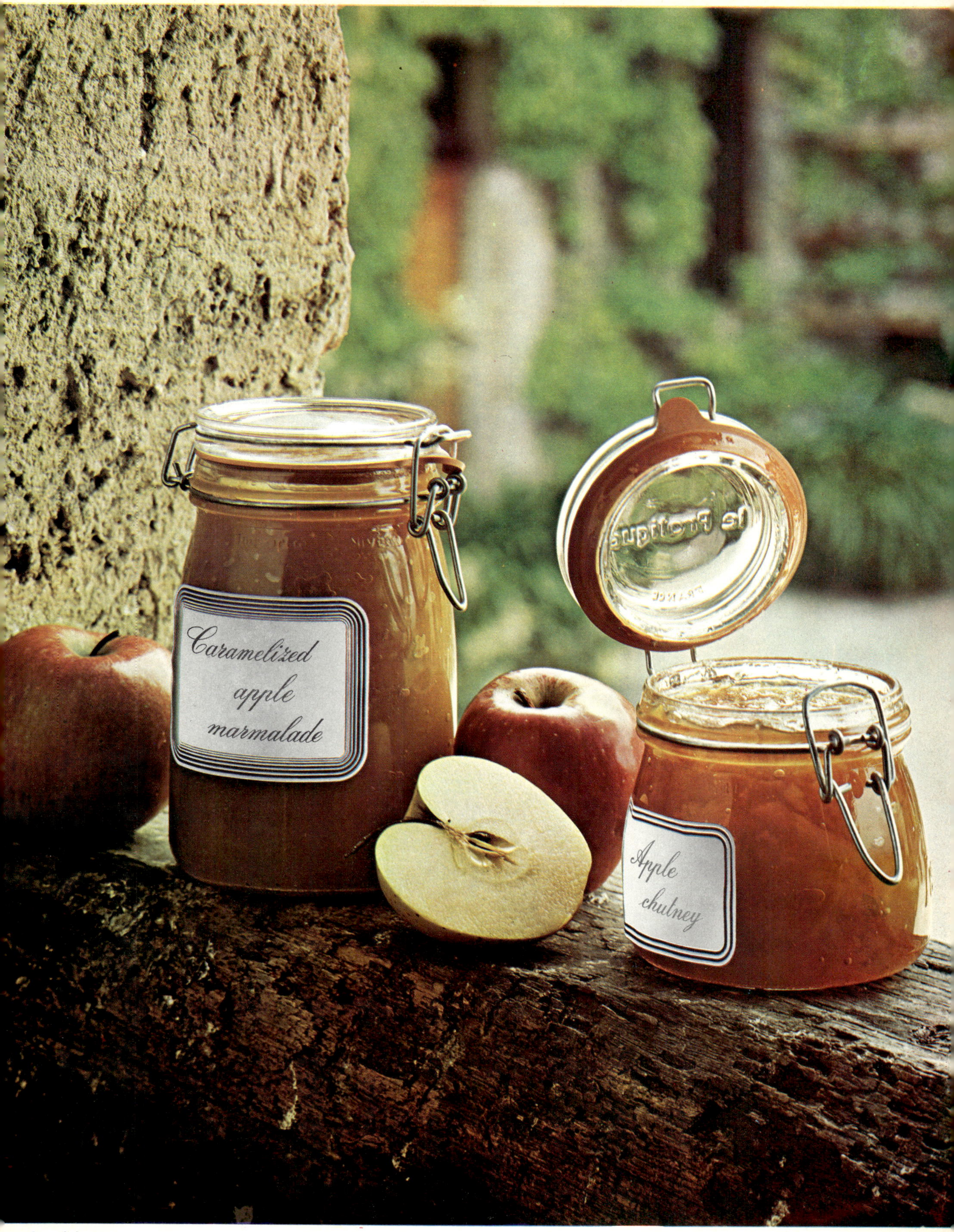
Caramelized apple marmalade
Apple chutney

Apricots in sugar syrup
Apricots in alcohol
Apricot marmalade
Apricots in Marsala syrup

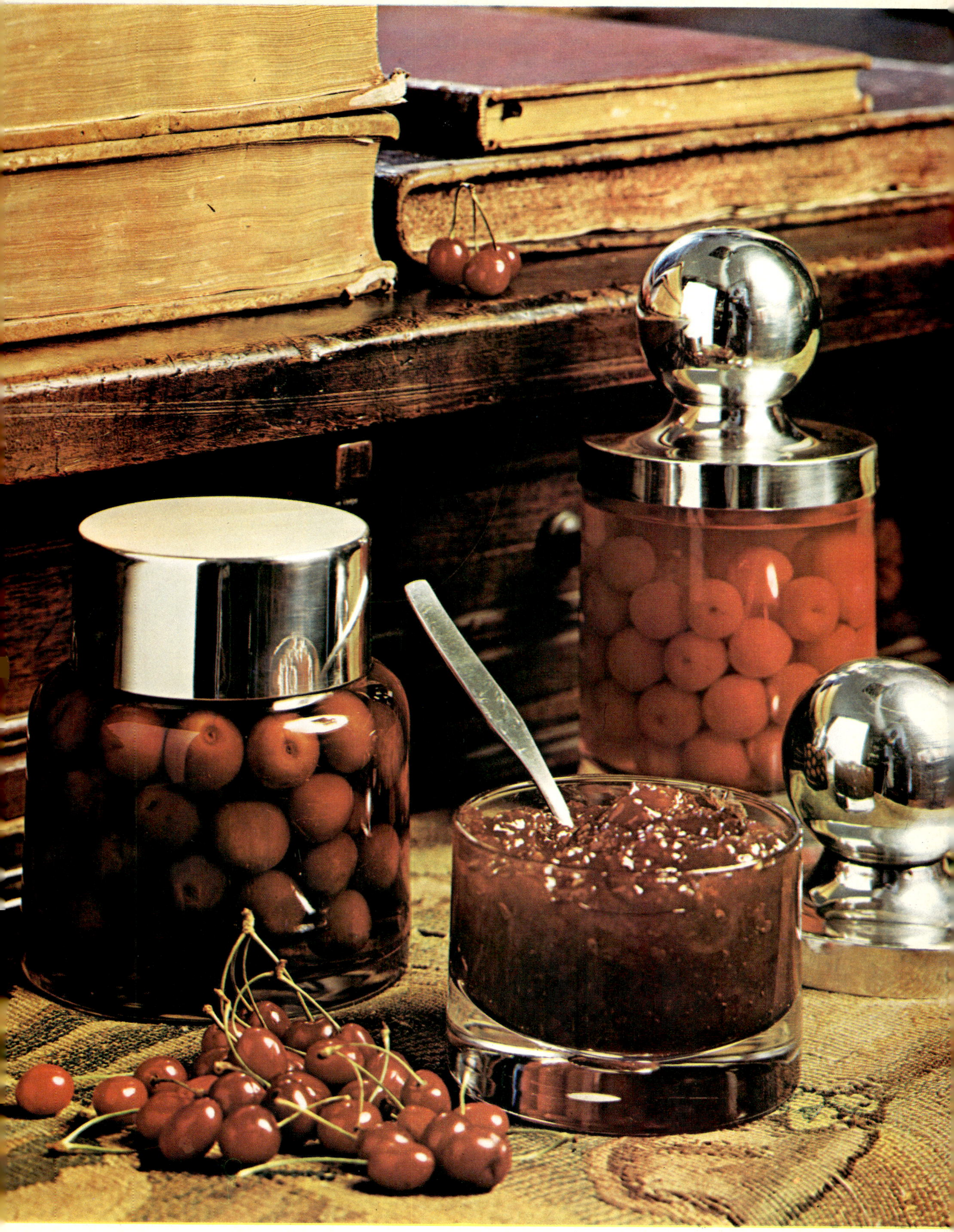

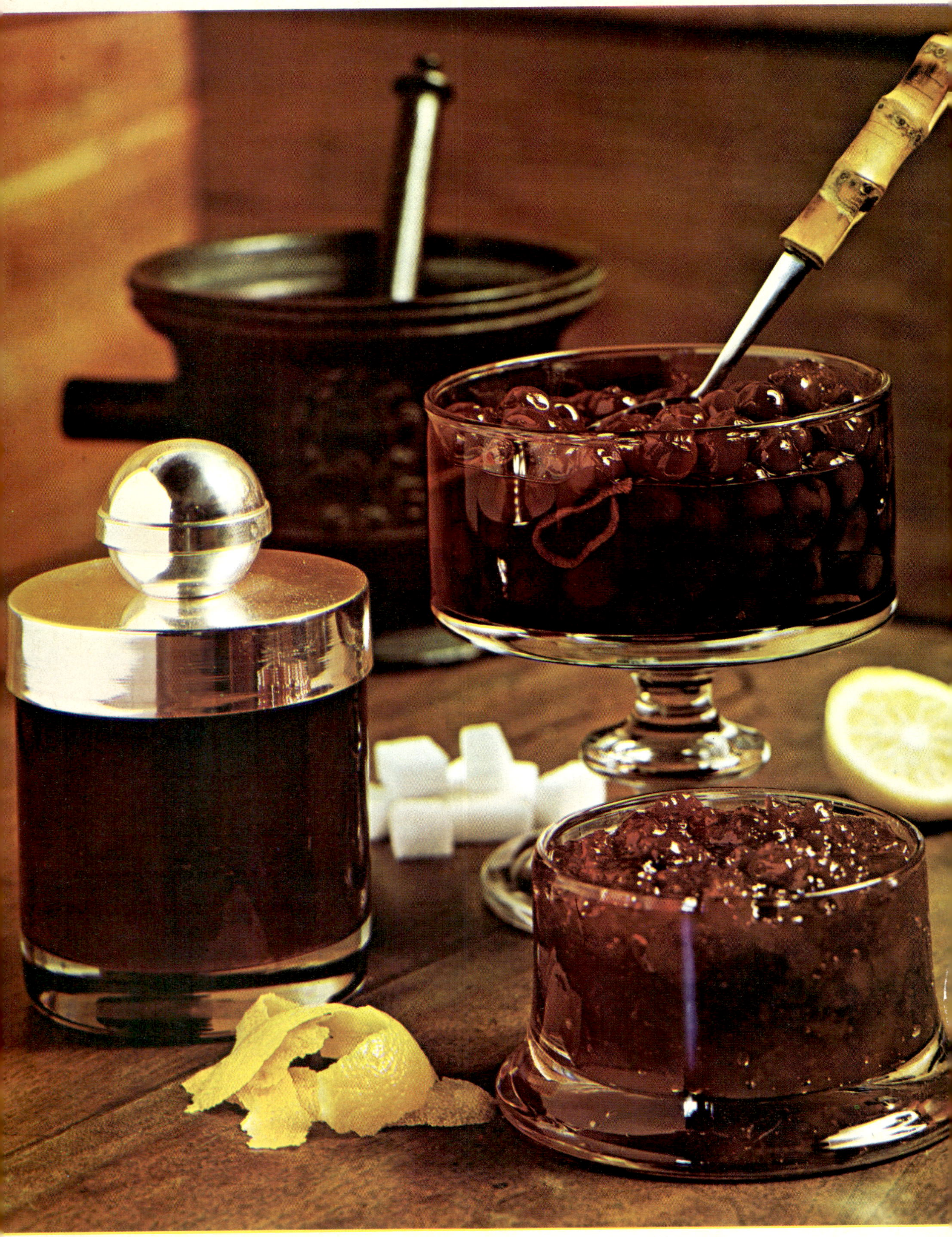

Bittersweet cherries "dolce garbo"

Served with boiled meat, duck, turkey, etc., and also as an hors d'oeuvre, as with olives.

Ingredients:
2 pounds soft Bing (dark-sweet) cherries
1 quart best quality white vinegar
1¼ cups sugar
10 cloves
Grated rind of 1 lemon

Preparation:
Wash cherries and cut stems to within a sixteenth of an inch. Dry cherries and then puncture them in two or three places with sewing needle. Put them into sterilized jars.

Boil vinegar with sugar, cloves and lemon rind for fifteen minutes. Cool until lukewarm. Strain and pour over cherries covering them completely. Seal jars and store in a cool, dark, dry place. Let stand one month before eating.

Cherries in red wine

Ingredients:
5 pounds ripe, perfect Bing (dark-sweet) cherries
1 quart red wine
2 cups water
1¾ pounds (3½ cups) sugar
Grated rind of 1 lemon
4 cinnamon sticks

Preparation:
Wash cherries and remove stems carefully to prevent tearing away skin. Pack cherries into sterilized jars. Boil wine, water, sugar, lemon rind and cinnamon sticks for five minutes. Strain. Cool syrup and pour it over cherries until syrup is one inch below top of cherries. Seal jars and sterilize them for fifteen to twenty minutes in a boiling water bath (see page 9). Cool jars in water in which they were sterilized; then check to see that covers are tight. If not, tighten lids and sterilize again in a boiling water bath for fifteen to twenty minutes. Store jars in a cool, dark, dry place.

Cherry nectar

Ingredients:
5 pounds sour cherries
1 ¾ pounds (3 ½ cups) sugar
Several one-inch pieces stick cinnamon
Several whole cloves

Preparation:
Select one pound of softest cherries. Wash and pit them and press them through a sieve or food mill. Set pulp aside. Break open pits, remove seeds. Mince seeds. Cut stems of remaining cherries to within an eighth of an inch. Wash and drain cherries thoroughly. Place cherries in sterilized jars, sprinkling each layer with sugar. Add a clove, some minced cherry seed and a piece of cinnamon to each jar. Pour cherry pulp over cherries and seal jars. Keep in a cool, dark, dry place.

At first cherries will float, then gradually as pulp becomes alcoholic, cherries will sink to the bottom of the jar. Let stand three months before eating.

Cherries in syrup

Ingredients:
7 pounds hard, ripe, perfect sour cherries
1 pound (2 cups) sugar
1 quart water
Rind of 1 lemon, in large pieces
Several drops maraschino liqueur or cherry brandy

Preparation:
Wash cherries in cold water and drain, being careful not to bruise cherries. Remove stems and spread them out to dry on paper towels. After they have dried, place them in sterilized jars.

Prepare syrup by bringing sugar, water and a few pieces of lemon rind to a boil. Let boil for three to four minutes and then cool. Strain syrup and pour over cherries in jar, covering them to 1 inch below the top. If you want cherries to have a more pronounced aroma, add a drop or two of maraschino or cherry brandy to each jar. Seal jars and sterilize them for twenty to thirty minutes in a boiling water bath (see page 9).

Store in a cool, dark, dry place.

Cherries in liquor

Ingredients:
2 pounds firm, perfect Bing (dark-sweet) cherries
1 pound (2 cups) sugar
½ cup water
Grappa, vodka or other brandy
Several pieces lemon rind
Several small cherry leaves

Preparation:
Wash cherries. Cut stem off to within a sixteenth of an inch. Let cherries dry on paper towels. Arrange them in sterilized jars.

Prepare syrup by boiling sugar and water for three minutes. Cool and pour over cherries filling jars half way. Add grappa or brandy to cover. Add a piece of lemon rind and a few small cherry leaves to each jar. Seal jars and store in a cool, dark, dry place.

It is advisable to wait for at least three months before tasting cherries to allow them to absorb the alcohol.

Wild cherries in rum

Cherries preserved in this manner may be used to decorate desserts or eaten as an aid to digestion; if the liquor is not used in other recipies, it may be drunk as a beverage.

Ingredients:
6 pounds perfect, not overly ripe wild cherries
1¼ cups sugar
Cinnamon sticks
Pieces of lemon peel
Light rum
Grain alcohol

Preparation:
Wash cherries and dry with a clean cloth, removing stems or cutting them off about an eighth of an inch from end of fruit. Put cherries in well-washed and perfectly dry jars. Divide sugar among jars. Add 1 cinnamon stick and 1 piece of lemon peel to each jar. Pour rum into sterilized jars to within an inch of top of cherries, then add enough alcohol to cover them completely. Seal jars and place them in sunlight for a week. Once each day gently shake and turn jars upside down so that cherries are moved and sugar dissolved. At end of week, store them in a cool, dark place. The cherries may be eaten after a month.

Wild cherry jam

Ingredients:
7 pounds ripe, perfect and pitted wild cherries
3 pounds (6 cups) sugar
½ cup water
Grated rind and juice of 1 lemon
¾ cup maraschino liqueur

Preparation:
Wash and pit cherries. Put sugar and water in a saucepan large enough to hold cherries. Bring to a boil, stirring occasionally to prevent sticking. Add cherries, lemon rind and juice. Stir mixture and let boil slowly, skimming foam from top with a spoon. When syrup has thickened to 238°F. (soft ball) on a candy thermometer, (a couple of drops on a plate held on an incline should run down very slowly,) remove saucepan from heat. Stir in maraschino and pour hot preserves into sterilized jars. Seal jars and keep them in a cool, dark place.

Wild cherry jelly

Ingredients:
5 pounds ripe, perfect, pitted wild cherries
1 pound fresh currants
1 quart water
Grated rind and juice of 1 lemon
5 pounds (10 cups) sugar

Preparation:
Wash and pit cherries into a stainless steel or enamel pot (aluminum must not be used). Add stemmed currants, water, and lemon rind. Bring to a boil and boil slowly for ten minutes, mixing and skimming foam occasionally with a wooden spoon. Remove from heat after ten minutes. Line a strainer with a double thickness of cheesecloth. Allow fruit to drip juice without pressing into a large bowl. Pour strained mixture back into pot. Stir in sugar and lemon juice. Bring to a boil. Skim foam from mixture until jelly has taken on a fine blood-red color. Remove from heat and pour into sterilized jars, immediately sealing them airtight. Store in a cool, dark place.

Candied wild cherries in rum

Ingredients:
6 pounds ripe, perfect wild cherries
1 cup sugar
Juice and grated rind of 1 lemon
2 cups dark rum

Preparation:
Wash cherries well. Pick out about a pound of the ripest and softest cherries. Remove stems from remaining cherries and pack them in sterilized jars to within an inch of the top. Pass the pound of soft cherries through a sieve or food mill. Add sugar, lemon juice and lemon rind to pulp. With a wooden spoon, mix until sugar is dissolved. Pour syrup over cherries in jars. Then cover completely with rum. Seal jars, shake to blend and store them in a cool, dark place. The cherries may be used after about a month. The highly alcoholic syrup can be drunk as an aid to digestion.

Cherries preserved in this fashion may be flavored with bits of cinnamon stick or whole cloves placed in jars after covering cherries with rum.

Wild cherry syrup

Ingredients:
4 pounds very ripe, perfect wild cherries
Grated rind and juice of 1 lemon
4 pounds (8 cups) sugar

Preparation:
Wash and stem cherries. Force cherries through a sieve or food mill into a glass container. You should have about 6 cups pulp. Reserve 20 of the pits. Leave container covered in a cool place for a day and a half, stirring occasionally. Crack open reserved cherry pits. Remove seeds and mince them. Pour pulp into a pot, adding cherry seeds. Bring to a boil, adding lemon rind. As soon as pulp has come to a boil, remove it from heat and strain it through cheesecloth. Pour it into the pot again and stir in sugar and lemon juice. Bring it to a boil again, stirring and skimming foam for not more than two minutes. Remove from heat and cool mixture quickly by standing pot in a bowl of ice water. Pour into sterilized bottles and seal.

Sterilize filled bottles for five to ten minutes in a boiling water bath (see page 9). Cool and store in a cool, dry place.

Chestnut or marron glaces

Ingredients:
2 pounds large and perfect marrons or chestnuts
2 pounds (4 cups) sugar
2 cups water
1 tablespoon glucose (sold in drug stores) or clear corn syrup

Preparation:
The making of marron glaces is rather simple; however, both skill and patience are required.

Cook chestnuts (see CHESTNUT BALLS IN RUM). Meanwhile, in a stainless steel or copper pan large enough to hold marrons in a single layer, stir sugar, water and glucose. As soon as this syrup boils, remove it from heat, but keep it warm. Drain and peel marrons while warm, removing both outer and inner skins. A few will crumble, but you should end with about 1¼ pounds of whole chestnuts.

As chestnuts are peeled, place them in the warm syrup one by one. After all the chestnuts have been placed in the syrup, cover pot and let stand for a day. Meanwhile the sugar will penetrate chestnuts. The next day, warm syrup with chestnuts over low heat. Heat until it just starts to boil. Remove from heat and take out chestnuts one by one with a fork and place them in a sieve so that syrup that drains from them may be collected. Now return all the syrup to pan. Boil for two minutes. Remove from heat and put chestnuts back in syrup carefully. Cover pot and let stand for another day.

On the next day repeat the operation: After reheating the syrup just to the boiling point, remove chestnuts; boil syrup for two minutes, return chestnuts to pot when syrup is hot, cover and let stand for another day.

Repeat this operation two more times, making sure, however, that syrup which has to penetrate the marrons does not become too thick or crystallize. This can be determined by its hardness when cold. Should it be hard as lollipop candy, add a few drops of hot water to syrup while boiling it without the chestnuts.

After 4 days heat syrup in order to remove chestnuts which by now should be thoroughly impregnated by the sugar. Place chestnuts in a single layer on a rack set over wax paper. Leave to dry for two days, then pack in an airtight container. Store in a cool, dry place.

Chestnut preserve in brandy

Ingredients:
3 pounds chestnuts
Fennel, some seeds or a stalk
1 bay leaf
2 pounds (4 cups) sugar
1½ cups water
1 pinch grated lemon rind
1 pinch grated orange rind
¼ cup brandy for each 4 cups chestnut puree

Preparation:
Cook chestnuts (see CHESTNUT BALLS IN RUM) with fennel (seeds or stalk) and bay leaf. Drain and peel while warm. Place in a pot (not aluminum) and stir in sugar, water and lemon and orange rinds. Bring to a boil slowly, stirring carefully to keep chestnuts from sticking. While stirring crush chestnuts. Continue to cook slowly and when chestnuts have been almost reduced to a pulp and reached the consistency of jam, remove from heat and measure. Stir in required amount of brandy. Pour immediately into sterilized jars. Pour ¼-inch thick layer of additional brandy over preserve in jars and seal. Store in cool, dry place.

Chestnut marmalade with rum

Ingredients:
3 pounds chestnuts or 1 pound 12 ounces dried, shelled chestnuts
1 orange rind in large pieces
1 lemon rind in large pieces
3½ cups sugar
1 cup water
⅓ cup dark rum for each 4 cups chestnut puree

Preparation:
Cook fresh chestnuts (see CHESTNUT BALLS IN RUM) with orange and lemon rinds. If you are using dried chestnuts, let them soak for half a day in cold water to cover. Drain, add lightly salted cold water and cook with orange and lemon rind. When fresh chestnuts are easily pierced, drain and peel while warm. Press fresh or dried chestnuts through a sieve or food mill. The resultant puree should weigh about 2 pounds (4 cups). Put puree into a stainless steel or copper pot, stirring in sugar and water. Bring to a boil, very slowly, stirring and skimming foam. When chestnuts are the consistency of a thickish puree, stir in rum. Remove marmalade from heat and pour it into sterilized jars. Seal jars and store in cool, dry place.

Chestnut balls in rum

These are not really and truly chestnuts, but exquisite delicacies that may be eaten like chocolates or used to decorate sweets.

Ingredients:
1 pound perfect chestnuts
1 cup sugar
¼ cup water
2 tablespoons cocoa
⅓ cup rum or brandy
½ teaspoon vanilla
1 teaspoon grated lemon rind
Pinch cinnamon

Preparation:
Cook chestnuts in a large quantity of water until easily pierced and tender. Drain. Peel, and while they are still warm force them through a sieve, food mill or potato ricer into a pot. You should end with about 11 ounces of puree. Dissolve ¼ cup of the sugar in water. Stir this syrup, cocoa, rum, vanilla and lemon rind into chestnut puree. Mix rapidly so that puree does not become lumpy. Bring mixture to a boil, stirring constantly. The paste should be very thick and rather smooth. Remove from heat and let cool until warm enough to handle. Keep paste warm while shaping chestnuts balls. Mix remaining sugar with cinnamon. Using the palms of the hands, make balls of chestnut paste about the size of hazel nuts. Roll each ball in sugar and cinnamon mixture and place on waxed paper in a single layer. Leave exposed to dry air for a couple of days or until firm and dry. Store in airtight containers in a cool, dry place.

Chestnuts in syrup

Marrons are excellent for decorating cakes or other sweets. They are also very good served as a dessert with whipped cream.

Ingredients:
6 pounds large, perfect chestnuts (marrons)
Rind of 1 orange
Fennel (several seeds or a stalk)
4 cups water
3½ cups sugar
Rind and juice of 1 lemon
Several ½-inch pieces vanilla bean

Preparation:
Boil unpeeled chestnuts in a large pot of water to which has been added rind of an orange in large pieces and a few seeds (or a stalk) of fennel. While marrons are cooking, prepare syrup by boiling water, sugar and lemon juice for two to three minutes. Remove from heat and cool. When marrons are easily pierced and tender, drain and cool. Carefully and patiently peel away both outer and inner peels. Add marrons one by one to sterilized jars. Don't be concerned if some of them break. Add a piece of lemon rind and a piece of vanilla bean to each jar. Cover marrons with cooled syrup. Seal jars and sterilize in a boiling water bath (see page 9) for twenty minutes. Store in cool, dry place.

Plain currant jelly

Ingredients:
6½ pounds currants removed from bunch
7 pounds (14 cups) sugar
Rind of 2 lemons, in large pieces
Juice of 2 lemons

Preparation:
Wash, prepare and dry currants as in CURRANTS IN GRAPPA. Press berries through a very fine sieve or a double thickness cheesecloth, crushing them with a wooden spoon. The juice should be collected in a large bowl of glass or earthenware. Stir in sugar, lemon rind and juice. Mix with a wooden spoon and set aside for two hours, stirring often until sugar is dissolved. Remove lemon rind. Pour into sterilized jars and leave them exposed in the sun, protected only by a layer of cheesecloth, for three days. Altogether, the jars must remain in hot sun for fifteen to twenty hours. Finally, seal jars and store them in a cool, dark, dry place.

Rose compote of currants

The bunches of currants preserved in this manner are served with roast game.

Ingredients:
5 pounds fresh currants in bunches
3 cups white vinegar
2 cups dry white wine
1 pound, 12 ounces (3½ cups) sugar
4 whole juniper berries
Grated rind and juice of ½ lemon
1 handfull rose petals

Preparation:
Select the best bunches of currants; discard any spoiled berries. Wash in lots of cold water, but don't let berries remain in water very long. Drain and spread bunches out on a cloth to dry in the open air. When currants are dry, arrange them in sterilized jars. In a pot boil vinegar, wine, sugar, juniper berries and grated lemon rind and juice. Boil for about three minutes then remove from heat and stir in rose petals, already washed and with yellowish part removed. Cover pot and let cool. Strain syrup through a sieve and pour over currants in jars, covering them. Seal and store in a cool, dark, dry place. After about a week check to make sure that the level of the marinade still remains over the currants. If not, open jar and add white vinegar until berries are covered. Seal again and store.

Bittersweet currant sauce

This sauce is a good accompaniment to roast game.

Ingredients:
3½ pounds red, ripe, unblemished currants
2 cups red or white wine vinegar of best quality
1 pinch ground cinnamon
2 whole cloves
Grated rind of 1 lemon
1½ pounds (3 cups) sugar

Preparation:
Wash, prepare and dry currants as in CURRANTS IN GRAPPA. Place berries in a glass or ceramic bowl. Pour vinegar over currants and add cloves, cinnamon and lemon rind. Let stand for two hours, then pour the whole mixture in a pot and bring it to a violent boil while skimming foam. Reduce heat and boil slowly for about fifteen minutes, skimming foam constantly. Stir in sugar and continue to boil slowly, skimming foam and stirring until sauce reaches a consistency a little less thick than that of jam. Taste, and if you prefer the sauce a little sweeter, add more sugar. Pour hot sauce into sterilized jars. Seal and store in a cool, dark, dry place.

Currants in grappa

Ingredients:
3½ pounds unblemished and not too ripe fresh currants
½ pound (1 cup) sugar
1 quart grappa, vodka, or other brandy

Preparation:
Wash currants and with the fingers carefully pull them from the stems without breaking berries. Let them dry on paper towels for one hour. Arrange them in sterilized jars sprinkling them with sugar. Cover currants with grappa or brandy. Seal and store in a cool, dark, dry place. The currants will be ready after about two months. They may be served as an aid to digestion or to garnish fruit cups, over ice cream or slices of plain cake.

Elderberry jam

This is a little known and insufficiently appreciated preserve, though it can certainly hold its own with the others.

Ingredients:
6½ pounds elderberry bunches
5 pounds (10 cups) sugar
Grated rind and juice of 1 lemon
1¼ cups water

Preparation:
Pick bunches when elderberries are perfectly ripe and black—toward beginning of September. Wash rapidly in cold water and remove berries from the stems. Drain and let dry on paper towels. Put elderberries, sugar, lemon rind and juice and water in a pot. Bring to a boil, stirring with a wooden spoon and skimming foam. Boil slowly until mixture becomes thick and jam-like. Remove from heat and pour while hot into sterilized jars. Seal and store in a cool, dark, dry place.

In addition to its use as a jam, it is very pleasant and tasty as a refreshing drink in the heat of summer. Just mix a spoonful in a glass of ice cold water.

Elderberry syrup

Elderberry syrup is served diluted in cold water as a refreshment or in hot water as an aid to digestion.

Ingredients:
3 pounds elderberries
2½ pounds (5 cups) sugar
Juice of 1 lemon

Preparation:
Prepare berries as in ELDERBERRY JAM. Place in a glass or earthenware bowl and stir in sugar and lemon juice. Cover and let stand at room temperature in a dry place for one day. On the next day, press mixture through a stainless steel strainer or food mill. Collect juice, which should be about four cups, and bring to a boil in a pot that is not aluminum. Boil slowly and stir occasionally with a wooden spoon and skim foam. Boil until syrup reaches consistency of honey. Cool syrup quickly by putting pot into ice water, stirring constantly to keep syrup from crystallizing. When cold, pour syrup into sterilized bottles and store in a cool, dark, dry place.

Fig compote

Ingredients:
2 pounds perfect fresh figs, not too ripe
1 pound (2 cups) sugar
Grated rind and juice of 2 lemons
Dash ground cinnamon (optional)
Liquor (optional)

Preparation:
Remove stems and cut figs into halves. Place in layers in a large pot, sprinkling each layer with sugar, lemon rind and juice. Cover and let stand for a couple of hours. Bring it to a slow boil over low heat for one hour, stirring frequently with a wooden spoon to prevent sticking. Set aside for twelve hours, then boil mixture over very low heat again for one hour, stirring constantly. Cool and then put in sterilized jars. Seal jars and sterilize for ten minutes in a boiling water bath (see page 9). Keep in a cool, dark, dry place.

If you wish, you can flavor compote with cinnamon or with your favorite liquor.

Convent figs

Ingredients:
7 pounds ripe, firm, fresh figs
2½ cups walnut meats
3 pounds (6 cups) sugar
Grated rind and juice of 2 lemons
1½ cups brandy, about
Small amount water

Preparation:
Carefully wash figs, trim off stems and place them on paper towels and dry them in the sun for thirty minutes. Cut figs into halves. Press a piece of walnut in the center of each half, trying to bury it in pulp of fig. Arrange fig halves in sterilized jars tight against one another and making layers of them. Sprinkle a handful of sugar over each layer, some of the lemon rind and juice and some of the brandy. When jars are full (the last layer of figs should be at least a half-inch from top of jar) add a couple of tablespoons of boiling water to the figs so that there will be some syrup when figs are served. Seal jars and sterilize them for forty-five minutes in a boiling water bath (see page 9). Store in a cool, dark, dry place.

Dried figs in liquor

Ingredients:
Dried figs
Walnut meats cut in quarters
Sugar
Liquor (grappa, vodka, or rum)

Preparation:
In addition to regular dried figs, you can use figs that you have dried yourself by stringing a thread through the stems and hanging them up to dry in the open air in sunlight for several days.

Remove stems and cut figs in half and stuff a quarter piece of walnut meat into pulp. Try to shove nut half way into fig. Arrange figs tightly against one another in the jars with walnut downward. Sprinkle a tablespoon of sugar and 3 tablespoons liquor over each layer. Seal jar and wait a few days so that liquor can be slowly absorbed. Open jars and add enough liquor to cover figs. Seal jars and store in a cool, dark, dry place.

Fig and brandy preserve

Ingredients:
5 pounds ripe fresh figs in perfect condition
2 pounds (4 cups) sugar
Several pieces lemon rind, chopped
3 tablespoons (1½ ounces) brandy
Juice of ½ lemon

Preparation:
Remove stem from figs and peel thinly if skin is thick. Chop figs, put them in a large kettle (not an aluminum kettle, however). Let stand one hour. Add sugar, lemon rind and simmer gently, stirring constantly with a wooden spoon and skimming foam as needed. When mixture has desired thick consistency, stir in brandy and lemon juice. Continue cooking, stirring constantly until thick. Pour into sterilized jars while still hot and seal immediately. Store in a cool, dark, dry place.

Grape jam

Ingredients:
8 pounds firm, unbruised and not overly ripe grapes
4 pounds (8 cups) sugar
Juice of 1 lemon

Preparation:
Wash grapes and pull off stems. Put grapes in a pot that is not made of aluminum. Stir in sugar and lemon juice. Bring to a boil slowly, stirring and skimming foam. As grapeskins gradually float to the top, lift them off with a slotted spoon and place them into a sieve held over the pot. Press juice out of skins with the back of a spoon. Discard skins. Allow mixture to boil slowly until jam is thick. Pour hot into sterilized jars. Seal and store in a cool, dark, dry place.

Mix grape jam with some plum jam to make an excellent spread. In fact, the sweet flavor of the grape jam is made more tart with the flavor of the plum jam.

Grapes in syrup

Preserved in this way, the grapes can be used to make tarts, fruit cups and the like.

Ingredients:
8 pounds white or dark grapes (in either case they should be hard-skinned and not recently sprayed)
6 cups water
2 pounds (4 cups) sugar
Several large pieces lemon rind
Several very tender grape leaves

Preparation:
Wash bunches of grapes. With a pair of scissors snip off grapes, leaving only a sixteenth of an inch of the stems. Spread grapes on a cloth to dry in sun for about one hour. In a saucepan boil water, sugar and lemon rind for two minutes. Cool. Arrange grapes carefully in sterilized jars, discarding any that have split. To each jar add a piece of lemon rind (removed from syrup) and a well-washed grape leaf or two. Pour in hot syrup to three-quarters. Seal and sterilize in a boiling water bath (see page 9) for fifteen to twenty minutes. Store in a cool, dark, dry place.

Grapes in alcohol (or in liquor)

Ingredients:
5 pounds large white grapes with hard skins
¼ cup water
1 pound, 2 ounces (2¼ cups) sugar
1 quart pure alcohol (or brandy or other liquor) at 90 proof (45% alcohol)
4 or 5 large pieces lemon rind

Preparation:
Wash, prepare and dry grapes as in GRAPES IN SYRUP. Arrange grapes carefully in sterilized jars. In a saucepan boil water and sugar for two minutes. Cool. Pour some of the syrup into each jar, dividing it equally. Then fill jars with alcohol or whatever liquor you prefer. Add a piece of lemon rind to each jar. Seal and store in a cool, dark, dry place.

Sultana grapes in grappa

This is a very simple preparation, but highly appreciated after a good meal.

Ingredients:
2 pounds sultana grapes
Several pieces vanilla bean
Several pieces stick cinnamon
Several large pieces lemon rind
About 1 quart grappa or other brandy

Preparation:
Wash, prepare and dry grapes as in GRAPES IN SYRUP. Place grapes in sterilized jars. Add a piece of vanilla bean, a small piece of cinnamon stick and a piece of lemon rind to each jar. Cover grapes completely with grappa or other brandy. Seal and store in a cool, dark, dry place. Serve them after one month.

The same procedure may be used with dates, dried prunes, dried apricots, dried cherries, dried peaches, dried pears, etc.

Grape juice

Ingredients:
7 pounds perfect muscat grapes*
½ cup sugar
Juice of 1 lemon
½ cup honey or 1 cup wine
Dash ground cinnamon (optional)

*Can also be made with red, white or purple grapes, each yielding a different color juice.

Preparation:
Choose grapes that have just been picked. Wash grapes and remove from stems. Press grapes through a very clean sieve to extract juice and discard seeds and skins. To juice that you collect (it should run to about nine cups) add sugar, lemon juice and honey (or wine or cinnamon.) Stir until sugar is dissolved. Pour juice into sterilized bottles or jars and seal. Sterilize in a boiling water bath (see page 9) for fifteen minutes and then let cool in the water in which they were sterilized. Store in a cool, dark, dry place.

Plain grape juice

Ingredients:
7 pounds perfect white grapes
1 pound 8 ounces (3 cups) sugar

Preparation:
Wash, stem and extract juice from grapes as in GRAPE JUICE. Pour juice into a non-aluminum pot. Boil juice for five minutes. Stir in sugar. Strain juice through a clean linen cloth or double thickness cheesecloth. Cool and pour into sterilized jars or bottles. Seal and sterilize in a boiling water bath (see page 9) for fifteen to twenty minutes. Cool in water. Store in a cool, dark, dry place.

This grape juice makes a pleasant beverage in the morning with breakfast.

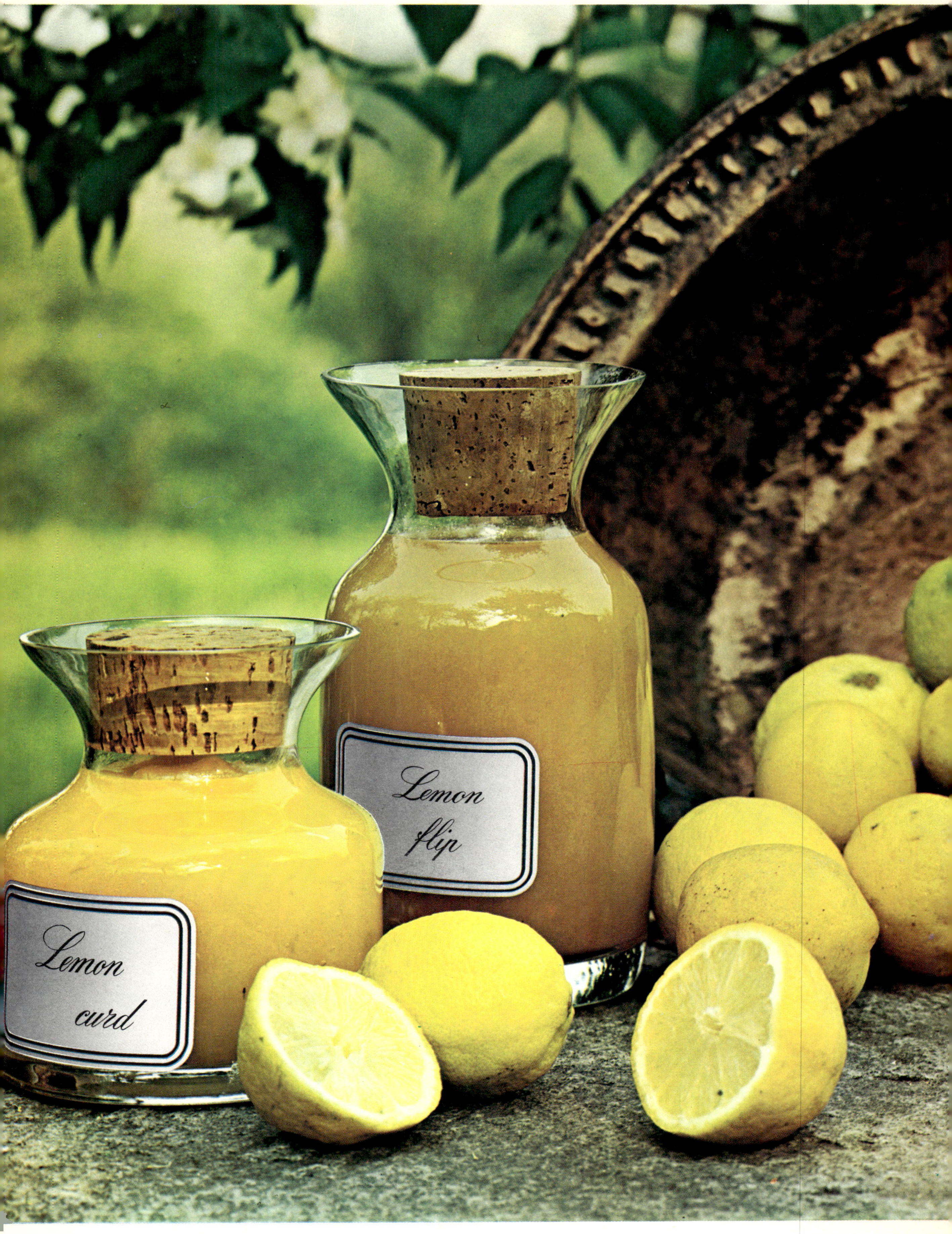
Lemon flip
Lemon curd

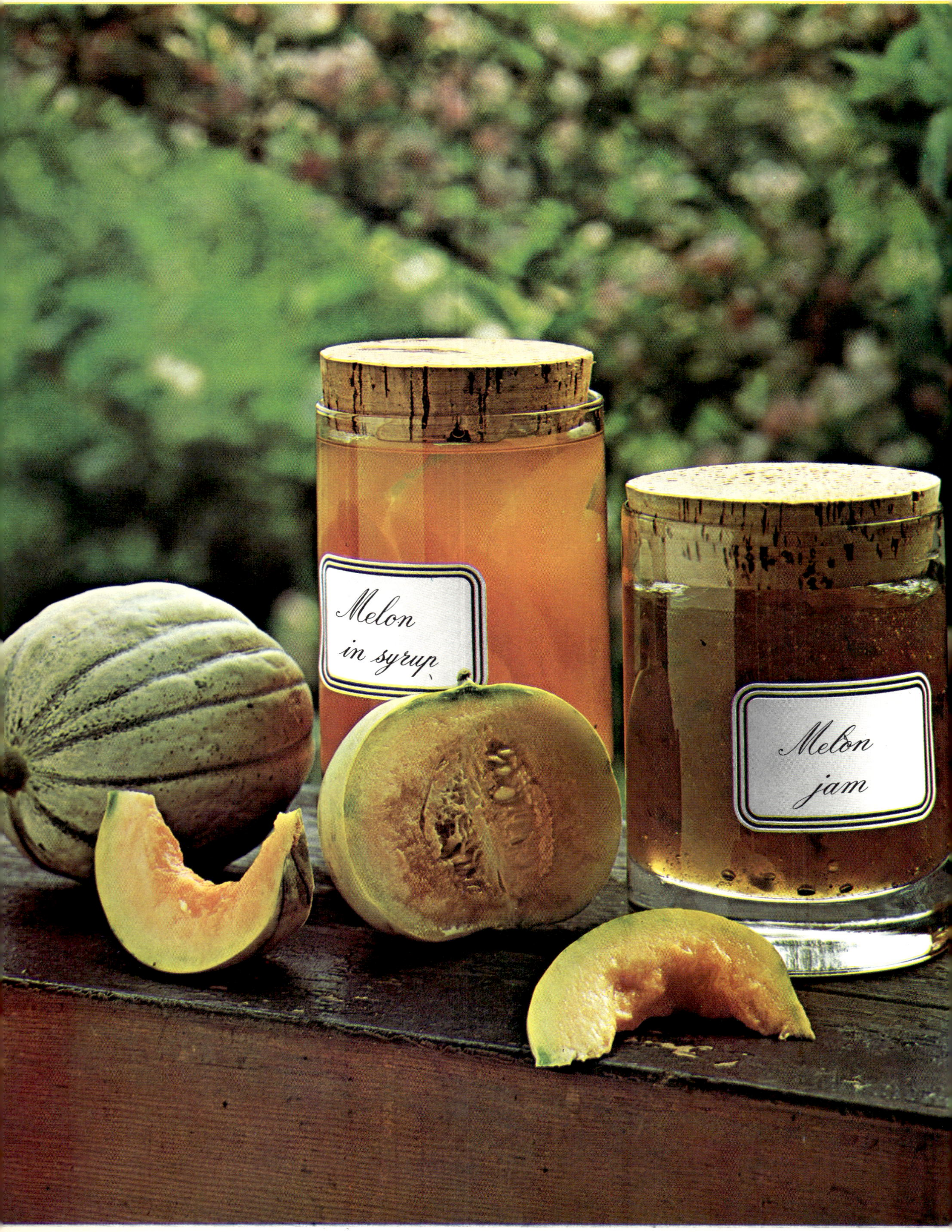
Melon in syrup
Melon jam

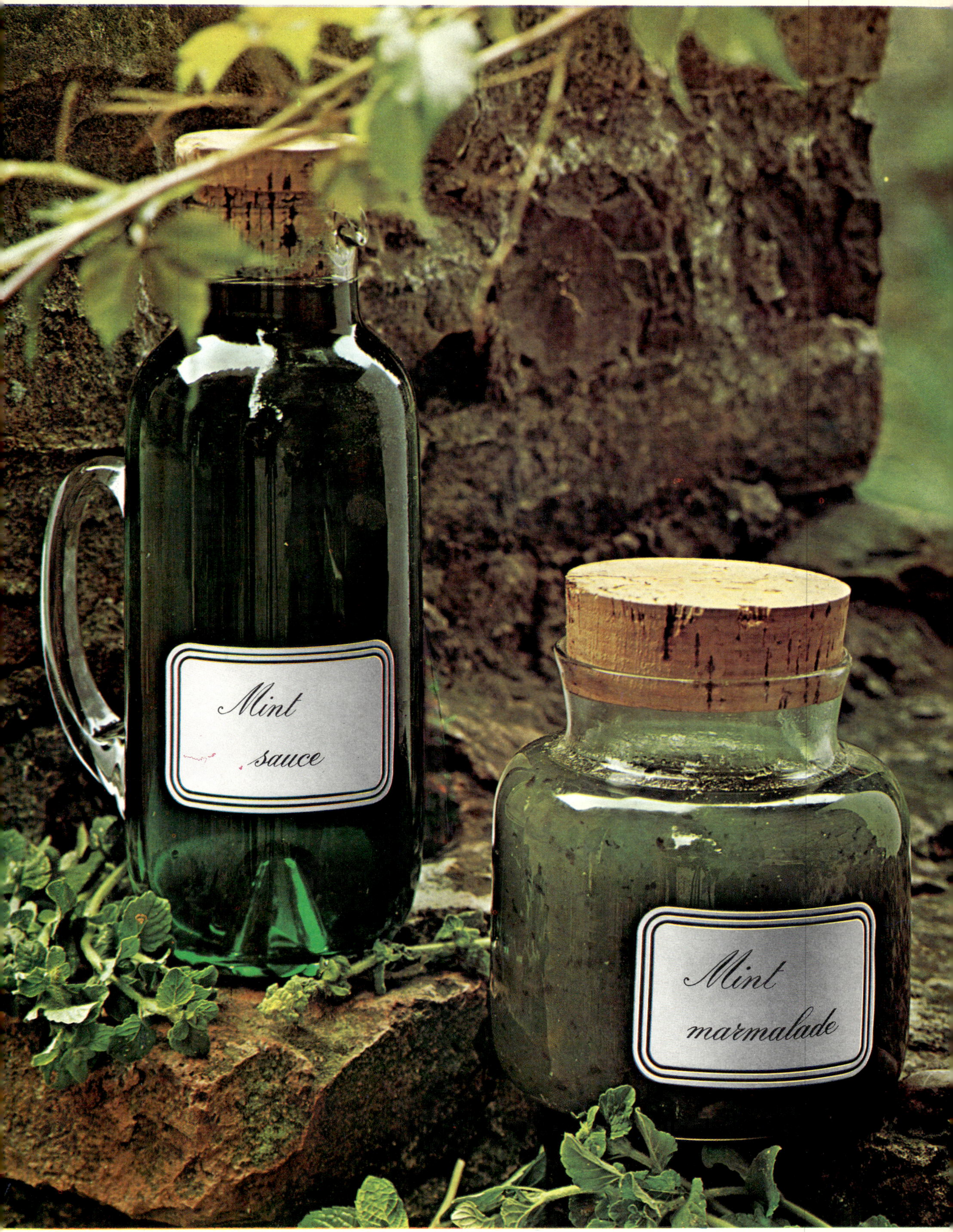
Mint sauce
Mint marmalade

Orange syrup
Orange wedges in alcohol
Orange marmalade
Orange jelly

Grapefruit jelly

Ingredients:
5 juicy grapefruits
4 rennet apples (sour cooking green)
2 cups water
2 pounds (4 cups) sugar

Preparation:
Peel grapefruit, leaving no white inner skin, as in GRAPEFRUIT WEDGES IN SYRUP. Dice grapefruit and membranes into a bowl. Peel, core and dice apples. Put grapefruit, apples and water into a pot. Bring to a boil and cook slowly until apples are mushy. The apples act as a natural thickening agent for the jelly. Press through a stainless steel food mill or a sieve. Force through as much pulp as possible. If you want a clear jelly, you will have to filter only juice through a double thickness cheesecloth, but there is a great deal of waste. Stir in sugar and bring to a boil for ten to fifteen minutes. Jelly is ready when a drop placed on a plate becomes firm on cooling. Pour immediately into sterilized jars. Seal and store in a cool, dark, dry place.

Grapefruit wedges in syrup

Grapefruit wedges in syrup go well mixed with wedges of other fresh citrus fruits or in fruit cups.

Ingredients:
8 pounds large, flavorful grapefruit
2 pound (4 cups) sugar
3½ cups water

Preparation:
Peel grapefruit with a very sharp or serrated knife, right down to the pulp, leaving no traces of bitter white inner skin. With knife section grapefruit, removing membrane and leaving sections whole. Squeeze membranes to remove all juice. Place wedges in sterilized jars, pouring juice over them. Heat sugar and water to a boil until syrup becomes clear. Cool syrup. Cover grapefruit with syrup. Seal and sterilize in a boiling water bath (see page 9) for ten to fifteen minutes. Store in a cool, dark, dry place.

Serve sections with syrup or use syrup as a base for a refreshing beverage.

Bitter lemon jam

This jam is an excellent aid to the digestion. Its pleasantly bitter robust flavor makes it ideal in the preparation of exotic desserts.

Ingredients:
2 pounds lemons
2 quarts peeled, sliced apples
3 pounds (6 cups) sugar
1 quart water
Brandy or some other liquor (optional)

Preparation:
Wash lemons. Slice lemons in quarters lengthwise, removing ends and seeds. Then slice each quarter crosswise with a very sharp serrated knife to keep from squeezing juice from slices. Put all the ingredients except brandy into a *non*-aluminum pot and bring slowly to a boil. When mixture is boiling stir and skim foam. Continue cooking, stirring constantly, until water has evaporated and mixture is thick and gelatinous. If desired stir in one-half cup brandy or other liquor for flavoring. Pour hot jam into sterilized jars. Seal tightly and store in a cool, dark, dry place.

Lemon curd

This can by no means be called a genuine marmalade; nevertheless, it has a very high and unequalled nutritive value. Children especially like it for its delicate and unmistakable flavor.

Ingredients:
Grated rind of 1 lemon
Juice of 8 large lemons
8 ounces (1 cup) soft sweet butter
2 pounds (4 cups) sugar
12 eggs, lightly beaten

Preparation:
Grate rind of one of the lemons into a heavy bottomed stainless steel pot (aluminum absolutely must not be used). Add lemon juice, butter and sugar. Stir over low heat until butter has melted and mixture is lukewarm. Beat in eggs. Stir slowly over low heat until marmalade becomes thick and a beautiful golden color. Make sure that marmalade does not boil. As soon as the first wisp of steam is seen, which indicates that mixture is on the verge of boiling, remove pot from heat at once and pour marmalade into sterilized jar and seal. After jar has cooled, store in a cool, dark, dry place. It will keep for at least three months in a dry place.

Lemon flip

Ingredients:
Grated rind of 2 lemons
1 cup sugar
1 cup water
2 eggs
½ cup lemon juice, strained
½ cup dry Marsala wine (sherry or port may be substituted)

Preparation:
Mix lemon rind with sugar in a glass or ceramic bowl. Bring the water to a boil and stir into bowl. Cool. Beat in eggs, one at a time. Beat in lemon juice and Marsala. Strain. Pour into bottles and seal. Store in refrigerator.

Because of its tonic properties, it may be served at breakfast, and as part of a convalescent's diet. Warmed in a double boiler, it is an excellent warm beverage in the winter months; served cold, it is excellent in the summer.

Lemon syrup

This syrup is served as a beverage when mixed with plain or carbonated mineral water

Ingredients:
2¼ cups lemon juice
Grated rind of 2 lemons
1 pound, 6 ounces (2¾ cups) sugar

Preparation:
Strain lemon juice through a fine sieve into a pot (do not use steel or aluminum). Stir in lemon rind and sugar. Heat until a sort of light, transparent skin forms on the surface, but do not boil. Strain syrup through double thickness cheesecloth. Cool and pour into sterilized bottles and seal with a bottle capper. Store in a cool, dark, dry place.

It is advisable to use small bottles like those used for Coca-Cola or 7-Up and that take regular bottle caps.

Lemons in oil

Ingredients:
2 pounds lemons
2 teaspoons coriander seeds, crushed
1 teaspoon peppercorns, crushed
2 bay leaves, crushed
1 teaspoon grated fresh ginger
Olive oil, as needed

Preparation:
Choose lemons that have not been treated with biphenyl (you can be certain if you buy them directly from the grower) and that have a few fresh, green leaves on them. Wash the lemons quickly in cold water, dry and arrange them in sterilized glass jars. Add coriander, peppercorns, bay leaves and ginger to jars. Add also the green leaves. Seal and let them stand for one day. Pour in enough olive oil to cover lemons. Seal jars again and wait two months before using lemon-flavored oil. This oil is used to add flavor to sauces, salads, etc., while the lemons are used in the preparation of various dishes such as Chicken Morocco Style or as relish or a garnish.

Grated citrus rind

This mixture of grated citrus rind and sugar can be used to flavor all kinds of desserts.

Ingredients:
4 ounces grated orange and lemon rind
½ cup sugar

Preparation:
Before using the oranges and lemons make absolutely sure that they were not sprayed with biphenyl.

If possible use a dry stainless steel grater over a large clean plate or platter. In grating, do not grate into white underlayer. Mix grated rinds with sugar. Pour mixture into clean, dry jars about the size of herb containers. Store in a cool, dry place.

Grate rinds before you squeeze oranges for juice or before you eat them as fruit.

This grated citrus rind mixture is especially good for adding flavor to cakes, pie fillings, cookies, sauces, puddings, breads, pancakes, French toast, waffles, etc.

Flavored sugar cubes

Ingredients:
A quantity of sugar cubes
Citrus fruits (lemon, orange, citron, grapefruit, tangerines)

Preparation:
Rub sugar cubes one by one on the skin of the citrus fruit, taking care not to break cubes. You can get ten flavored cubes from each piece of fruit. Keep cubes in clean, sealed glass jars.

The cubes are useful in preparing certain flambee'd sauces, crepes suzette, etc., to which they give a delicious aroma. Also delicious served with hot tea.

Melon jam

Ingredients:
7 pounds ripe, perfect melons
6 cups water
Juice of 4 lemons
Rind of 1 lemon, in large pieces
2 pounds (4 cups) sugar
1 cup brandy

Preparation:
Peel and seed melons and chop pulp. The yield should be about 2 pounds. Put pulp in a pot *not* made of aluminum and add water. Add lemon juice and rind. Bring to a slow boil for thirty minutes or until melon becomes transparent. Stir in sugar and continue cooking, stirring frequently with a wooden spoon until mixture becomes thick like jam. Remove lemon rind. Stir in brandy. Pour hot into sterilized jars. Seal and store in a cool, dark, dry place.

Melon preserve

The pieces of melon and the syrup can be used in fruit cups, with a serving of ice cream, or simply served as a dessert sprinkled with liquor.

Ingredients:
7 pounds well-flavored melons (not watermelon)
4 pounds (8 cups) sugar
Juice of 2 lemons

Preparation:
Scrub melons carefully with a brush under cold, running water. Cut melons in half horizontally and remove seeds. Slice into wedges and peel off skin with a sharp knife. You should end with about four pounds fruit. Cut wedges crosswise into slices about a quarter of an inch thick. The slices must be quite dry. Arrange the slices in sterilized jars, alternating a layer of melon with a layer of sugar of the same thickness. Sprinkle with a few drops of lemon juice. Seal jars and sterilize in a boiling water bath (see page 9) for fifteen to twenty minutes. Store in a cool, dark, dry place.

Melon in syrup

Ingredients:
7 pounds well-flavored but not overly ripe melons (not watermelon)
Water
2 pounds, 4 ounces (4½ cups) sugar
Juice of 2 lemons
Port wine (optional)

Preparation:
Halve melons and remove seeds. Cut melon into large wedges or into cubes, slicing off skin and softest parts. Approximately four pounds of cleaned fruit will be left. In a pot heat two quarts water with one cup sugar and juice of one lemon to a boil. Drop in pieces of melon. Remove pot from heat and let melons stand in syrup for five minutes. Drain reserving one quart of liquid. Place melon on a rack and place in sun until dry. In a pot combine remaining sugar, reserved cooking liquid and remaining lemon juice. Bring to a boil. Place dried melon pieces in sterilized jars. Pour boiling syrup into jars covering the melons to three-quarters. If desired, add a few drops of port wine to each jar. Seal jars and sterilize in a boiling water bath (see page 9) for thirty minutes. Store in a cool, dark, dry place.

Melons alla certosina

Ingredients:
4 pounds peeled, cubed melon (not watermelon)
White wine and water (as needed)
Grated rind and juice of 2 lemons
3 pounds (6 cups) sugar
1 piece vanilla bean
8 peppermint leaves
8 anise seeds (optional)
95% grain alcohol (as needed)

Preparation:
Put melon cubes in a pot. Cover with a mixture of half white wine and half water and grated rind and juice of one lemon. Boil slowly for about three minutes, then remove from heat and let fruit cool in syrup. Drain and reserve one cup of the cooking liquid. Discard remainder. Drain cubes on paper towels. Pour sugar into a large pot and add one cup reserved cooking liquid. Bring to a boil, stir until clear and then boil one minute. Stir in melon. Pour entire contents of pot into a glass or ceramic bowl and add vanilla, mint leaves and anise seeds. Place bowl in a cool place and let stand for one day. Replace melon and syrup in pot and bring to a boil for two minutes. Drain melon cubes, reserving syrup, and put cubes in sterilized jars, placing some of the mint leaves and anise seeds in each jar (discard vanilla). Add a pinch of remaining grated lemon rind to each jar. Return reserved syrup to heat and boil it until it is the consistency of honey. Pour hot syrup over melon cubes. Add enough alcohol to each jar to cover melon cubes. Seal and store in a cool, dark, dry place.

Mint marmalade

The flavor of this marmalade is especially suited to the summer months because of the sensation of coolness that it gives. If diluted with water, it yields an excellent syrup.

Ingredients:
2 pounds peeled, sliced apples
Juice of 2 lemons
Grated rind of 1 lemon
4 to 8 ounces tender peppermint leaves, the exact quantity depending on how strong you want the flavor to be, finely chopped
1½ pounds (3 cups) sugar

Preparation:
Drop apples in a bowl of cold water to which has been added the juice of one of the lemons. Drain apples and place in an untinned copper pot. Add lemon rind and mint leaves. Bring to a boil slowly, stirring and skimming foam until apples are tender and mushy. Press mixture through a sieve or food mill. This will yield a green puree. Replace in pot and stir in sugar and remaining lemon juice. Boil again, stirring and skimming until marmalade becomes thick. Pour while hot into sterilized jars. Seal and store in a cool, dark, dry place.

Mint sauce

Ingredients:
2 cups finely chopped mint leaves
¾ cup confectioners' sugar
1 quart wine vinegar
½ teaspoon salt
Few grains pepper

Preparation:
Combine ingredients in a saucepan. Stir to dissolve sugar. Bring to a boil over medium heat. Pour while hot into sterilized jars. Seal and store in a cool, dark, dry place.
　　Good sauce for lamb or veal.

Mint jelly

Ingredients:
Tart, firm apples
1 cup (firmly packed) mint leaves
Sugar
Green food coloring

Preparation:
Wash apples thoroughly and remove stems. Slice apples and place in a large kettle. Add about half as much water as apples and bring to a boil. Simmer until apples are soft. Place fruit and juice into a sieve lined with double thickness cheesecloth and let juice drip into a bowl. Pour one cup boiling water over mint leaves and let stand for one hour. Strain mint through another sieve, pressing juice from mint. Measure apple juice and add two tablespoons of the mint juice to each cup of apple juice. Bring to a boil then add three-quarters cup sugar for each cup juice. Stir to dissolve sugar and boil over high heat skimming foam, until a small amount dropped on a cold plate becomes firm. Add food coloring to desired tint and pour jelly into sterilized glasses. Cover with lids. Store in a cool, dark, dry place.

Orange sections in syrup

Ingredients:
15 oranges
2 pounds (4 cups) sugar
9 cups water
¾ cup kirsch

Preparation:
With the fingers remove rind from oranges and save rind from 2 of the oranges. (Note that this rind should not have been sprayed with biphenyl.) Pull sections of orange apart leaving membrane intact. Arrange sections in sterilized jars, packing them in tightly.

In a saucepan combine sugar, two rinds that you reserved, and water. Bring to a boil and boil for five minutes. Remove from heat and cool to lukewarm. Stir in kirsch and remove orange rind. While syrup is lukewarm, pour it into jars covering sections completely. Seal jars and sterilize in a boiling water bath (see page 9) for fifteen or twenty minutes. Store in a cool, dark place.

Orange jelly

Delicious candies for children can be made from this jelly; merely cut it into small cubes and roll them in sugar.

Ingredients:
3 orange rinds
5 juicy oranges, about
4 green apples, about
3 cups water
3 cups sugar

Preparation:
Slice off rind as thinly as possible, removing only the top orange layer of rind, and dice oranges. You should have 1¼ pounds (2¼ cups) pulp and juice. Peel, core and dice apples. This also should amount to about 1¼ pounds (2¼ cups). Combine apples, oranges, orange rind, and water in a pot. Bring to a boil, allowing the mixture to cook slowly until apples, which serve as a natural thickening agent, are completely cooked. After the mixture is cooked strain it through a sieve or food mill. Force the pulp through as well. You should have about 4 cups. Pour back into saucepan. Stir in sugar. Boil for about twenty minutes stirring occasionally to prevent sticking. When it is thick like jam, remove from heat and pour it immediately into sterilized jars. Seal and store in a cool, dry place.

Orange marmalade

Ingredients:
7 or 8 juicy oranges
2 cups peeled, minced green apples
3 cups sugar

Preparation:
With a sharp knife remove only the colored part of the rind of two oranges, taking care to avoid white underpeel. Mince colored rind. With a sharp knife peel all the oranges, taking care to remove all the white skin. Cut sections into pieces, removing seeds and fibrous portion at the center of the sections. Put orange pieces in an enamel or stainless steel pot. Add apple (the pectin in the apples acts as a thickening agent) and sugar. Bring to a boil. Cook for about five minutes, without skimming. When apples are cooked, remove from heat and force through a strainer or food mill. Stir in minced rind. Put whole mixture back in pot and boil for about fifteen minutes over a low heat and skimming foam constantly. After marmalade has reached consistency of honey, remove from heat and pour into sterilized jars. Close and store in a cool, dry place.

Orange and lemon marmalade

Ingredients:
1¼ pounds oranges
1¼ pounds lemons
3 cups sugar

Preparation:
Before using oranges and lemons make absolutely sure that they have not been sprayed with biphenyl.

With a sharp knife slice off colored portion of rind as thinly as possible. Cut into thin ¼-inch wide strips. Set aside. Remove thick, white inner peel and cut fruit pulp into large pieces directly into an enamel, stainless steel or untinned copper pot large enough to hold all the fruit comfortably. Add sugar and rind. Bring to a boil, lower heat and simmer, stirring and skimming foam with a wooden spoon. When marmalade is thick, pour it hot into sterilized jars with airtight closures. Seal jars immediately and store them in a cool, dry place.

Orange wedges in alcohol

The wedges are used to garnish cakes or other desserts. The liquor may then be used as an aid to digestion; it should be kept in closed bottles.

Ingredients:
2 pounds ripe, firm-fleshed oranges
1½ cups sugar
4 or 5 whole cloves
4 or 5 sticks cinnamon
Grappa (vodka or brandy)

Preparation:
It is absolutely essential that oranges were not sprayed with biphenyl.

Wash oranges in running water and dry them. With a sharp knife cut oranges into wedges, following natural direction of orange sections. Each orange will yield six to eight wedges. As each wedge is cut, arrange it in a sterilized jar, pressing and shifting the pieces so that jar is packed as tightly as possible. Divide sugar into as many parts as you have jars and sprinkle it in. Add two whole cloves and a stick of cinnamon to each jar. Pour in grappa or brandy to cover orange wedges. Seal jars and store them in cool, dry place. The wedges may be used after about a month.

Orange sauce

This sauce is a perfect accompaniment to canard a l'orange or to roast turkey.

Ingredients:
3 juicy oranges
2 lemons
1¼ cups sugar
⅓ cup white wine
1 cup thick, flavorful meat sauce or beef gravy
1 pinch salt
1 pinch pepper
¼ cups curacao

Preparation:
With a sharp knife slice off the colored part of rind of oranges and lemons. Cut them into narrow strips. Cover with water and boil for 5 minutes. Drain and let dry. Squeeze juice from oranges and lemons. Put sugar in an enamel or stainless steel pot. Add white wine and let boil over a low heat until sugar takes on a blondish color. Stir occasionally. As soon as sugar is golden yellow remove from heat and stir in rinds and juice from oranges and lemons and meat sauce. Bring to a slow boil, skimming foam constantly. Boil for at least 5 minutes, until mixture is slightly thickened. Stir in salt and pepper. If sauce is too liquid, bind it with a teaspoon of cornstarch mixed with a little white wine. When sauce has reached the proper consistency, about that of honey, remove from heat and stir in curacao. Stir well and pour it hot into sterilized jars. Seal and sterilize in a boiling water bath (see page 9) for about 10 minutes. Store in a cool, dry place.

Candied orange rind

Candied orange peel is used in making various desserts (for example, plum pudding,) decorating cakes, and in pastry making generally.

Ingredients:
8 ounces cleaned orange rinds
½ cup granulated sugar

Preparation:
Peel oranges with a very sharp knife slicing off only colored portion, leaving white underskin, which is somewhat bitter. Cut skin into thin strips. Put rinds in an enameled or stainless steel pan and add sugar and enough water to cover. Bring to a boil and boil very slowly for ten minutes. Remove from heat and set aside for twenty-four hours. Bring rinds to a boil again and boil for fifteen minutes. Remove from heat and set aside for another twenty-four hours. Remove rinds with a fork. Put sugar and water mixture back on heat and boil for five minutes. Put rinds back into syrup and set aside for a day. Boil sugar and water mixture, which will not be very thick, together with peels. Remove from heat and remove rinds from syrup and spread them out in a single layer to dry for a day. Afterwards lightly roll them in sugar. They will keep for a long time in glass jars in a cool, dry place.

Orange juice

Orange juice diluted with effervescent mineral water makes a superb thirst-quenching beverage in the summer.

Ingredients:
10 oranges
2 lemons
4 pounds (8 cups) sugar

Preparation:
It is absolutely essential that the oranges and lemons have not been sprayed with biphenyl.

With a sharp knife slice off colored part of rind from fruit and set aside. Squeeze out juice into a glass or ceramic container. Add rind and let mixture stand for a couple of hours. Pour sugar into a pot, untinned copper, if possible, and stir in juice. Boil slowly. Skim foam during boiling time, about four or five minutes. Remove from heat, strain through double thickness cheesecloth and pour into sterilized bottles still hot. Seal and store in a cool, dry place.

Orange syrup

Ingredients:
14 oranges
3 lemons
4 pounds (8 cups) sugar
2 cups water

Preparation:
With a sharp knife slice off the colored portion of rind from seven oranges, being careful not to include any of the bitter white portion. Place orange rind to soak in cold water to cover for three hours. Squeeze juice from lemons and all of the oranges. Boil sugar and water for 10 minutes until you have a thick syrup. Remove from heat. When syrup is almost cold stir in drained orange rind and juice. Boil for 15 minutes. Strain syrup to remove rinds. Bring to a boil again, stirring and skimming foam until syrup has almost the consistency of honey, about 30 minutes. This time varies as oranges and lemons vary in size and juice yield. Remove from heat and cool mixture quickly in ice water. Pour cooled syrup into sterilized bottles and seal, storing in a cool, dry place.

Peach marmalade

Ingredients:
11 pounds ripe, unbruised peaches
Rind of 1 lemon, in large pieces
Juice of 2 lemons
12 tender peach leaves
5½ pounds (11 cups) sugar

Preparation:
Wash the peaches carefully. Halve and remove pits. Dice peaches and place into a pot. Add lemon rind and juice and peach leaves. Bring to a slow boil, stirring and skimming foam. Boil slowly for five minutes or until peaches are mushy. Press through a food mill or sieve. Replace peach pulp in pot and stir in sugar. Bring slowly to a boil again, stirring constantly to prevent sticking. When marmalade is thick pour while hot into sterilized jars. Seal and store in a cool, dark, dry place.

Candied peaches

Ingredients:
11 pounds unblemished, not too ripe peaches
Juice of 4 lemons
Rind of 2 lemons, in large pieces
1 quart water
10 pounds (20 cups) sugar

Preparation:
Peel, halve and dry peaches as for PEACHES IN SYRUP. Heat water, sugar, remaining lemon juice and lemon rind. Stir and boil syrup until it becomes clear. Add peach halves and let boil in syrup for one minute. Remove from heat and set aside in a cool place for one day. The next day heat pot until syrup just starts to bubble. Remove peach halves with a slotted spoon, placing them in another pot, if possible, exactly the same size as the first. Boil syrup that remains in the first pot for three to five minutes. Remove from heat and pour hot syrup over peach halves in the other pot, removing lemon rind. Allow to stand for another day. Repeat this operation at least three times until peaches have absorbed all, or almost all, the syrup. When peaches have become well-impregnated with syrup, heat to warm syrup left and remove peach halves. Place peaches on a rack set over a pan and allow them to dry in the sun for three to five days, turning halves over from time to time. When they are dry and the sugar on the surface has crystallized, pack peaches in wooden boxes lined with wax paper and store in a cool, dark, dry place. Candied peaches are used as a topping for ice cream, on iced cakes or as a decoration.

Peaches in syrup

Ingredients:
9 pounds firm, unbruised peaches with yellow flesh and, if possible, all the same size
Juice of 2 lemons
Rind of 1 lemon, in large pieces
2½ quarts water
3 pounds (6 cups) sugar

Preparation:
Heat a large pot of water with lemon juice and lemon rind added. When water boils, add peaches, a few at a time, leaving them in boiling water for thirty seconds. Remove peaches and place them in cold water. Remove and pull off skin. Place them on a dry cloth to dry one by one as they are peeled.

Cut peaches in half, remove pit and place cut side down on a tray. Put tray in sun for about one hour so that the peaches will dry completely. With a hammer break open pits and remove seeds. While peaches are drying boil water and sugar until syrup is clear. Arrange peach halves, cut side down, in sterilized jars, pressing down lightly and adding one peach seed to each jar. Cover them with hot syrup. Seal jars and sterilize in a boiling water bath (see page 9) for twenty to thirty minutes. Let jars cool in water in which they were sterilized and test to make sure that seal is perfect. Store in a cool, dark, dry place. They should be eaten within the year.

Peaches in alcohol

Ingredients:
2 pounds firm, ripe, unbruised peaches
Juice of 3 lemons
2 pounds (4 cups) sugar
Grain alcohol
Whole cloves (if desired)

Preparation:
Peel and halve peaches as in PEACHES IN SYRUP. Crack open pits and remove seeds. Sprinkle peach halves with remaining lemon juice to prevent browning. Arrange peaches in sterilized jars, cut side down, in layers, alternating with layers of sugar. Cover peaches with alcohol so that all empty spaces are filled and peaches are covered. If desired, add a peach seed and a few whole cloves to each jar. Leave a space of at least a half inch between peaches and lid. Seal and store in a cool, dark, dry place. Let stand three months before serving.

Peaches in vinegar

This is a rather unusual preserve. Nevertheless, served with boiled beef or duck, peaches in vinegar are truly delightful with their pleasant bitter-sweet flavor.

Ingredients:
2 pounds unbruised and not over-ripe peaches
Juice of 3 lemons
2 cups white vinegar
2 pounds (4 cups) sugar
5 whole cloves
1 piece stick cinnamon

Preparation:
Peel and halve peaches as in PEACHES IN SYRUP. Do not dry in sun but sprinkle with remaining lemon juice to prevent browning. Arrange peach halves in sterilized jars.

Meanwhile, boil vinegar and remaining ingredients in a pot that is not aluminum, for about ten minutes. Pour hot syrup through a sieve into jars and cover peaches. Seal jars and store in a cool, dark, dry place.

Pear jam

Ingredients:
2 pounds sound, ripe pears
Juice of 1 lemon
1 pound (2 cups) sugar
2 cups water
A few drops of some liquor

Preparation:
Peel, quarter and core pears and drop into cold water to cover. Add lemon juice. Drain pears, slice thinly into a large pot. Add sugar and water. Bring slowly to a boil, stirring occasionally. When pears are mushy and tender, beat with a stainless steel wire whip until well blended. Boil until mixture is thick like jam. Pour hot jam into sterilized jars. Add a few drops of liquor to jam for added flavor. Seal and store in a cool, dark, dry place.

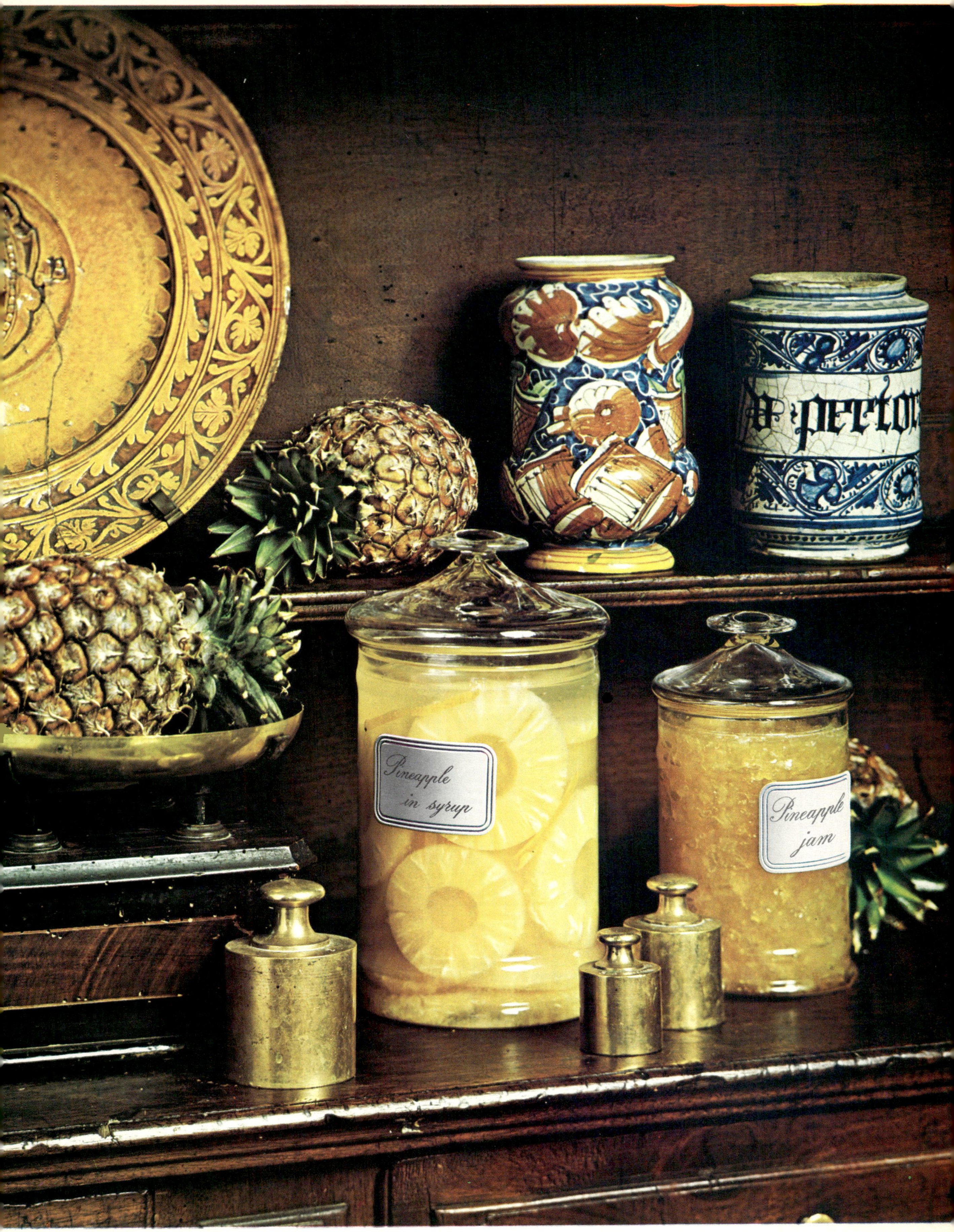

Pineapple in syrup
Pineapple jam

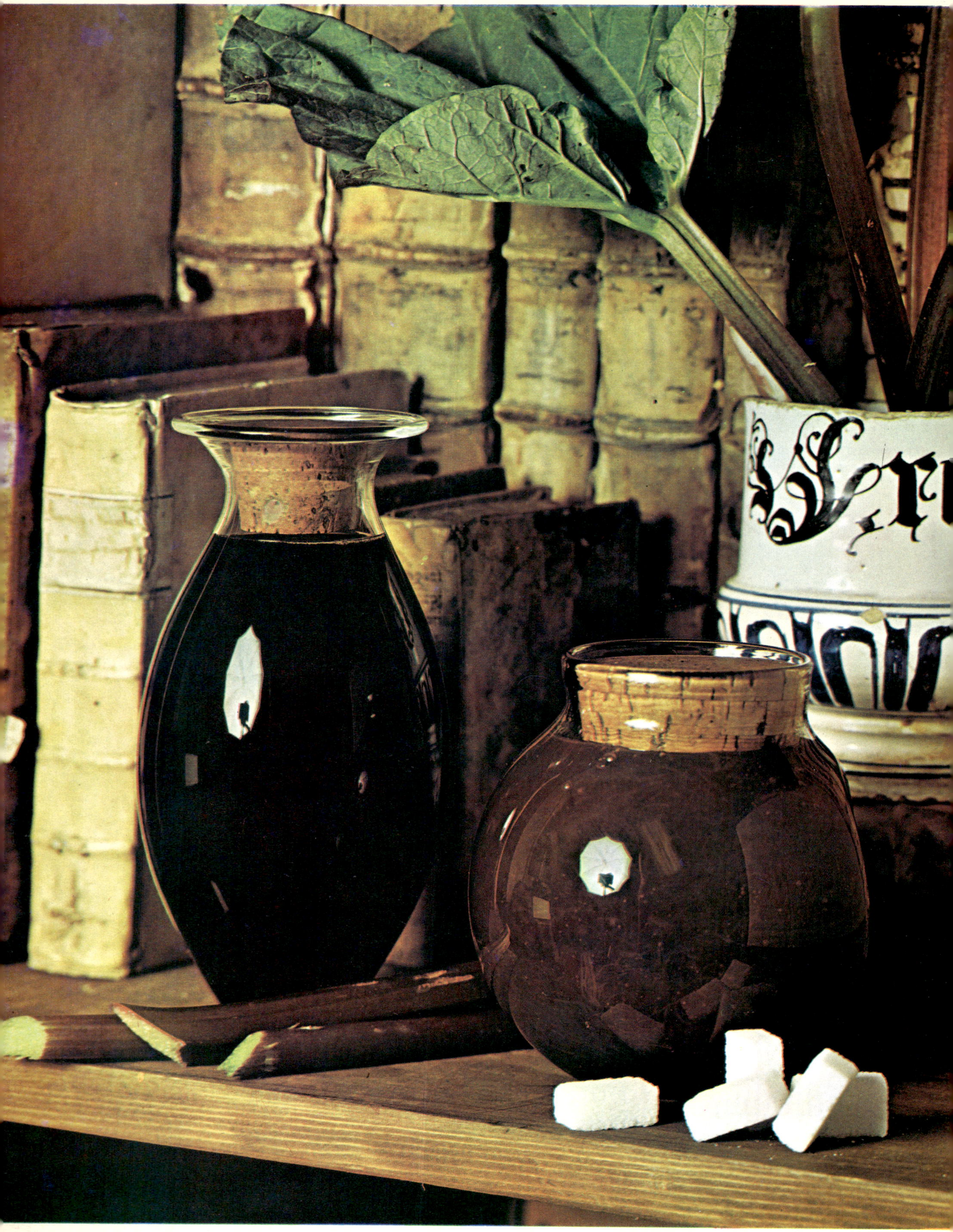

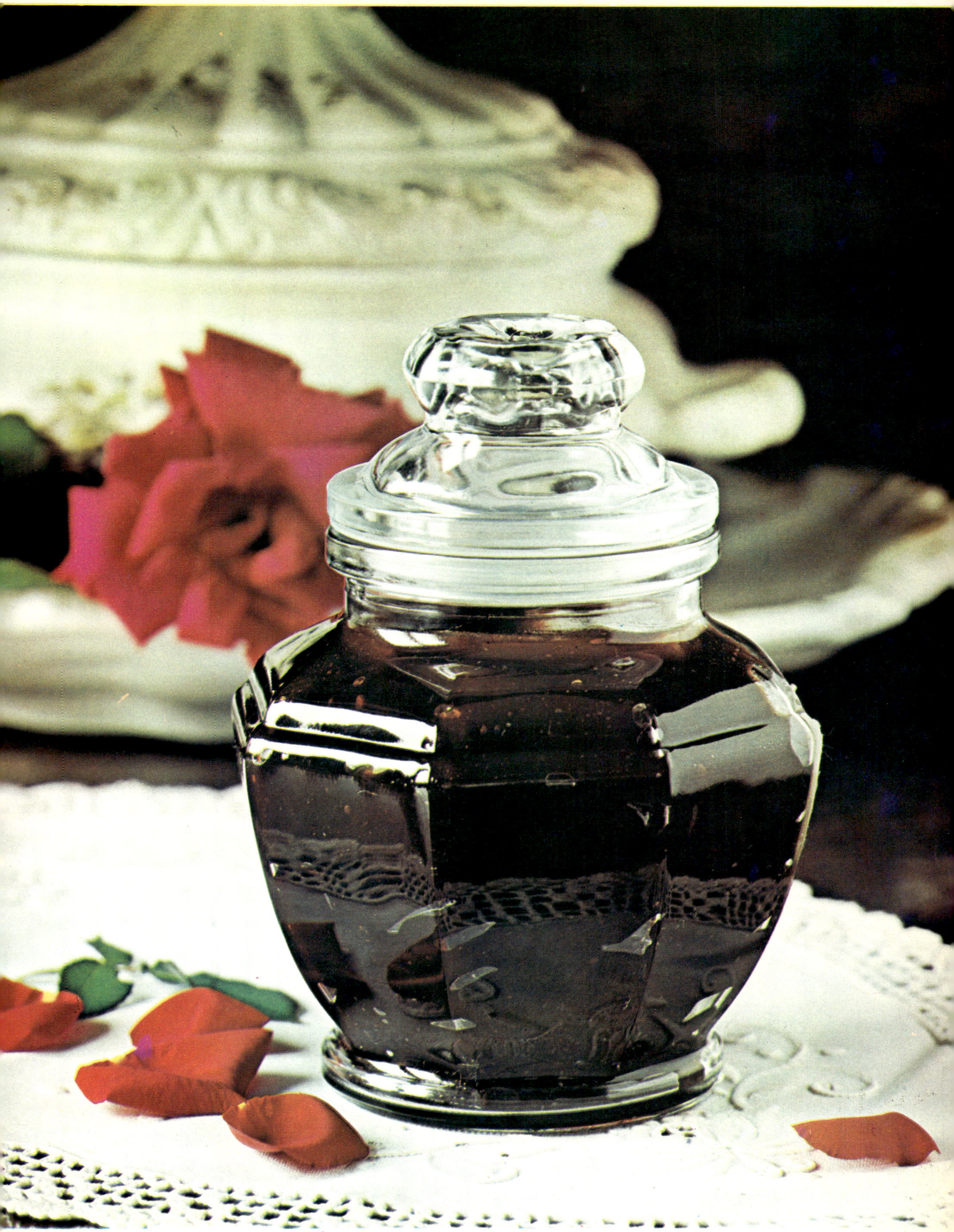

Strawberry jam

San Martino pear jam

Ingredients:
7 pounds San Martino pears (or other pears with a hard, dense pulp)
2 quarts dry white wine
1 cup water
Grated rind and juice of 1 lemon
Grated rind of 1 orange
2 pounds (4 cups) sugar
7 or 8 whole cloves
1 pinch ground cinnamon
1 cup honey
2 tablespoons dry mustard

Preparation:
Peel, quarter and core pears and place into a pot. In a bowl combine white wine, water, lemon rind and juice and orange rind. Pour over pears and add remaining ingredients. Bring to a boil slowly, stirring and skimming foam constantly. Boil until mixture is thick and jam-like. Pour hot jam into sterilized jars. Seal and store in a cool, dark, dry place.

This somewhat piquant jam goes well with boiled meats or roast game.

Pears in compote

Various sweets can be prepared from these pears, or they may be arranged around a roast of game as a garnish.

Ingredients:
8 pounds firm-fleshed pears
1 cup white vinegar
1 cup dry white wine
Grated rind and juice of 1 lemon
2 pounds (4 cups) sugar

Preparation:
Peel, quarter and core pears. Pour vinegar into a large pot that will hold all the pears. Add white wine and lemon rind and juice. Add pears and pour sugar over them. Cover pot and let stand for one hour. Remove lid and bring to a boil. Let pears cook slowly, stirring occasionally, for two hours, making sure pears remain under syrup. With a slotted spoon remove pears and place in sterilized jars. Cover them with syrup. If there is not enough liquid to cover, add equal parts of white vinegar and white wine heated to boiling. Seal jars and store in a cool, dark, dry place.

Pears in red wine

Pears in red wine may be served plain as a dessert or on a slice of pound cake or the like.

Ingredients:
7 pounds firm, small pears
Juice of 1 lemon
2 pounds (4 cups) sugar
2½ quarts red wine
Rind of 1 lemon, in large pieces
Whole cloves
Pieces stick cinnamon, 2 inches long

Preparation:
Peel, halve and core pears and put them in cold water to cover. Add lemon juice. In a pot combine sugar, wine and lemon rind. Bring to a boil and remove from heat. Remove lemon rind. Arrange drained pears in sterilized jars, putting a clove and a piece of cinnamon in each jar. Pour syrup over pears to within three-quarters of the top. Seal and sterilize jars in a boiling water bath (see page 9) for twenty minutes. Store in a cool, dark, dry place.

Marinated pears

These pears, which are the pride of the Russian housewives, can be served with roast game.

Ingredients:
7 pounds ripe, firm pears (preferably Kaiser or other hard cooking pear)
Juice of 3 lemons
4 to 5 quarts water
1 pound, 5 ounces (2⅔ cups) sugar
2 cups best quality vinegar (red or white)
8 whole cloves
5 juniper berries
¼ teaspoon ground cinnamon
1 pinch salt
Grated rind of 1 lemon

Preparation:
Peel, quarter and core pears, adding them to water to cover. Add juice of 1 lemon. In a pot combine water, one cup of the sugar and juice of second lemon. Bring to a boil, add drained pears and boil for two minutes. Remove pears with a slotted spoon. Set aside one quart of the syrup. Place pears on a clean cloth and set them in the sun for one or two days until they are perfectly dry and wrinkled. Put pears in sterilized jars. In a pot, combine vinegar and remaining ingredients along with grated lemon rind and juice of third lemon. Boil for two minutes and then cool. Strain and pour over pears in jars. If there is not enough syrup to cover pears, add some of the reserved pear syrup. Seal jars and store in a cool, dark, dry place.

Pears in chocolate

Ingredients:
7 pounds small, firm-fleshed pears
Grated rind and juice of 1 lemon
1 cup unsweetened cocoa
5 pounds (10 cups) sugar
2½ quarts water

Preparation:
Peel, halve and core pears and place them in cold water to cover. Add lemon juice. In a pot combine sugar, water and lemon rind and bring to a boil. Cool. Beat syrup gradually into cocoa. Strain to remove any lumps. Place drained pears in sterilized jars and cover them to three-quarters of the top with chocolate syrup. Seal jars and sterilize for twenty minutes in a boiling water bath (see page 9). Store in a cool, dark, dry place.

Pears prepared in this fashion are excellent served hot in their syrup and topped with whipped cream.

Pears "limara"

The syrup from these pears makes a delicious drink when cold.

Ingredients:
3 ounces (½ cup) slivered orange and lemon rind (make sure they haven't been sprayed with biphenyl)
3½ pounds Kaiser or other hard cooking pears, ripe and firm
Juice of 1 lemon
2⅔ cups water
1½ pounds (3 cups) sugar
Brandy (optional)

Preparation:
With a sharp knife slice off colored part of orange and lemon rind. Cut rind into long, very thin strips. Peel, quarter and core pears. The yield should be about one quart. Place quartered pears in cold water to cover. Add lemon juice. In a pot combine water, sugar and orange and lemon rinds and boil for three to four minutes. Add pears. Boil again and then remove immediately from heat. Let pears remain in syrup until cool, keeping pot covered. When pears are cold, remove with a slotted spoon and place in sterilized jars, adding orange and lemon rinds to each jar. Bring remaining syrup to a boil and boil for five minutes. Pour boiling syrup into jars, covering pears. If you wish, add a few drops of brandy to each jar. Seal and sterilize for twenty to twenty-five minutes in a boiling water bath (see page 9). Store in a cool, dark, dry place.

Persimmon jelly

Ingredients:
6 pounds ripe persimmons
1 cup water
2 pounds (4 cups) sugar
Rind of 1 lemon, cut into large strips

Preparation:
Wash and stem persimmons. Halve them, remove all the pulp and press it through a strainer or food mill. Weigh the resultant pulp; it should be about 2 pounds (4 cups). Boil water, sugar and lemon rind until 238° F. (soft ball) on a candy thermometer. At this point remove lemon rind and stir in persimmon pulp. Continue cooking over a low heat until mixture becomes gelatinous. Test by letting a drop fall on a dry plate; cool and then lift one edge of the plate; if drop remains rounded, jelly is ready. Remove from heat and pour hot into sterilized jars. Seal and store in cool, dry place.

Persimmon marmalade

Ingredients:
4 pounds ripe persimmons
1 apple
Grated rind and juice of 1 lemon
3 pounds (6 cups) sugar
1 piece vanilla bean, 2 inches long
¼ cup orange liqueur

Preparation:
Wash and stem persimmons. Cut into halves and scoop out pulp. Place pulp into an enamel or stainless steel pot. Peel apple core and dice. Add apples, lemon rind and juice to persimmons. Bring to a boil. Let mixture boil for three or four minutes, skimming foam. Remove from heat and press mixture through a sieve or food mill. Put puree back in pot. Stir in sugar and vanilla bean. Bring mixture to a boil again. Boil slowly so that froth comes to surface. Remove with a spoon. During cooking keep stirring and skimming marmalade until it thickens to the right consistency. Remove from heat and stir in liqueur. Remove vanilla bean. Pour marmalade hot into sterilized jars. Seal and store in a cool, dry place.

Pineapple jam

Ingredients:
5 pounds pineapple
2 green apples
4 pounds (8 cups) sugar
Grated rind and juice of 1 lemon

Preparation:
Remove top and bottom of pineapple, slice off outer skin and remove fibrous core with an apple-corer or pineapple corer. Cut pulp into ½ inch cubes. Peel and core apples and cut them into ½ inch cubes. Put fruit into a mixing bowl, sprinkle with sugar, lemon rind and lemon juice. Mix thoroughly, cover and let stand for five or six hours. Afterward, pour mixture into a stainless steel or untinned copper pot. Bring to a very slow boil, skimming foam and mixing with a wooden spoon. Cook slowly until jam reaches proper consistency. A small amount spooned onto a plate should be thick and spreadable when cooled. Stir occasionally to prevent sticking. Pour hot jam into sterilized jars and seal them. When jam has cooled, store jars in a cool, dark place.

Bittersweet pineapple jam

Though served with all roasts, it should be used judiciously, for it is designed to enhance rather than submerge the natural flavor of the food.

Ingredients:
1½ cups sugar
1½ cups white vinegar
5 or 6 juniper berries
3 whole cloves
1 piece stick cinnamon
2 or 3 dried hot peppers
3 cups drained pineapple chunks in syrup or diced fresh pineapple
½ cup Sultana raisins
1 teaspoon dry mustard
Grated rind and juice of 1 lemon

Preparation:
Pour sugar and vinegar into a pot large enough to hold all ingredients. Crush juniper berries and wrap them in piece of cheesecloth, together with cloves, cinnamon stick and peppers. Tie cheesecloth. Boil spices for a few minutes in vinegar and sugar mixture. Add pineapple, raisins, mustard and lemon rind and juice. Let mixture come to a boil again. Boil very slowly for about half an hour, stirring frequently, and removing cheesecloth bag after fifteen minutes. After jam has thickened (see PINEAPPLE JAM) remove from heat and while it is still hot, pour into sterilized jars. Seal jars immediately. After they have cooled, store in a cool, dark place.

Pineapple in kirsch

Ingredients:
5 firm pineapples
Juice of 1 lemon
8 cups water
3 cups sugar
Rind of 1 lemon, cut into strips
4 cups kirsch

Preparation:
Peel pineapple with a sharp knife, slice and cut the slices into 1 inch chunks, discarding fibrous core in center. Put pieces on a large platter and sprinkle with lemon juice.

Bring water and sugar to a boil. Add pineapple pieces, bring to a boil and boil for 1 minute. Remove from syrup with a slotted spoon and let cool. Put pieces in sterilized jars, adding a piece of lemon rind to each jar. Cover pineapple with kirsch. If you do not have enough kirsch to cover, add a syrup made from 1½ cups sugar and ½ cup water and brought to a boil for one or two minutes.

Seal jars and store them in a cool, dry place. Syrup in which pineapples have been parboiled makes an excellent beverage, or it may be used in other preparations for sauces, compotes or other desserts.

Pineapple in syrup

Ingredients:
5 or 6 firm, fresh pineapples
2 pounds (4 cups) sugar
6 cups water
Rind of 1 lemon, cut into strips
¾ cup maraschino liqueur

Preparation:
When buying pineapples, make sure that the cluster of leaves is not dry.

Cut skin off pineapples. Cut into slices ¼ inch thick. Remove the hard central fibrous core using a sharp knife or rounded cookie cutter.

The pineapples may be prepared in a number of ways. We give the simplest though least orthodox method.

Prepare syrup by boiling sugar and water for five minutes. Arrange pineapple slices in sterilized jars (obviously, the pineapple slices should be of a diameter slightly smaller than the openings of the jars). Add a piece of lemon rind and a few drops of maraschino to each jar. Cover slices with hot syrup and seal jars. Sterilize them for 30 to 35 minutes in a boiling water bath (see page 9). Store in a cool, dark place.

Prickly pear marmalade

This marmalade is used in making pastries in Sicilian and Sardinian as well as in Moroccan and Arab cooking.

Ingredients:
7 pounds prickly pears
1 cup water
Rind of 1 lemon, in large pieces
2 pounds (4 cups) sugar
Juice of ½ lemon

Preparation:
Wash and peel prickly pears. Cut pulp into pieces and put in an untinned copper pot. Add water and lemon rind. Bring to a boil and stirring constantly, boil slowly for five minutes. Press mixture through a sieve or food mill. Your sauce should have the consistency of honey. Pour puree back in pot, add sugar and bring to a slow boil, stirring constantly and skimming foam. When marmalade has a thick consistency, remove from heat and stir in lemon juice. Pour hot into sterilized jars, sealing them. Store in a cool, dark, dry place. The color of the prickly pear marmalade will depend on variety of prickly pear used.

Prickly pear compote

Ingredients:
6 pounds good, ripe prickly pears
1½ quarts (6 cups) currant syrup
¾ cup dry white wine
Rind of 1 lemon, in large pieces
Juice of 2 lemons

Preparation:
Wash and peel prickly pears. Slice them in half and place them one by one in a large skillet. Pour cold currant syrup and white wine over them. Add lemon rind and juice. Cover skillet and bring to a boil. Lower heat and simmer for five minutes. Remove from heat and remove lemon rind. While prickly pears are still hot, arrange them tightly in sterilized jars. Over each layer, pour some of the hot cooking syrup. Fill jars to within about an inch of the top, then cover prickly pears completely with remaining syrup. Seal jars and sterilize for about twenty minutes in a boiling water bath (see page 9). Store in a cool, dark, dry place.

Plum jam

Ingredients:
6½ pounds pitted, ripe greengage plums
3½ pounds (7 cups) sugar
Grated rind and juice of 1 lemon

Preparation:
Wash plums. Cut into halves and remove pits. Dice plums and put them into a pot that is not made of aluminum. Stir in sugar and lemon rind and juice. Bring slowly to a boil, stirring and skimming foam. Boil slowly until mixture is thick. Pour hot into sterilized jars. Seal and store in a cool, dark, dry place.

This jam is an excellent filling for tarts.

Black plum marmalade

Ingredients:
9 pounds ripe, unblemished blue plums
Grated rind and juice of 1 lemon
1 cup water
4 pounds (8 cups) sugar

Preparation:
Wash plums well. Stem, cut in half and remove pits. Place halves into a stainless steel pot. Add lemon rind and juice and water. Bring to a boil slowly and boil for about five minutes until the plums are mushy. Press plums through a food mill or sieve. Replace puree in pot and stir in sugar. Bring to a boil, stirring and skimming foam. When marmalade is thick, pour while hot into sterilized jars and store in a cool, dark, dry place.

Plum jelly

Ingredients:
6½ pounds very ripe, red plums
Grated rind and juice of 1 lemon
4½ pounds (9 cups) sugar

Preparation:
Wash plums. Cut into halves and remove pits. Press through a sieve or food mill. You will end with about eight cups pulp. Pour into a pot that is not aluminum. Stir in lemon rind and juice and sugar. Bring to a boil slowly, stirring and skimming foam until a few drops of the mixture when dripped on a plate become firm. Pour while hot into sterilized jars. Seal and store in a cool, dark, dry place.

Brandied plums

Ingredients:
2 pounds small, firm, unblemished blue plums
2 cups water
2 tablespoons loose tea
1 tablespoon crumbled mint leaves
1 vanilla bean
Rind of 1 lemon, in large pieces
½ cup sugar
1 quart brandy

Preparation:
Wash and dry plums. Bring water to a boil and add tea and mint leaves. Cool. Add plums. Let stand for three hours to absorb flavor of tea and mint leaves, stirring them gently on occasion. Remove the plums with a slotted spoon and prick them in five or six places with a needle. Arrange them in sterilized jars. To each jar add a few bits of vanilla bean, a piece of lemon rind and some of the sugar. Cover plums with brandy. Seal jars and store in a cool, dark, dry place. The plums may be served after about three weeks.

Prunes in syrup

Ingredients:
5 pounds small, unblemished blue plums ("mirabelles" for preference)
1 quart water in which prunes have been cooked
1¾ to 2¼ cups sugar
Juice of 1 lemon

Preparation:
Rub plums clean with a cloth. Puncture them in five or six places with a needle. Place plums in a bowl and pour boiling water over them. Let stand until water becomes lukewarm. Drain plums, reserving one quart of water for making syrup. Spread plums out in the sun to dry. When they are dry, arrange them in sterilized jars. In a pot combine sugar with reserved water. Bring to a boil and pour hot syrup over plums covering them to three-quarters. The plums themselves will give off a large amount of juice during processing. Add a few drops of lemon juice to each jar. Seal and sterilize in a boiling water bath (see page 9) for about fifteen minutes. Store in a cool, dark, dry place.

Bittersweet prunes

Bittersweet prunes are served as an antipasto or as an accompaniment to boiled meats and wursts.

Ingredients:
6½ pounds small blue plums ("Burbank" if possible)
2 pounds (4 cups) sugar
2 teaspoons ground cinnamon
1 lemon
1 quart white vinegar
5 or 6 whole cloves

Preparation:
Wash plums without removing stems. Mix all ingredients except plums in a non-aluminum pot and bring to a boil. Add plums. Boil for five minutes and remove from heat. Cover and let plums stand for half a day. Drain them carefully, replace liquid in pot and boil for about ten minutes. Put plums in a large bowl and pour boiling liquid over them. Let stand covered for five or six hours. Repeat the operation until there is enough liquid to cover plums. Drain and place plums in sterilized jars. Replace liquid in pot and boil again. Pour hot syrup over plums through a strainer until plums are covered with liquid. Let fruit cool in jars, then seal. Store in a cool, dark, dry place.

Quince delight

Ingredients:
2 pounds quinces
Grated rind and juice of 2 lemons
½ cup water
3 pounds (6 cups) sugar

Preparation:
Peel and core quinces. Put them in a bowl covered with cold water and the juice of one and one-half of the lemons to prevent darkening. Drain and place in large pot. Stir in water, juice of the remaining lemon half and lemon rind. Bring to a slow boil and stir constantly while cooking. When quinces are very soft press them through a strainer or food mill. Return puree to pot, stir in four cups of the sugar and bring mixture to a boil, stirring and skimming foam until it reaches the consistency of marmalade and is very smooth. (See CHERRY MARMALADE page 30.) While jam is still hot, pour it into molds or a shallow pan sprinkled with sugar. It should be a thickness of three-quarters of an inch. When it is cold cut it into whatever shapes please you using a sharp knife or small cookie cutters. Roll in remaining sugar and store in airtight containers.

Quince delight in brandy

Ingredients:
7 pounds ripe quinces
Grated rind of ½ lemon
Juice of 3 lemons
Water
2¼ pounds (4½ cups) sugar
½ cup brandy

Preparation:
Remove stems and any other unwanted bits from quinces and wash in cold water. Cut them into cubes, discarding seeds and place them in a large pot with lemon rind, lemon juice and enough water to cover. Boil slowly, stirring occasionally and skimming foam. If water evaporates before quinces are cooked, stir in additional boiling water. After quinces are tender, drain and press them through a sieve or food mill and measure pulp which should be about two pounds (four cups). Stir in four cups of the sugar and cook slowly, stirring until mixture becomes very thick. It should be stirred continually over lowest possible heat. Stir in brandy. Cook until thick as corn meal mush. Sprinkle a shallow pan with half of the remaining sugar. Pour in quince mixture, spreading it out to a thickness of about three-quarters of an inch. Sprinkle top with remaining sugar and place pan in a cool place. When mixture is cold and hardened, cut it into cubes or oblong or any other shape you wish using a sharp knife or cookie cutters. Roll the pieces in additional sugar and store them in a tin in a cool, dark, dry place.

Raspberry jam

Ingredients:
2 pounds ripe, perfect raspberries
1 pound, 6 ounces (2¾ cups) sugar
Juice of 1 lemon

Preparation:
Wash raspberries quickly in cold water and drain on paper towels. Place raspberries in a bowl (glass or some other material) and sprinkle over sugar and lemon juice. Let stand for two hours. Drain off liquid and put it in a pot of untinned copper. Boil rapidly until syrup is reduced to half its original volume. Add raspberries. Mix and skim foam with a wooden spoon. Boil slowly until a jam consistency. When jam is ready, pour it hot into sterilized jars. Seal jars. Store in a cool, dark, dry place.

Raspberry jelly

Ingredients:
5 pounds ripe, perfect raspberries
2 cups water
Grated rind and juice of 1 lemon
5½ pounds (11 cups) sugar

Preparation:
Rinse raspberries quickly and drain well. Place into a bowl and crush with a potato masher. Stir in water and lemon rind and juice. Let stand for two hours. Pour berries into a pot and boil them slowly for about ten minutes, skimming foam. Press mixture through a double thickness of cheesecloth, squeezing fruit pulp well in order to obtain as much puree as possible. Return puree to pot and stir in sugar. Bring to a boil again and stir and skim foam from jelly. As soon as the jelly has reached the proper consistency (test by letting a drop fall on a cold, dry plate; it should harden immediately, without leaving any traces of liquid) pour it into sterilized jars immediately. Seal and store in a cool, dark, dry place.

Raspberries in syrup

Ingredients:
5 pounds sound but not dead ripe raspberries
1 pound, six ounces (2¾ cups) sugar
Grated rind and juice of 1 lemon
1 quart water

Preparation:
If home grown, gather raspberries in the early morning hours. Pick carefully so that berries are not crushed. Preserve as soon as possible after picking. Rinse quickly and place on paper towels to dry.

Arrange dry raspberries in sterilized jars. Boil sugar, lemon rind and water for two to three minutes. Stir in lemon juice. Pour hot syrup over raspberries, covering them to three-quarters. Seal jars and sterilize for five minutes in a boiling water bath (see page 9). Do not, however, allow the water to boil too violently for the raspberries are very delicate. Store jars in a cool, dark, dry place.

Raspberry syrup

Ingredients:
5 pounds ripe, perfect raspberries
5½ pounds (11 cups) sugar
Juice of 2 lemons

Preparation:
Crush the raspberries placed into a glass or pottery bowl with a potato masher. Let raspberries ferment for two days or more, according to temperature of room in which fermentation is taking place. Stir pulp occasionally with a woden spoon. After fermentation has taken place (raspberries will have an alcoholic odor) press pulp through cheesecloth. Pour juice into an untinned copper pot. Stir in sugar and lemon juice. Bring mixture slowly to a boil, stirring and skimming foam for two minutes. Pour syrup into a glass or ceramic bowl and cool completely. Pour into bottles, seal and store in a cool, dark, dry place.

Rhubarb jam

Rhubarb jam makes an excellent filling for tarts.

Ingredients:
5½ pounds tender rhubarb
Juice of 1 lemon
3½ pounds (7 cups) sugar

Preparation:
Wash rhubarb in cold water. Dice rhubarb stalks, discarding any tough filaments. Put rhubarb in a pottery or plastic bowl. Stir in lemon juice and sugar. Let marinate at room temperature for twelve hours or overnight. The next day drain juice from the rhubarb into a pot and boil until reduced to half its original volume. Add rhubarb. Bring to a boil, stirring and skimming foam until thick. Pour while hot into sterilized jars. Seal and store in a cool, dark, dry place.

Rhubarb marmalade

Ingredients:
6½ pounds rhubarb
3 green apples
Rind of 1 lemon, in large pieces
Juice of 1 lemon
1 pinch ground ginger
4½ pounds (9 cups) sugar

Preparation:
Wash rhubarb and remove tough portions. Cut into one inch pieces and put in a pot. Peel, core and dice apples. Add apples, lemon rind and juice to rhubarb. Bring mixture slowly to a boil, stirring and skimming foam. Cook slowly for twenty to thirty minutes, stirring frequently. Stir in ginger. When rhubarb is reduced to a pulp, press it through a sieve or food mill. Replace puree in pot and stir in sugar. Bring to a boil again slowly. Cook at a slow bubble, stirring constantly until thick. Pour marmalade hot into sterilized jars. Seal and store in a cool, dark, dry place.

Rhubarb in syrup

Rhubarb in syrup is good for cakes, fruit cups and the like.

Ingredients:
4½ pounds 2-inch pieces trimmed rhubarb
Juice of 1 lemon
Rind of 1 lemon, in large pieces
A few pieces crystallized ginger
2½ pounds (5 cups) sugar

Preparation:
Wash and drain rhubarb. In a large pot heat a large quantity of water with lemon juice until boiling. Place rhubarb in a colander and dip into boiling water. When water reboils, remove colander and drain. Reserve one quart of the water in which rhubarb was boiled. Arrange rhubarb in sterilized jars. To each jar add a piece of lemon rind and a piece of ginger. In a pot heat reserved cooking water and sugar and boil until syrup clears. Pour hot syrup over rhubarb filling jars to three-quarters. Seal jars and sterilize in a boiling water bath (see page 9) for thirty to thirty-five minutes. Store in a cool, dark, dry place.

Rhubarb wine

This is not a true wine but a beverage common in the country districts of the Anglo-Saxon countries.

Ingredients:
4½ pounds trimmed, diced rhubarb
Rind of 1 lemon, in large pieces
Juice of 1 lemon
3 quarts water
1 pound (2 cups) sugar
Juice of 1 grapefruit
1 cup brandy

Preparation:
Place rhubarb in a glass or ceramic bowl (do not use metal) and add lemon rind and juice and water. Let stand in a cool place for four or five days, stirring the mixture at least twice a day. Strain mixture through a double thickness cheesecloth, crushing rhubarb to remove juice. Pour liquid obtained into a large jug or crock and stir in sugar, grapefruit juice and brandy. Cover and set aside for two weeks in a cool place. Pour into sterilized bottles and cap with a bottle capper. It is a tonic and an aid to digestion.

To obtain a different wine, proceed in this manner: Steam the diced rhubarb. When it is cooked, press it through a sieve or food mill into a glass or ceramic bowl. Stir in one and one-half quarts water, lemon rind and juice of one lemon and two cups sugar. Cool. Strain liquid through a double thickness cheesecloth and add one and one-half cups brandy. Let stand two weeks in a cool place. Pour into sterilized bottles and cap with a bottle capper. Store in a cool, dark, dry place.

Rose jam

Ingredients:
4½ pounds green apples
Grated rind and juice of 1 lemon
1 pound fresh, fragrant rose petals
1 cup water
3 pounds (6 cups) sugar

Preparation:
Peel, core and dice apples into a pot that is not made of aluminum. Stir in lemon rind and juice, washed and drained rose petals and water. Let stand covered thirty minutes. Bring to a boil slowly, stirring and skimming foam. When apples are mushy and soft, press mixture through a sieve. Replace puree in pot and stir in sugar. Bring slowly to a boil, stirring constantly. This jam should not be allowed to come to the heavy consistency of normal jam, for it tends to crystallize easily if the sugar is allowed to thicken too much. Therefore, when it reaches the consistency of honey pour it hot into sterilized jars. Seal and store in a cool, dark, dry place.

Rose jelly

Ingredients:
4½ pounds green apples
2 quarts water
Grated rind and juice of 1 lemon
5½ pounds (11 cups) sugar
1 pound fresh, fragrant rose petals with yellow bases removed

Preparation:
Peel apples, dicing them without removing core. In a pot combine water, lemon rind and juice. Add apples. Boil apples until they are mushy (about thirty minutes) stirring and skimming foam. Press apples through a double thickness cheesecloth, pressing juice out of the pulp well. Replace juice in pot, stir in sugar and bring again to a boil. Boil until syrup when dropped on a plate becomes solid on cooling. While syrup is still boiling stir in rose petals. Boil for two minutes. Strain jelly again through a double thickness cheesecloth, squeezing petals. Replace jelly in pot and boil it for one minute—no more. Pour immediately into sterilized jars and store in a cool, dark, dry place.

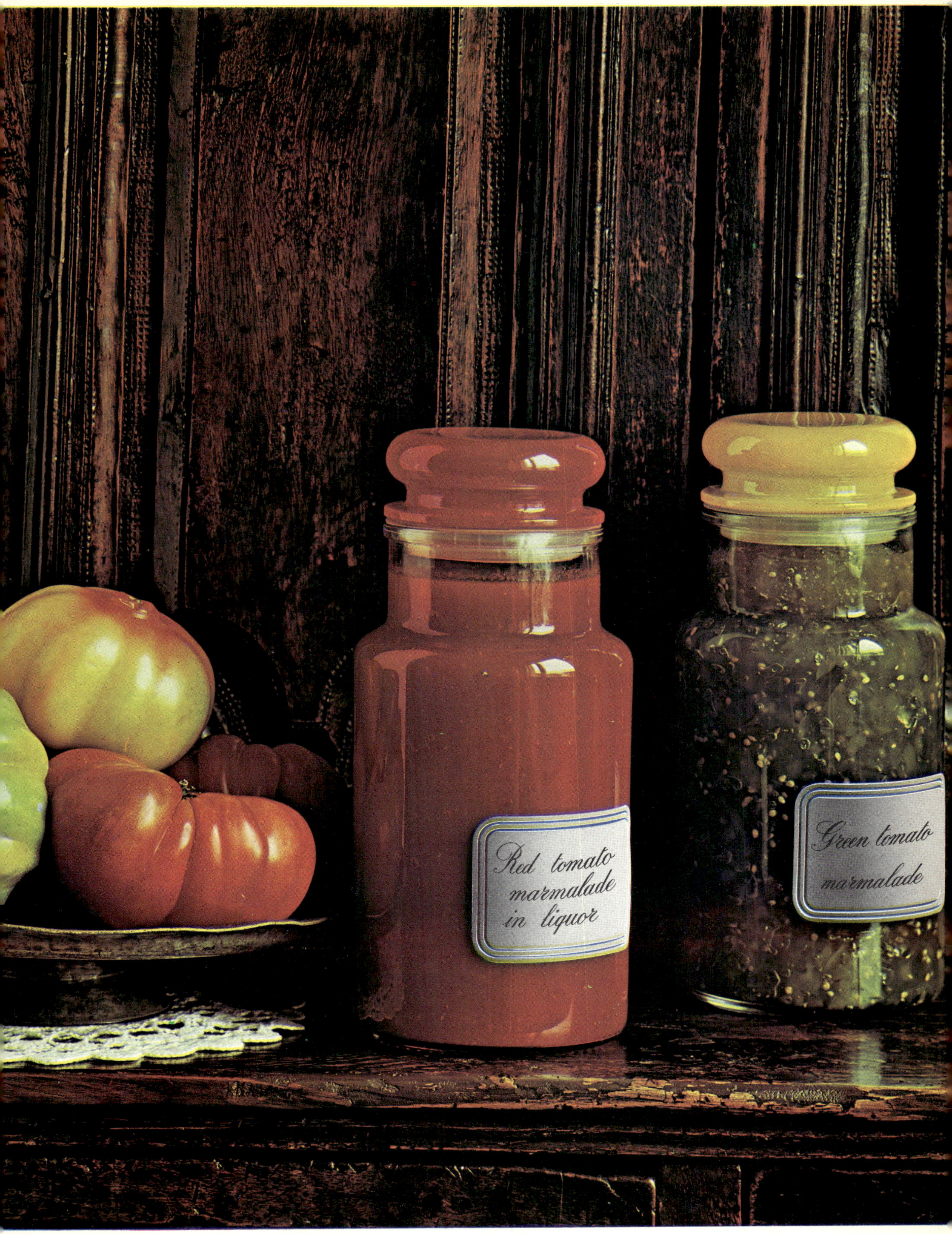
Red tomato marmalade in liquor
Green tomato marmalade

Coffee marmalade

Milk marmalade

Green beans with tomatoes

Plain canned green beans

Canned beans

Beans all' uccelletto

Strawberry jam

Ingredients:
7 pounds wild or garden strawberries
Grated rind and juice of 1 lemon
4 pounds (8 cups) sugar
1 cup water
½ cup maraschino liqueur

Preparation:
Select whole, sound, ripe berries. Hull and rinse berries quickly and dry on paper towels. Put berries in a glass or ceramic bowl. Add lemon rind and juice. Boil sugar and water in a pot stirring constantly until sugar is dissolved. Boil for three or four minutes. While hot pour syrup over berries in bowl. Mix berries and let stand for one hour. Pour berries and syrup into a pot and bring to a slow boil, stirring constantly. Cook until jam has the right consistency (see CHERRY MARMALADE). Stir in maraschino and while hot pour into sterilized jars. Seal jars and store in a cool, dark, dry place.

Strawberries in syrup

Used in compotes to make fillings for cakes and tarts; it is also useful as a garnish to fruit cups and various desserts

Ingredients:
4 pounds red, perfect and not too ripe wild or garden strawberries, all of the same size
1 pound (2 cups) sugar
1 quart water
Several pieces lemon rind
Small amount brandy (or grain alcohol)

Preparation:
Hull berries. Rinse berries rapidly so as not to absorb any of the water and place on a cloth to dry in the sun for an hour. Arrange dry berries in small sterilized jars.

Prepare a syrup by boiling sugar and water for three to five minutes. While still boiling, pour syrup over berries in jars, covering them to three-quarters. In each jar place a piece of lemon rind. Since strawberries are so delicate and a lengthy sterilization would spoil their consistency, it is advisable to pour a few drops of warm brandy or alcohol on the inside of the lids of the jars. Light brandy, and while alcohol is burning, slowly screw on cover. The alcohol will burn up the oxygen in the jar.

Now sterilize jars for about five minutes in a boiling water bath (see page 9). Check covers afterwards to make sure that they are tight.

Store in a cool, dark, dry place.

Strawberry custard

Ingredients:
2 pounds perfectly ripe and sound strawberries
4 pounds (8 cups) sugar
Grated rind and juice of 1 lemon
6 cups 45% grain alcohol

Preparation:
Hull strawberries and rinse quickly. Dry on paper towels. Mix berries with sugar in a large clean glass or ceramic bowl. Stir in lemon rind and juice. Let stand in a cool, airy place for two days, stirring them with a wooden spoon at least twice a day. Keep bowl covered with cheesecloth. Stir in alcohol. Strain mixture through double thickness of cheesecloth, pressing through pulp. Pour custard into wide-necked, small sterilized jars. Seal. Store in a cool, dark, dry place.

Strawberry juice

Strawberry juice is used for making ices, ice cream and the like. Add sugar to taste to juice, as desired.

Ingredients:
5 pounds fresh-picked perfect, ripe strawberries
Juice of 1 lemon

Preparation:
Wash strawberries in cold water and drain. Hull them and press them through a fine sieve or food mill. For every four cups pulp, add the juice of half a lemon. Mix and pour juice into bottles to within an inch of the top. Use bottle caps with the appropriate bottle-capping tool and sterilize for about one hour in a boiling water bath (see page 9). Let bottles cool in the same water, then store in a cool, dark, dry place.

Tangerine jelly

Ingredients:
3½ pounds rennet apples or quinces
3 cups water
Grated rind of 4 tangerines
Grated rind of 1 lemon
3½ pounds (7 cups) sugar
Juice of 10 tangerines

Preparation:
Cook peeled but not cored apples in two cups of the water, skimming foam. When apples are tender and mushy, strain through a double thickness of cheesecloth. Let it drip slowly so juice is clear. Pour juice into pot. Add tangerine rind and lemon rind. In another saucepan boil sugar with remaining water about five minutes or until clear. Pour syrup into apple juice. Stir in tangerine juice. Boil for one to two minutes. Remove from heat and let stand for fifteen minutes. Pour through a fine sieve to remove rinds. Replace in pot and boil again, skimming foam until a drop of jelly on a cold plate becomes firm. Pour hot into sterilized jars and seal. Store in a cool, dark, dry place.

Tangerine wedges in syrup

Ingredients:
3½ pounds perfect, firm tangerines
1 pound, 2 ounces (2¼ cups) sugar
1 cup water
Rind of 1 lemon, cut into large pieces

Preparation:
Peel tangerines and pull apart wedges. Remove white, threadlike membranes carefully without puncturing the wedges themselves. You should end with about two pounds fruit. Arrange wedges one by one in sterilized jars. Tap jars down on a padded surface to firm in the wedges. Place a piece of lemon rind in each jar. In a pot, combine sugar and water and bring to a boil. As soon as syrup begins to boil and sugar is dissolved, pour hot syrup into jars, seal and sterilize for ten to fifteen minutes in a boiling water bath (see page 9) and store them in a cool, dark, dry place.

For a less sweet preparation, proceed as follows: Stir one and one-half cups sugar into two cups water. Prepare syrup as above. Pour hot over sections, seal and process as above.

Candied violets

Ingredients:
4 ounces violets without stem and any green; they should be sweet-scented and without dried edges
11 ounces (1⅓ cups) sugar

Preparation:
The violets must be perfectly dry and not withered or faded. Arrange a layer of violets in a clean jar, sprinkle with sugar; then another layer of violets, also sprinkled with sugar, and so on. The last layer should be a layer of sugar. When jar is filled, seal it and put it in a cool, dark, dry place. Every day for a week, check violets and if sugar is not completely dissolved, stir very delicately with a bamboo skewer. After a week keep jars closed and store in a cool, dark, dry place. Use violets sparingly to flavor sweets, and keep the jar closed at all times. If sugar should crystallize, add a few drops of grain (95%) alcohol, or a coffee spoonful of good brandy.

These are not genuine candied violets, for the preparation has been greatly simplified; nevertheless, the flavor is better than genuine candied violets.

Violet syrup

This is a highly flavored syrup, suitable for flavoring sweets, ices, ice cream, etc.

Ingredients:
2 ounces highly perfumed violet petals
⅔ cup water
11 ounces (1⅓ cups) sugar

Preparation:
Put violet petals in a pottery or ceramic bowl. Bring water to a boil and pour it over violet petals. Let stand for two hours. Strain liquid through a double thickness cheesecloth into a bowl. Allow filtered liquid to stand for at least an hour in order for any particles to sink to the bottom of the bowl. Slowly pour this liquid (keeping back particles on the bottom) into a stainless steel or untinned copper pot. Stir in sugar and bring to a boil slowly. Continue boiling very slowly. When liquid is a little less thick than honey, cool it quickly by placing pot in ice water. Pour into a sterilized bottle and seal with a bottle capper. Store in a cool, dark, dry place.

Miscellaneous preserves

Red "summer" jam

Ingredients:
1 pound cherries (sweet or sour)
1 pound fresh currants
2 pounds strawberries
2 pounds bilberries (blueberries)
2 pounds raspberries
7 pounds (14 cups) sugar
1½ cups water
Juice of 1 lemon

Preparation:
Wash fruit. Stem and pit cherries, remove currants from the bunches, hull strawberries, wash bilberries and raspberries. Boil sugar and water in a large pot for three to five minutes until a thick syrup. Add cherries. Let boil for five minutes, then add remaining fruit. Boil entire mixture stirring with a wooden spoon and skimming foam until mixture is thick. Stir in lemon juice and pour while hot into sterilized jars. Seal and store in a cool, dark, dry place.

"Black Forest" jelly

Ingredients:
2 pounds currants (or bilberries—blueberries)
2 pounds raspberries
4 pounds (8 cups) sugar
Rind of 1 lemon in large pieces
1 pound wild strawberries

Preparation:
Press in a sieve currants (or bilberries) and raspberries, obtaining in all about seven cups thick juice. Pour juice into an untinned copper pot and stir in sugar and lemon rind. Bring to a boil very slowly, skimming foam during cooking. When mixture begins to thicken, stir more frequently and continue skimming foam. Cook until a drop on a cold plate solidifies. Stir in strawberries. Cook slowly, for five minutes, until strawberries are well blended with jelly. Remove lemon rind. Pour hot jelly into sterilized jars. Seal and store in a cool, dark, dry place.

Cooked wine

Ingredients:
5 pounds red and white grapes
8 ounces ripe black and white figs

Preparation:
In this recipe you can use any variety of grapes.

Wash grapes thoroughly and remove from stems. Put grapes through a fruit squeezer. Peel figs. Put grape juice and figs in a pot and simmer over very low heat for several hours or until very thick. Press through a very fine strainer and pour hot, cooked wine into sterilized jars. Seal and store in a cool, dark, dry place.

Slightly warmed, it is soothing for coughs and hoarseness.

Grandpa's preserve

Fruit preserved in this manner can be used to garnish sweets or as an aid to digestion. In addition, the syrup makes an excellent liqueur.

Ingredients:
11 pounds raspberries, cherries, blueberries, apricots, pears, plums and peaches
4½ pounds (9 cups) sugar
1½ cups water or enough to dissolve the sugar
4 quarts brandy

Preparation:
Clean fruit by wiping with a clean cloth or wash quickly in water. Drain fruit on paper towels. If necessary, pit or core fruit, cutting apricots and peaches in half and pears into wedges. Pack fruit firmly into sterilized jars.

In a saucepan boil sugar and water, stirring until syrup becomes clear. Remove from heat at once and let cool. Divide syrup equally among jars and pour over fruit. Fill jars with brandy. Seal and store in a cool, dark, dry place.

Fruit cup

Ingredients:
9 pounds fruit: apples, pears, peaches, apricots, gooseberries, cherries, pineapple
Juice of 1 lemon
2 quarts water
2 pounds (4 cups) sugar

Preparation:
Wash fruit. Peel, core and pit all the fruit. Dice into bite-size pieces and mix pieces with lemon juice. Spoon into sterilized jars filling them to within one inch of top.

Boil water and sugar for a few minutes or until clear. Pour while hot into jars, covering fruit completely. Seal and sterilize in a boiling water bath (see page 9) for twenty minutes. Store in a cool, dark, dry place.

Milanese mustard

This mustard goes excellently with boiled or grilled meats.

Ingredients:
5 pounds mixed fruits (pears, apples, apricots, peaches, grapes, etc.)
1 pound, 5 ounces (2⅔ cups) sugar
1 cup dry white wine
Juice of ½ lemon
2 whole cloves
Pinch of ground pepper
Grated rind of 1 orange
Pinch ground cinnamon
1 tablespoon dry mustard
Brandy (optional)

Preparation:
Wash, peel, core or pit fruit. Dice fruit. In a large pot combine sugar, wine and lemon juice and heat to a boil. Stir in fruit and remaining ingredients except dry mustard and brandy. Boil slowly stirring mixture occasionally for about ten minutes. Press mixture through a sieve or a food mill. Replace puree in pot and stir in mustard mixed with a few drops of white wine. Cook at a boil slowly until thick. Pour while hot into sterilized jars. Seal and store in a cool, dark, dry place.

For a change of flavor, stir in a small glass of brandy before pouring into jars.

Red tomato marmalade in liquor

This marmalade is used mostly in the preparation of sweets and tarts.

Ingredients:
7 pounds firm-pulped tomatoes
Grated rind of 1 lemon
Juice of 2 lemons
4 pounds (8 cups) sugar
½ cup liquor to taste (rum, brandy, etc.)

Preparation:
Wash tomatoes. Remove cores and cut them into halves. Squeeze each half to remove seeds and liquid. Put tomato halves in a pot not made of aluminum. Stir in lemon rind and juice. Bring to a boil, stirring occasionally and skimming foam repeatedly. Let boil for about five minutes, then press through a sieve. Replace pulp in pot and stir in sugar. Continue cooking, stirring and skimming foam until tomatoes are thick, clear and red. Stir in liquor. Pour while hot into sterilized jars. Seal and store in a cool, dark, dry place.

Green tomato marmalade

This marmalade is good for cakes, tarts, etc.

Ingredients:
2 pounds green tomatoes
12 ounces (1½ cups) sugar
Grated rind and juice of ½ lemon
Pinch of salt

Preparation:
Remove cores and cut into wedges. Place in a blender and whirl until coarsely chopped. Put tomatoes in a bowl and stir in sugar, lemon rind and juice and salt. Let this mixture stand for four hours covered. Pour into a pot and bring to a boil. Stir and skim foam constantly. When mixture is thick, pour while hot into sterilized jars. Seal and store in a cool, dark, dry place.

Coffee marmalade

This marmalade is particularly adapted to breakfast because of its stimulating quality.

Ingredients:
2 cups water
1 tablespoon best ground coffee
1 pound green apples
Grated rind and juice of 1 lemon
12 ounces (1½ cups) sugar
1 vanilla bean
Brandy or some other liqueur (optional)

Preparation:
Heat water to boiling. Pour boiling water over coffee, then filter. Slice whole apples and place them in a saucepan with lemon juice and sugar. Stir constantly over a low heat for five minutes or until apples are mushy. Pour in coffee, vanilla and lemon rind. Continue cooking very slowly, stirring constantly. When mixture is thick, press apples, which by now should be a glistening black, through a sieve. Replace in pot and boil for one to two minutes. Pour while hot into sterilized jars. Seal and store in a cool, dark, dry place.

If you like, marmalade may also be flavored with brandy or some liqueur. This should be stirred into mixture just before pouring it into jars.

Milk marmalade

Ingredients:
2 pounds (4 cups) sugar
4 cups milk
Rind of 1 lemon, in large pieces

Preparation:
Mix sugar with cold milk in a pot that is not aluminum. Add lemon rind. Bring mixture very slowly to a boil, stirring with a wooden spoon for about an hour and a half. Check constantly during cooking to make sure that heat is very low since mixture tends to stick and burn easily. When mixture is thick, slightly less than that of normal marmalade, remove from heat. Remove pieces of lemon rind and pour hot mixture into sterilized jars. Seal jars and store in a cool, dark, dry place.

If you wish, you can make delicious candies from this mixture by leaving it on heat longer to become quite thick. Pour it out on an oiled cookie sheet, leveling the paste with an oiled spatula, to about the thickness of half an inch. When mixture is completely cold and hardened, break into pieces and wrap in plastic wrap to keep from becoming sticky.

Old-fashioned jam

Ingredients:
3½ pounds white, perfectly mature grapes
3 pounds small pears
8 ounces (1 cup) sugar
Rind and juice of 1 lemon
Pinch of ground cinnamon

Preparation:
Wash grapes. Remove stems and press through a sieve or food mill. You should have about six cups juice. Put juice in a stainless steel pot and boil slowly until reduced to about half its original volume, stirring and skimming foam. You should have about three cups liquid.

Wash, peel and cut pears into quarters or wedges, removing core. You should end with about four cups pears.

To hot grape juice add pear wedges, sugar, lemon rind and juice and cinnamon. Cook at a slow boil, stirring constantly until thick. Pour while hot into sterilized jars. Seal and store in a cool, dark, dry place.

Indian marmalade

Use as an accompaniment or flavoring for roast fowl and meat or to add a touch of flavor to pilaff.

Ingredients:
7 pounds green apples
2 pounds pears
2 teaspoons curry powder
Grated rind and juice of 1 lemon
1 cup white wine
1 celery heart, minced
3 walnut halves, chopped
4½ pounds (9 cups) sugar

Preparation:
Peel, core and dice apples and pears. Place them in a pot and stir in curry powder, lemon rind and juice, wine, celery and walnuts. Boil, stirring and skimming foam frequently. Let boil for fifteen minutes then press the whole mixture through a sieve or food mill. Replace puree in pot. Stir in sugar, bring to a boil, stirring and skimming foam until marmalade is thick. Pour while hot into sterilized jars. Seal and store in a cool, dark, dry place.

Chinese jam

Ingredients:
11 ounces fresh, fragrant rose petals
3 pounds (6 cups) sugar
Juice of 1 lemon
2 pounds mature, unblemished peaches
2 pounds red plums

Preparation:
Remove yellowish base of the rose petals. Bring a pot of water with a pinch of salt to a boil. Place rose petals in a colander and submerge in boiling water for thirty seconds. Remove from boiling water and submerge at once in cold water. Remove from cold water. Drain and dry on paper towels. Place on a cookie sheet and sprinkle three-quarters cup of the sugar and lemon juice over them. Let stand for two hours.

Wash, halve and pit peaches and plums. Dice and place in a pot that is not made of aluminum. Stir in remaining sugar; set aside for one hour. Coarsely chop sugared rose petals and stir them into peaches and plums. Bring to a boil slowly. Continue cooking while stirring and skimming foam until mixture is thick. Pour while hot immediately into sterilized jars. Seal and store in a cool, dark, dry place.

Wine jelly

Ingredients:
2 pounds peeled, sliced but not cored rennet (or green) apples (or quinces)
6 cups good, red wine
Grated rind of 1 lemon
Juice of 2 lemons
4½ pounds (9 cups) sugar

Preparation:
Combine apples or quinces, 1 quart of the wine and lemon rind and juice of one lemon in a pot that is not made of aluminum. When the apples are cooked and mushy (if using quinces, the cooking time will be longer, therefore one cup of water should be added with the wine) press mixture through a sieve lined with a double thickness cheesecloth, pressing fruit well. You should end with about seven cups of thick and slightly cloudy liquid. Replace in pot and stir in remaining wine, sugar and remaining lemon juice. Bring to a boil slowly, stirring and skimming foam. The liquid will become clear and little by little it will begin to thicken like an ordinary jelly (this takes thirty to thirty-five minutes). Boil slowly until a drop of the liquid on a cold, clean plate becomes firm on cooling. Pour jelly while hot into sterilized jars. Seal immediately and store in a cool, dark, dry place.

Vegetables

Plain artichokes

Ingredients:
5 pounds small artichokes
Juice of 1 lemon
Salt, as necessary
Peppercorns
Bay leaves

Preparation:
Wash artichokes well and remove tough outer leaves and keep only pale green, tender, inner part and a small piece of the stem, carefully peeled. Trim tips of leaves with scissors. As each artichoke is prepared, drop it into a bowl of warm water to which lemon juice has been added. When all the artichokes are prepared, arrange them in sterilized jars, pressing and squeezing so as to get the greatest number possible in each jar. Add one teaspoon salt to each quart, several peppercorns and a bay leaf. Cover artichokes with boiling water. Seal jars and sterilize in a boiling water bath (see page 9) for one hour, then let jars cool in the same water. Store in a cool, dark, dry place.

Before serving artichokes, rinse them with cold water, then saute them with oil and parsley.

Artichokes Italian style

These can be served as an antipasto or as a vegetable course.

Ingredients:
9 pounds small artichokes
3 quarts water
1 quart olive oil
1 cup lemon juice
1 garlic clove
20 peppercorns
2 whole cloves
2 bay leaves
1 sprig thyme
Several cumin seeds
2 tablespoons salt

Preparation:
Wash, prepare and soak artichokes as in PLAIN ARTICHOKES. Cut artichokes into halves. Put water in an untinned copper pot. Add olive oil, lemon juice, garlic, peppercorns, cloves, bay leaves, thyme, cumin and salt. Bring to a boil. Add artichokes to pot and boil over high heat. Cook until artichokes are tender but still firm. If cooking water evaporates before artichokes are done, add boiling water to keep up level of liquid. Remove artichokes with a slotted spoon. Pack in sterilized jars. Strain cooking liquid and pour over artichokes to cover. Seal jars and sterilize in a boiling water bath (see page 9) for 1 hour. Store in a cool, dark, dry place.

Pickled artichokes

Ingredients:
2 pounds small artichokes
Juice of 1 lemon
1 quart white wine vinegar
6 peppercorns
3 whole cloves
2 bay leaves
Olive oil, as needed

Preparation:
Wash, prepare and soak artichokes as in PLAIN ARTICHOKES. Put vinegar, peppercorns, cloves and bay leaves in a pot not of aluminum. When vinegar boils, add artichokes and let them boil for two or three minutes if they are small, an additional minute if they are large. Remove from heat and let cool in vinegar. With a slotted spoon, put artichokes in sterilized jars. Strain liquid and pour over artichokes. Carefully pour in a layer of oil to float on the surface and cover artichokes. Seal jars and store in a cool, dark, dry place.

Artichokes in oil

Ingredients:
2 pounds small artichokes
Juice of 1 lemon
1 quart water
1 quart white wine or vinegar
Several peppercorns
Several bay leaves
Several whole cloves
2 teaspoons salt, as needed
Olive oil, as needed

Preparation:
Wash, prepare and soak artichokes as in PLAIN ARTICHOKES. Cut largest globes in half. In a pot not made of aluminum, boil water, wine, peppercorns, bay leaves, cloves and salt. When mixture is boiling rapidly, add drained artichokes. Let liquid come to a boil again. Lower heat and simmer gently for about five minutes. Drain and place to dry between two clean cloths so that they do not come into direct contact with the air which tends to discolor them. When artichokes are dry, arrange them in sterilized jars, adding two peppercorns and a bay leaf to each jar. Cover artichokes with oil. Seal and check the level of the oil for several days, adding more oil if needed to keep artichokes covered. Store in a cool, dark, dry place.

Plain asparagus

Ingredients:
2 pounds asparagus
Salt

Preparation:
Lightly peel tough parts of the stalks of asparagus and as you complete each one put it in cold water. Cut off tough bottoms so that each spear will fit one inch below top of jar. Arrange them in sterilized jars with the points up. Add one teaspoon salt to each quart jar. Cover with boiling water, leaving one inch headspace. Seal jar. Process according to pressure canner method (see page 9) at ten pounds pressure; twenty-five minutes for half-pint and pint jars or thirty minutes for one-and-one-half pint and quart jars.

Before eating asparagus, wash it in a large quantity of cold water, then saute in foaming butter and serve with grated Parmesan cheese.

Store jars in a cool, dark, dry place.

Asparagus in vinegar

Ingredients:
7 pounds perfect asparagus spears
Boiling salted water
About 2 quarts white wine vinegar
6 peppercorns
Several sprigs of fresh tarragon

Preparation:
Clean and wash asparagus carefully, cut off tough stem, leaving only the spears. Tie spears in small bunches and cut length long enough to fit the size of the jars. Bring large quantity of salted water to a boil. Place asparagus in a colander and place into boiling water two to three minutes. Remove colander and drain. Untie asparagus and place on paper towels to drain thoroughly. When asparagus is dry, arrange asparagus in sterilized jars, with tips upward. Bring vinegar and peppercorns to a boil. Remove peppercorns. Pour while hot over asparagus until covered. Put a sprig of tarragon in each jar. Seal and store in a cool, dark, dry place.

If you want a somewhat less sharp asparagus, add about one cup water to vinegar before boiling.

Basil leaves in oil

Ingredients:
Basil leaves (perfect leaves, picked before flowering)
Olive oil

Preparation:
Wash sprigs of basil in cold water, shake off excess water and hang them up for an hour to dry. Remove only the green leaves. They must be absolutely dry. Pack them into small sterilized jars, pressing down lightly. When you have formed a layer of leaves, add olive oil to cover. Lightly pressing down on leaves eliminates any air that is trapped in jar. Continue until jar is filled. Press down final layer, then cut a piece of wax paper to cover leaves and keep them pressed down under the oil. Seal well and store in a cool, dark, dry place.

Aside from using the basil leaves, you can also use the oil for cooking or salads.

Basil leaves in salt

Ingredients:
8 ounces basil leaves
Salt
Olive oil as needed

Preparation:
Wash, dry and prepare basil as in BASIL LEAVES IN OIL. Weigh leaves after removing from stems. Put a layer of leaves into sterilized jars then a layer of salt, using the proportion of a handful of leaves to each teaspoon salt. The top layer must be salt. Press down gently on the leaves to press out most of the air between leaves. Pour a layer of olive oil over the top to cover leaves and seal jars. Store in a cool, dark, dry place.

When you use leaves, remember they are highly salted and do not use usual amount of salt in the food being prepared.

Beans Roman style

Ingredients:
2½ pounds fresh shelled beans (lima, butter, soy beans) weigh beans after shelling
1 carrot, shredded
1 celery stalk, sliced
1 clove garlic
2 onion
3 whole cloves
1 bay leaf
2 tablespoons olive oil
1½ cups peeled, chopped tomatoes
1 tablespoon chopped parsley
½ cup dry white wine
Salt and pepper, as needed

Preparation:
Heat a pot with enough salted water to cover beans. Add carrot, celery, garlic, one whole onion studded with the three cloves and bay leaf. When water boils, add beans and cook until tender but still crisp. Reserve half of the water in which beans were cooked. Drain beans removing flavoring vegetables.

Pour oil into a skillet. Slice remaining onion and add. Saute until onion is brown. Add tomatoes and parsley and cook for one minute. Add beans, white wine, salt and pepper to taste. Simmer for two or three minutes until ingredients have formed a sauce that well covers beans. If sauce is too thick, add some of the water in which beans were cooked. Pour while hot into sterilized jars.

Seal jars and sterilize by pressure canner (see page 9) at ten pounds pressure; pints, forty minutes; quarts, fifty minutes. For soy beans process as above; pints, fifty-five minutes; quarts, one hour and five minutes. Store in a cool, dark, dry place.

Beans all'uccelletto

Ingredients:
1½ cups (approximately) olive oil
1 onion, chopped
1 clove garlic
2 sage leaves
2 peeled tomatoes, chopped
5 pounds fresh, shelled beans (lima, butter or soy beans)
Salt, as needed
Pepper, as needed
1 pinch sugar
Chicken stock, as needed

Preparation:
Pour two tablespoons of the oil in a skillet. Saute onion, garlic and sage leaves until onion is golden. Stir in tomatoes and beans and simmer ten minutes. Add salt, pepper to taste and a pinch of sugar. Add chicken stock or boiling water to cover beans. Simmer until beans are just tender. Taste and add salt if necessary. Cool. Pour into sterilized jars. Cover with a thin layer of remaining olive oil. Seal jars and sterilize in the same manner and the same length of time as in BEANS ROMAN STYLE. Store in a cool, dark, dry place.

Beans all'uccelletto are served with stews, tripe, etc., bringing them to a boil and sprinkling freshly chopped parsley over them.

Capers in salt

Basil in salt

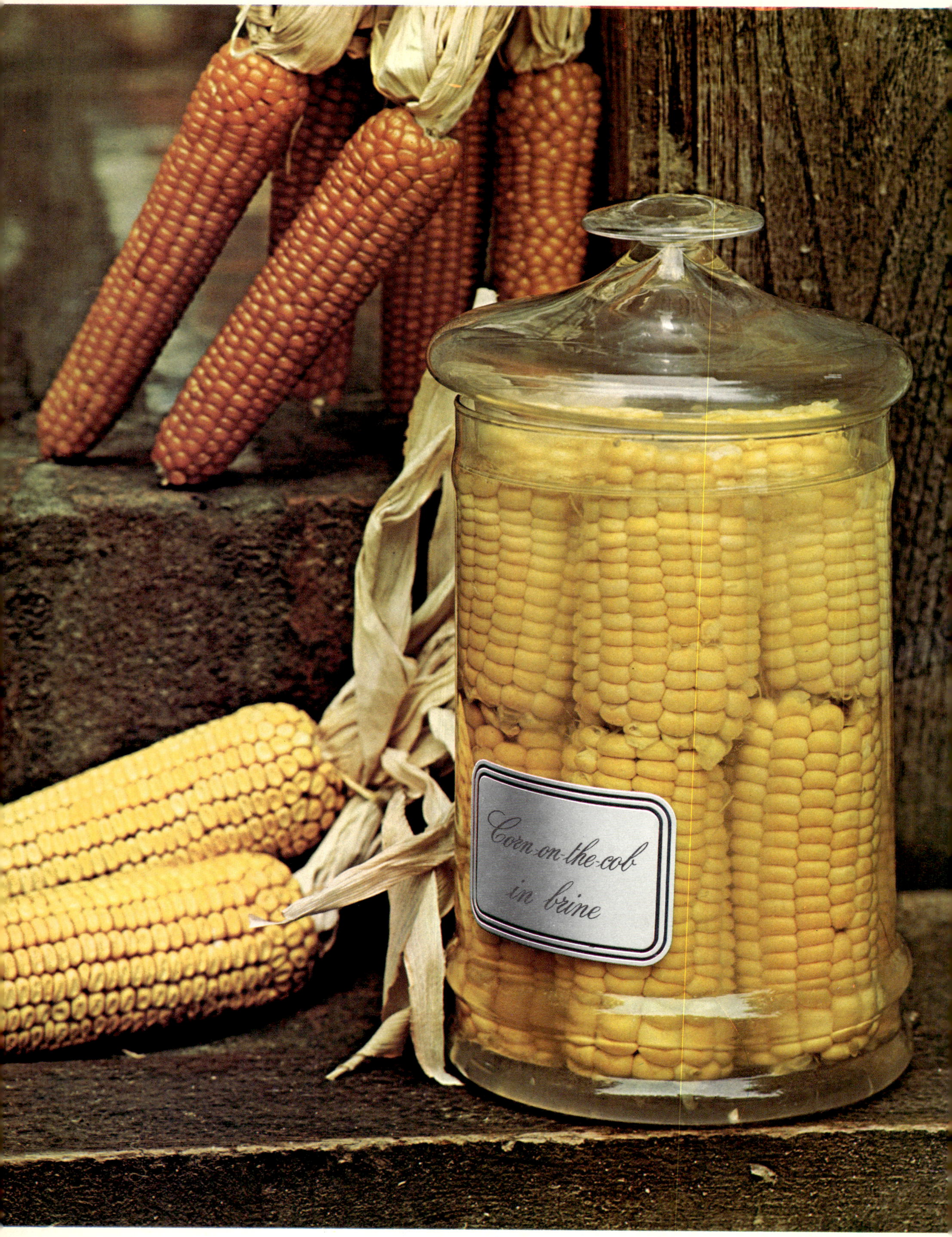
Corn-on-the-cob
in brine

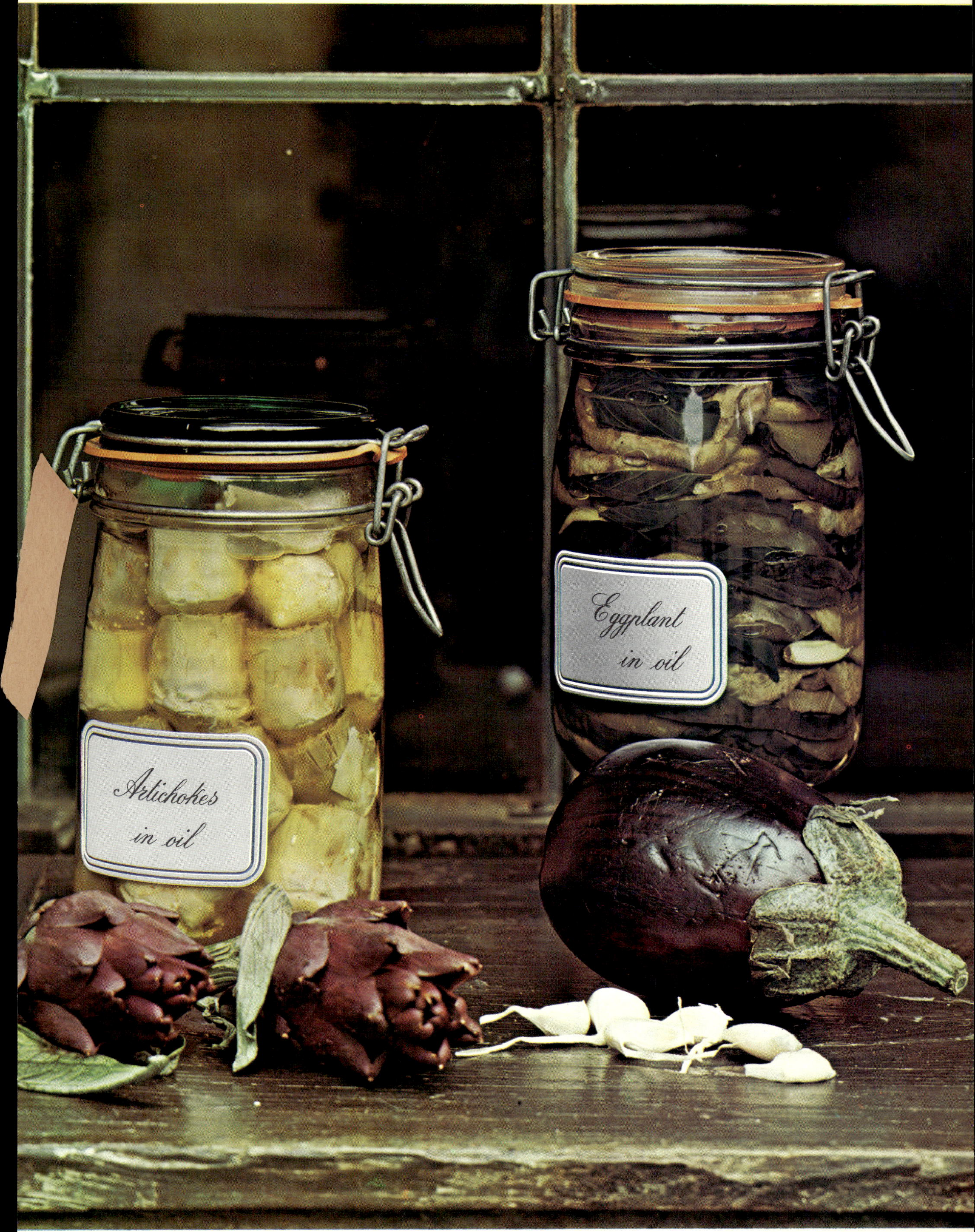
Artichokes in oil
Eggplant in oil

Dried mint

Beans in oil

Served as an antipasto, a vegetable course or in salads.

Ingredients:
3 pounds fresh, shelled beans (lima, butter or soy)
Salt, as needed
Several sage leaves
Several bay leaves
1 clove garlic
Several peppercorns
Best quality olive oil, as needed

Preparation:
Put beans in a pot and cover with cold water. Bring very slowly to a boil. Add salt to taste, sage, bay leaves, garlic and several peppercorns. When beans are almost tender, drain and remove sage, bay leaves, garlic and peppercorns. Put beans in sterilized jars and cover with olive oil. Make sure that you have the very best quality of oil, because the flavor of the beans depends upon it. Seal jars and sterilize in the same manner and the same length of time as in BEANS ROMAN STYLE. Store in a cool, dark, dry place.

Canned beans

These are served by draining off the liquid in which they have been preserved and cooking in any way you prefer.

Ingredients:
7 pounds fresh, shelled beans (lima, butter or soy)
1 carrot
1 stalk celery
2 onions
2 whole cloves
1 sprig thyme
Several rosemary leaves
1 bay leaf
1 small piece salt pork (2 ounces)
Several fresh basil leaves
Pepper, as needed
Salt, as needed
Olive oil, as needed

Preparation:
Cook beans as in BEANS ROMAN STYLE adding carrot, celery stalk, onions studded with cloves, thyme, rosemary, bay leaf and salt pork to water. Drain beans reserving cooking water and discarding flavoring vegetables and salt pork. Let beans cool, and pack in sterilized jars. Add several basil leaves to each jar. Cover with reserved cooking water which has been seasoned to taste with salt and pepper. Pour a thin layer of olive oil on top and seal jars. Sterilize in the same manner and the same length of time as in BEANS ROMAN STYLE. Store in a cool, dark, dry place.

Plain canned green beans

Ingredients:
5 pounds young, tender green beans or wax beans
Salt, as needed

Preparation:
Break off both stem and tip ends. Fill a large pot (untinned copper is best) with water and heat until boiling. Add green beans and two tablespoons salt and boil rapidly for two minutes. Drain and spread them out on trays to cool. Arrange green beans in sterilized jars and cover them with boiling water. Add one teaspoon salt to each quart jar and sterilize in a pressure canner (see page 9) at ten pounds pressure; pints for twenty minutes, quarts for twenty-five minutes. Store in a cool, dark, dry place.

When it comes time to serve the beans, drain off the water in which they were preserved, wash them in cold water and saute them in butter or cook them in some other way.

Green beans, home style

Ingredients:
5 pounds green beans or wax beans
1 cup olive oil
1 onion, chopped
Several cloves garlic
2 cups peeled, chopped tomatoes
Salt, as needed
Pepper, as needed
Pinch of sugar

Preparation:
Remove ends, string and wash beans. Heat oil with onion and garlic in a large skillet until golden brown. Add tomatoes and let boil for two to three minutes. Add beans, salt, pepper to taste and pinch of sugar. Stirring occasionally, cook beans for eight to ten minutes over a low heat. Let cool. Put beans in sterilized jars, seal and sterilize as in PLAIN CANNED BEANS. Store in a cool, dark, dry place.

They should be eaten within six months. When preparing them for serving, remove from jar and boil for a minute or two, or you may heat them in a double boiler over low heat.

Pickled green beans

Ingredients:
5 pounds green beans or wax beans
White wine vinegar, as needed
Olive oil, as needed
Several bay leaves
Several peppercorns

Preparation:
Remove tips of the beans and string them if necessary. Heat enough vinegar to cover beans until boiling and then add beans. Boil rapidly for two minutes and drain. Spread beans out on a clean cloth to dry, then arrange them in sterilized jars and cover them with oil. Put a bay leaf and a couple of peppercorns in each jar. Seal jars. Store in a cool, dark, dry place.

These are served as hors d'ouevres, along with other pickled foods.

Green beans with tomatoes

Ingredients:
5 pounds fresh green beans or wax beans
1 onion, chopped
Olive oil, as needed
2 cloves garlic, left whole
4½ cups peeled, chopped tomatoes
7 or 8 fresh basil leaves
Salt, as needed
Pepper, as needed

Preparation:
Remove the tips from beans and wash in cold, salted water. Drain and spread out to dry on towels. Brown onion in two tablespoons of oil. Add garlic, tomatoes and basil leaves. Boil slowly, stirring, for four or five minutes. Add beans and let the mixture come to a boil. Add salt and pepper to taste. Remove garlic. Cool beans and place them in sterilized jars covering beans completely. Seal jars and sterilize by pressure canner method (see page 9) at the same pressure and time as for PLAIN CANNED GREEN BEANS. Store in a cool, dark, dry place.

When beans are served, add a pinch of sugar to sweeten acid taste of tomatoes.

Sweet-sour green beans

Ingredients:
2 pounds perfect green beans or wax beans
Salt, as needed
3 cups white vinegar
½ cup sugar
1 bay leaf
3 fresh basil leaves
2 whole cloves
1 stick cinnamon

Preparation:
Wash, remove tips and cut beans into two-inch lengths. Drop beans into boiling salted water to cover and boil for two minutes. Drain and spread out to dry on a clean cloth. Place beans in sterilized jars. Boil vinegar with remaining ingredients for one minute. Cool and strain. Pour over beans covering them completely. Seal jars and store in a cool, dark, dry place.

Serve as an hors d'ouevre mixed with mayonnaise thinned with cream.

Marinated beets

Ingredients:
4½ pounds small, red beets
2 tablespoons salt
1 quart white or red wine vinegar
5 whole peppercorns
1 or 2 bay leaves
5 or 6 fresh basil leaves

Preparation:
Use small, sweet, round beets. Cut off the greens (which boiled and sauteed in oil and garlic can be served as a vegetable.) Wash beets several times and boil them in salted water to cover, uncovered, for about an hour, or until easily pierced. Let beets cool in cooking water. Drain, reserving about one cup of the water. Let water stand undisturbed so that it becomes almost clear. Peel beets and leave whole. Arrange them in sterilized jars. In a pot combine reserved water, salt, vinegar, peppercorns, bay leaves and basil. Bring to a boil for one to two minutes. Pour while hot into jars to cover beets. Seal jars and store in a cool, dark, dry place.

Beets in vinegar

This can be served in a salad alone or mixed with other vegetables.

Ingredients:
*7 pounds beets
Salt
2 quarts vinegar
Several whole peppercorns
Several whole juniper berries
2 whole cloves
1 stick cinnamon
1 onion, cut into halves
Several celery stalks, left whole
Herbs to taste*

Preparation:
Prepare and cook beets as in MARINATED BEETS. Peel beets and dice them. In another pot boil three cups water, 1 tablespoon salt, vinegar, peppercorns, juniper berries, cloves, cinnamon stick, onion, celery stalks and herbs as desired for five minutes. Put beets in sterilized jars. Strain vinegar and while hot pour over beets covering them. Process by the pressure canner method (see page 9) at ten pound pressure for thirty minutes for half pints and pints and thirty-five minutes for one-and-one-half pints and quarts.

Store in a cool, dark, dry place.

Braised cabbage

Cooked in this style and put in an airtight container, the cabbage will keep for about a week in the refrigerator.

Ingredients:
*5 pounds green cabbage
½ pound salt pork in slices
4 carrots, sliced
2 onions
2 cloves
A bouquet garni consisting of thyme and bay leaves
Beef broth, as needed*

Preparation:
Remove dry, spoiled leaves. Cut cabbage into quarters, wash carefully and drop into boiling lightly salted water and boil for ten minutes. Drain and peel off leaves. In a pot (preferably of terracotta,) put down a layer of salt pork. Add the carrots, sliced; the whole onions, with a clove stuck in each one; and bouquet garni. Cover with cabbage leaves and barely cover with beef broth. Cover. Cook over low heat for about two hours. Put cabbage leaves in a glass or porcelain container with an airtight lid, removing onions and bouquet garni. Store in the refrigerator. Will keep only one week.

Plain savoy cabbage

When the cabbage is used, remove the necessary quantity from the jar, keeping what is left over in the refrigerator, and cook in any way that you please.

Ingredients:
7 pounds cleaned Savoy cabbage
Salt, as needed
Rind of 1 lemon, in large pieces
Juice of 1 lemon
2 bay leaves
3 green apples peeled, cored and sliced
10 peppercorns
5 or 6 juniper berries (optional)
1 cup dry white wine, about

Preparation:
Cut cabbage head in quarters and remove core. Shred leaves into very thin strips. Place strips in salted water to cover. Let stand in the water for a few moments, then drain in a colander. Heat large quantity of salted water with lemon rind and juice and bay leaves to boiling. Add cabbage and boil for a minute. Drain and remove lemon rind and bay leaves. Place cabbage in sterilized jars in layers placing several slices of apple on each layer, together with several peppercorns, juniper berries and a dash of white wine. Press down lightly. Fill jars in this way, making sure that cabbage is rather moist and allowing one-half inch head space. If necessary, add some salted water that has been boiled and cooled. Seal the jars and sterilize by pressure canner method (see page 9) at ten pounds pressure: Pints thirty minutes; quarts thirty-five minutes. Store in a cool, dark, dry place.

Pickled savoy cabbage

This is a Venetian variant of the traditional German sauerkraut.

Ingredients:
3 or 4 firm green cabbages
Course salt, as needed
1 teaspoon sugar
Several peppercorns
Several juniper berries
Several bay leaves
Several sprigs of fresh tarragon
Several fresh basil leaves
Several teaspoons chopped shallots
White wine vinegar, as needed

Preparation:
Trim cabbage and wash. Chop coarsely. Heat a large amount of salted water and sugar to boiling. Add cabbage and boil for three or four minutes. Drain and spread cabbage out on clean towels in the sun to dry. Sprinkle cabbage liberally with salt, peppercorns, juniper berries, bay leaves, tarragon, basil and sprinkle evenly over cabbage. Turn cabbage so that it absorbs the flavorings well. Dry for four hours. Put cabbage in a terracotta or ceramic container or in a clean, wooden keg. On every two inch layer of cabbage sprinkle a teaspoon shallots, a pinch of coarse salt and moisten with vinegar. Press down and cover with vinegar. Cover cabbage with a plastic or glass disc with a weight on top to keep cabbage under vinegar. Cover container and store in a cool, dark, dry place. The cabbage will be ready after a month.

Sauerkraut

Ingredients:
4 pounds tender green cabbage
8 juniper berries
8 cumin seeds
8 sprigs tarragon
Several bay leaves
1 sprig basil and 1 pinch thyme
Several peppercorns
11 ounces (1⅓ cups) salt

Preparation:
Remove tough outer leaves. Wash these leaves and set aside. Cut cabbage in half and remove core. Using a very sharp knife, cut cabbage into fine strips (or you can use a cabbage grater). Put cabbage in a large bowl and mix well with herbs and peppercorns. After about one-half hour, put one-quarter of the cabbage into a crock or wooden keg large enough to hold all the cabbage. Sprinkle with one-quarter of the salt. Continue this way ending with the salt. Cover with reserved cabbage leaves, then cover cabbage leaves with several thicknesses of cheesecloth. On the cheesecloth put a clean board cut approximately to the shape and size of the crock or keg, and on this put a weight heavy enough so that the juices come just above the top surface of the board. Store in a cool, dark, dry place and let ferment for about fifty days. During this period, a grayish liquid will form, each time it does, skim it off.

After two months sauerkraut is ready to eat. Each time you take out a portion, clean the edges of the container and the board with a cloth. Sauerkraut is good both raw and cooked (be careful not to overcook it.)

Capers in salt

These capers are used to add flavor to sauces or other preparations.

Ingredients:
4½ pounds capers
4½ pounds coarse salt

Preparation:
If you are picking capers yourself, make sure that you take them before buds open and with an eighth of an inch stem. Wash, drain and put them in the sun for about two hours to dry. Put a layer of coarse salt on the bottom of sterilized jars and cover with a layer of capers. Alternate in this way until jar is filled. Seal jar and store in a cool, dark, dry place.

When you are ready to use capers, wash off salt with cold water, changing it several times. Remember that whatever dish you are preparing should be salted after capers are added. The capers are also excellent dressed simply with olive oil and grated orange or lemon rind.

Capers in vinegar

Ingredients:
2 pounds capers
Salt, as necessary
1 quart white vinegar
Several cloves
1 bay leaf
1 fresh basil leaf

Preparation:
Pick, wash and dry capers as in CAPERS IN SALT. Put in a bowl and sprinkle generously with salt. Let stand for two days. Put capers into small sterilized jars. Pour vinegar in a pot and add cloves, bay leaf and basil. Boil for two minutes. Pour hot over capers and seal. Store in a cool, dark, dry place.

Before using capers, rinse them with cold water to remove vinegar. Serve them dressed with olive oil or mixed into a sauce, salad or sandwich.

Plain carrots

Ingredients:
5 pounds small, tender carrots
1 pinch sugar
Salt, to taste

Preparation:
Scrape carrots. Cut lengthwise into quarters and, if they are very long, cut each strip in half. Add carrots to boiling salted water for ten to fifteen minutes. Drain and let cool. Arrange them in sterilized jars. Add one teaspoon salt to each quart jar. Cover them with boiling water, leaving a headspace of one inch. Put a pinch of sugar in each jar. Seal and sterilize according to pressure canner method (see page 9) at ten pounds pressure, twenty-five minutes for one-half pints and pints, thirty minutes for one-and-one-half pints and quarts. Store in a cool, dark, dry place.

The carrots may be served plain, with a dressing of oil, lemon, salt, and pepper, after being warmed for a moment in boiling water, or they may be browned in oil, butter and parsley. Either way, they make a good vegetable course with roast meat. They may also be added to a vegetable soup with fresh greens.

Pickled carrots

Ingredients:
2 pounds carrots
White vinegar, as needed
Several basil leaves
Several peppercorns
Pinch of sugar

Preparation:
Cut carrots in the shape you like, diced, sliced or cut into strips. Boil in water to cover for five to six minutes, drain and let dry. Place carrots in sterilized jars and cover with vinegar. Add a leaf or two of basil, several peppercorns and a pinch of sugar. Seal jars and store in a cool, dark, dry place.

These carrots can be served as hors d'oeuvres or, finely chopped, in the preparation of piquant sauces for boiled meats, or as an ingredient in Russian salad, together with other boiled or pickled vegetables such as potatoes, peas and celery.

Pickled cauliflower

Pickled cauliflower is served as an hors d'oeuvre together with boiled meats.

Ingredients:
5 pounds perfect cauliflowers
Rind of 1 lemon, in large pieces
Juice of 1 lemon
White wine vinegar, as needed
Several peppercorns
Several bay leaves
Salt, to taste

Preparation:
Remove the green leaves from cauliflower. Break flowrets from stem. Keep flowrets the size of a walnut. Place flowrets in a bowl of heavily salted cold water for about two hours. Boil a large quantity of salted water with lemon rind. Drain cauliflower and add to water along with lemon juice. Boil for two to three minutes. Drain and dry flowrets on paper towels. Arrange them in sterilized jars. Boil enough vinegar to cover flowrets together with a few peppercorns, bay leaves and salt to taste (about one teaspoon for each quart jar) for one minute. Strain and pour it hot covering cauliflower. Let cool uncovered. Seal and store in a cool, dark, dry place.

If you do not want the cauliflower to be too sharp, add one cup water to vinegar before boiling.

Plain celery

Used in preparing soups, omeletes, braised meats, etc.

Ingredients:
5 pounds celery
Salt, as needed
Juice of 1 lemon
Several peppercorns

Preparation:
Select the tenderest stalks, including the hearts, and cut stalks long enough to fit jar, allowing one inch head space. Wash celery and drain water. Place stalks in boiling salted water to cover. Add half of the lemon juice and boil for two or three minutes. Remove celery with a slotted spoon and drain in a colander. Allow to cool. Boil two quarts water and then cool. Pack celery vertically in sterilized jars. Add one teaspoon salt to each quart. Cover with boiled and cooled water, allowing one inch head space. Put two peppercorns and a few drops of remaining lemon juice in each jar. Seal and sterilize by pressure canner method (see page 9) at ten pounds pressure: Pints for thirty minutes; quarts for thirty-five minutes. Store in a cool, dark, dry place.

Sweet celery relish

Ingredients:
2 pounds white, tender celery
2 cups sugar
Juice of 1 lemon

Preparation:
Wash and trim only the heart of the celery and discard tough, stringy stalks. Remove leaves. Cut celery in thin slices. Place celery in a pot and add cold water until level is half an inch above celery. Cook covered over a low heat until almost all water is gone and celery is tender but still firm. Stir in sugar and lemon juice. Let stand one hour, stirring occasionally. Reheat pot to boiling, stirring until sugar has thickened. When mixture is thick and jam-like (the pieces of celery, however, should retain their shape), pour it hot into sterilized jars. Seal and store in a cool, dark, dry place.

This relish is an accompaniment to boiled meats, roasted game, duck and so on.

Pickled celery

This pickled celery can be used as an hors d'oeuvre together with other pickled vegetables or in combination with other vegetables in Russian salad.

Ingredients:
5 pounds green or white celery
2 teaspoons salt
Juice of 1 lemon
Several peppercorns
2 cloves garlic
1 bay leaf
Several whole cloves
White wine vinegar, as needed
Several fresh basil leaves

Preparation:
Use only inner white tender stalks. Remove leaves and cut stalks to fit jars, or into three to four inch pieces. Wash celery in cold water. Heat enough water to cover celery with salt, lemon juice, peppercorns, garlic, bay leaf and cloves until boiling. Add celery and cook for five minutes. Drain and spread out on clean towels to dry for several hours. Place celery in sterilized jars and cover with vinegar. Add two basil leaves and several peppercorns to each jar. Seal and store in a cool, dark, dry place.

Celery in oil

This is served as an hors d'oeuvre.

Ingredients:
5 pounds white celery
1 quart white vinegar
2 teaspoons salt
Peppercorns
Bay leaves
1 stick cinnamon, broken into pieces
Whole cloves
Olive oil, as needed

Preparation:
Use only tender inner stalks. Remove leaves and wash and drain. Spread celery out on clean cloth to dry. Cut stalks into three inch lengths, each half inch wide. Put pieces of celery in a skillet and cover them with vinegar. Add salt, cover and simmer for about fifteen minutes or until celery is tender but still firm. Drain celery and spread out on a cloth in the sun to dry. Pack celery in sterilized jars, adding to each jar several peppercorns, a bay leaf, a piece of cinnamon stick and a clove. Cover celery with oil. Seal and store in a cool, dark, dry place.

Corn preserved for vegetable courses

Ingredients:
5 pounds young and tender corn on cob
Salt, as needed
2 cups water

Preparation:
For cream style corn, pick corn when kernel is still very immature and milky. Shuck corn, remove silk and wash quickly. Drain and dry. Remove kernels without getting some of the cob using a sharp serrated knife. Scrape corn to remove all pulp. Put kernels in a large stainless steel pot, salt lightly and add water. Bring very slowly to a boil, stirring with a wooden spoon. Boil gently for five to ten minutes (the length of cooking time depending on the milkiness of the kernel). Corn is ready when kernels have become thick and creamy. Pour while still hot into small sterilized jars leaving one inch headspace. Seal and sterilize by pressure canner method (see page 9) at ten pounds pressure: Pints, one hour, and twenty-five minutes. Do not use quarts. Store in a cool, dark, dry place.

To prepare whole kernel corn, prepare corn as for cream style corn, but do not scrape cob to remove pulp. Measure corn and place in a pot. Add one teaspoon salt and two cups boiling water to each quart of corn. Boil three minutes. Pack while hot into sterilized jars leaving one inch head space. Seal and sterilize by pressure canner method (see page 9) at the same pressure and time as for cream style corn.

Corn on the cob in brine

Ingredients:
5 pounds very small, young tender corn on cob
1 quart water, about
Salt, as needed
½ cup sugar
2 to 3 bay leaves
Several peppercorns
Rind of 1 lemon, in large pieces
Juice of ½ lemon

Preparation:
Shuck ears, cut off any stem and remove silk. Trim length of ears to fit into large jars. Place corn into salted, boiling water to cover and boil for three or four minutes. Drain and spread ears out on a clean cloth in an airy place to dry for two hours. Put ears in large sterilized jars. Boil one quart water, two teaspoons salt, sugar, bay leaves, peppercorns and lemon rind for two minutes. Stir in lemon juice. Strain. Cool, then pour over ears in jars. Prepare more water mixture if necessary. Seal and sterilize by pressure canner method (see page 9) at the same pressure and time as in CORN PRESERVED FOR VEGETABLE COURSES. Store in a cool, dark, dry place.

To serve, put the ears in boiling water for several minutes, let them dry, then brown in butter.

Pickled baby ears of corn

Ingredients:
10 to 12 baby ears of corn
Salt, as needed
½ cup sugar
8 peppercorns
3 whole cloves
1 sprig tarragon
1 quart white vinegar

Preparation:
Pick the ears while they are still milky, without leaves and about three to four inches in length. Clean and remove any hard kernels. Cover ears with boiling salted water for one minute, then drain and dry on a clean cloth. Arrange in sterilized jars. Heat sugar, peppercorns, cloves, one teaspoon salt, tarragon and vinegar to a boil. Boil for two minutes. Strain and pour hot over ears until covered. Seal jars. Store in a cool, dark, dry place.

These are served as an hors d'oeuvre like other pickled vegetables.

Cucumbers in oil

Ingredients:
7 pounds small, firm cucumbers
Coarse salt
4 bay leaves
15 basil leaves
15 tarragon leaves
4 cloves garlic
2 or 3 small peppers (sweet) cut into strips
10 small onions, left whole
2 quarts vinegar
1 cup white wine
Olive oil, as needed

Preparation:
Wash and dry cucumbers and put them in a glass bowl. Sprinkle with salt. Let stand for one-and-one-half days in a cool place, stirring them occasionally with a wooden spoon. Drain cucumbers and dry on paper towels for two to three hours. Place in sterilized jars, adding bay leaves, basil, tarragon, garlic, sweet peppers and onions, all divided equally between jars.

Bring vinegar and white wine to a boil and pour it while hot covering cucumbers. Let cool, seal jars and let stand for ten days. Pour off vinegar, leaving flavoring agents, and cover cucumbers in oil. Seal and store in a cool, dark, dry place.

Cucumbers in brine

Ingredients:
7 pounds small pickling cucumbers
2¼ cups regular salt
Rind of 1 lemon, in large pieces
Several fresh basil leaves
Several fresh tarragon leaves
Some peppercorns
½ cup sugar
2 bay leaves
1 cup coarse salt

Preparation:
Clean, wash and dry cucumbers. Put them down in a layer in a glass bowl. Sprinkle with regular salt and add lemon rind. Cover the bowl and let stand for a day. Drain cucumbers and put them on a clean cloth in sun to dry. When they are dry, put them in layers in a glass jar or crock (*not* in a metal container), alternating the layers with a few basil leaves, tarragon leaves and peppercorns. When jar is filled to within two inches of the top, boil three quarts water with sugar, bay leaves and coarse salt. Let liquid cool and then pour it over cucumbers, covering them completely. Keep cucumbers submerged with a plate or a piece of wood or plastic cut to the right size. Cover jar and keep in a cool, dark, dry place. The grayish water that rises to the surface does not mean that the cucumbers have spoiled, but are being pickled properly. Before serving, rinse pickles with cold water.

Pickled cucumbers

Ingredients:
7 pounds small pickling cucumbers
Coarse salt, as needed
2 quarts best white wine vinegar
Some peppercorns
Several bay leaves
5 or 6 whole cloves
Several fresh basil leaves
2 sprigs fresh tarragon

Preparation:
Clean and wash cucumbers and put them in a plastic bowl large enough to hold them all, adding a handful of coarse salt for each two pounds cucumbers. Let them stand for several hours so that some of the water is extracted from them. Drain cucumbers and return them to the plastic bowl. Boil enough vinegar to cover cucumbers with peppercorns, bay leaves, cloves, basil and tarragon. Pour boiling vinegar over cucumbers. Set aside for one day. Drain vinegar into a pot and boil it again. Taste it and if not sufficiently salty, add salt. Pour vinegar boiling over cucumbers again and let stand another day, removing cloves. If necessary add more vinegar until cucumbers are covered. On the third day pour vinegar and cucumbers into a pot that is not made of aluminum and boil until cucumbers are half done. Let cool and put cucumbers into sterilized jars and cover with vinegar. Seal and store in a cool, dark, dry place.

Plain eggplant

Ingredients:
9 pounds eggplant
5 or 6 fresh basil leaves
1 cup salt
1 tablespoon freshly ground pepper

Preparation:
Rub eggplant with a clean, dry cloth and cut, unpeeled, into three-quarter inch cubes. Mix basil leaves, salt, and pepper with eggplant. Place in a colander, set into sink and drain for four hours. Put cubes in sterilized jars, pressing down lightly until they are within half an inch of the top. Cut a disc of wax paper and lay it on the surface of the eggplant cubes. Seal and sterilize by pressure canner method (see page 9) at ten pounds pressure: Pints, thirty minutes; quarts, forty minutes.

When serving, as a vegetable course or as an hors d'oeuvre, dress the cubes with oil and lemon or saute them in oil, butter and chopped parsley. Before adding salt, taste to make sure you do not oversalt them.

Pickled eggplant

Ingredients:
7 pounds purple, medium-sized, firm eggplants
Salt, as needed
Pepper, as needed
Juice of 1 lemon
Several fresh basil leaves
Several parsley sprigs
Several bay leaves
Peppercorns (or chili peppers) to taste
White vinegar, as needed
Olive oil, as needed

Preparation:
Wash, slice and drain eggplant as for EGGPLANT IN OIL. Heat water to boiling adding lemon juice. Add eggplant slices a few at a time and boil for one minute. Remove with a slotted spoon. Spread eggplant out on a cloth to dry in the sun. Arrange slices in sterilized jars, adding basil, parsley, a piece of bay leaf and a few peppercorns (or pieces of chili pepper) to each jar. Cover eggplant with vinegar. Seal jars. Check after a few days to make sure eggplant is still under vinegar. If some of the vinegar has been absorbed, pour in additional vinegar. Then pour a film of olive oil over vinegar. Seal again. Store in a cool, dark, dry place.

Eggplant cubes

Ingredients:
2 pounds eggplants
Salt, as needed
Pepper, as needed
White vinegar, as needed
Olive oil, as needed
2 cloves garlic
½ cup chopped parsley
Several fresh basil leaves
Pinch of oregano

Preparation:
Wash, cube and drain eggplants as for PLAIN EGGPLANT. Heat enough vinegar to cover eggplant until boiling. Immerse cubes, a small amount at a time for one minute. Drain. Heat one-quarter cup olive oil in a skillet and saute garlic until brown. Add eggplant and saute for two minutes. Stir in parsley, basil and oregano. Season to taste with salt and pepper. Put eggplant into sterilized jars and cover with fresh olive oil. Seal and sterilize by pressure canner method (see page 9) at same pressure and time as for PLAIN EGGPLANT. Store in a cool, dark, dry place.

Eggplant cubes are served as a vegetable course with roast meats.

Eggplant a la chanterelle

Ingredients:
7 pounds eggplant
Salt, as needed
Pepper, as needed
White vinegar, as needed
Olive oil, as needed
4 to 5 cloves garlic, chopped
⅓ cup preserved capers, chopped
4 cups peeled and chopped tomatoes
1 tablespoon chopped parsley
1 pinch oregano
Several fresh basil leaves

Preparation:
Choose firm, very small eggplants. Remove stems and wash and dry. Cut eggplants into one-half inch cubes and place in a colander set in the sink. Sprinkle cubes with salt and pepper. Drain for two hours. Mix half water and half vinegar, enough to cover eggplant, and bring to a boil. Add cubes and when water reboils, drain. Heat one cup olive oil in skillet and saute garlic until golden. Add eggplant, capers, tomatoes, parsley, oregano and basil. Cook over high heat for three to four minutes. Place cubes in sterilized jars. Add fresh olive oil to cover. Seal and sterilize by pressure canner method at same pressure and time as in PLAIN EGGPLANT. Store in a cool, dark, dry place.

When you are ready to serve the eggplant, saute the cubes in a skillet, adding a pinch of sugar to cover the bitter flavor.

Plain canned Celery
Plain canned Peas
Plain canned Asparagus

Piquant onions

Onions, Venetian style

Bittersweet onions

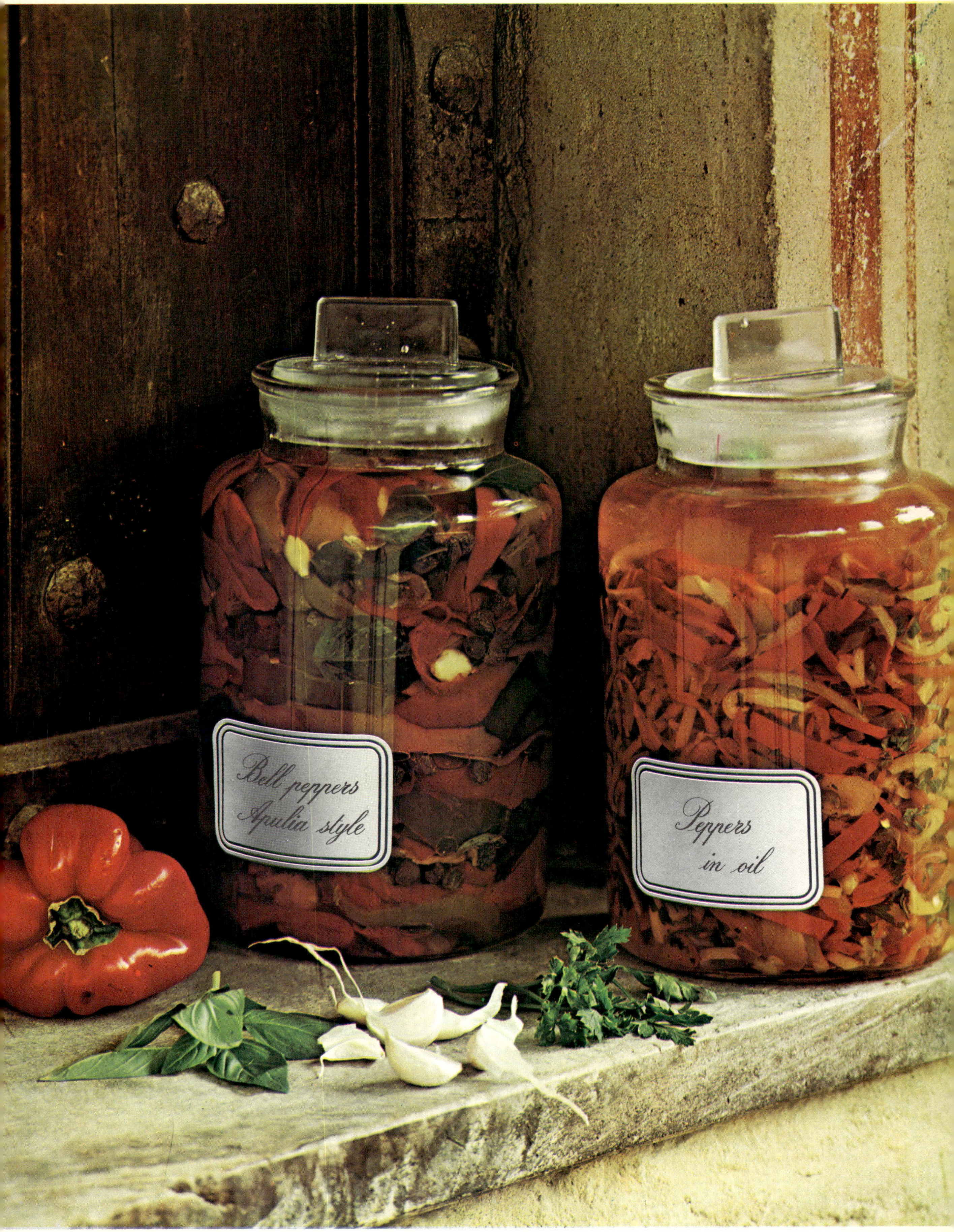
Bell peppers
Apulia style
Peppers
in oil

Pepper relish

Dried eggplant

Ingredients:
Small firm eggplants in any quantity you like
Salt, as needed
Some bay leaves
Some peppercorns

Preparation:
Remove stems from eggplants and clean with a cloth. Cut lengthwise in slices about one-quarter inch thick. String slices on pieces of string about a yard long. Prepare salted boiling water (two tablespoons salt for every quart water) adding bay leaves and peppercorns. Let garlands of eggplant boil in this mixture for two minutes, then drain and hang strings up in sun to dry. Dry in direct sunlight. Store them in small boxes covered with cheesecloth in a cool, dark, dry place.

In order to cook dried eggplant, soak in warm water for five minutes, then saute in oil and garlic. Sprinkle with chopped parsley and serve.

Eggplant in brine

Dressed with olive oil, eggplant in brine is served as an hors d'oeuvre.

Ingredients:
11 pounds eggplant
Coarse salt, as needed
6 to 7 cloves garlic
10 chili peppers
20 fresh basil leaves
2 teaspoons crumbled oregano
Olive oil, as needed

Preparation:
Wash and slice eggplant as for DRIED EGGPLANT. Dip slices, only a few at a time, into salted boiling water for one minute. Place slices in a colander or wicker basket. Place a weight on top and let them drain for a day. Arrange the eggplants in wide-mouth crock or glass jar. Make a layer of eggplant, then one of salt, another of eggplant, then a layer of a couple of pieces of garlic, chili pepper, some basil leaves, oregano and more salt; repeat layering until jar is filled and last layer is salt. Place a heavy wooden or plastic disc cut to the size of the opening on top of eggplant. After a few days the liquid given off by the eggplant will appear above disc. Spoon off liquid and remove lid. Cover top with oil. Cover and store in a cool, dark, dry place.

Eggplant in oil

Ingredients:
2 pounds small, firm eggplants
Salt, as needed
Pepper, as needed
White vinegar, as needed
Several fresh basil leaves
Several cloves garlic
Olive oil, as needed

Preparation:
Wash eggplants in cold water and dry them. Remove stems and cut them in crosswise slices about a quarter of an inch thick (if you wish, you can also peel the eggplant). Sprinkle slices with salt and pepper and place them in a colander set into the sink to drain overnight. Heat enough vinegar to cover slices, until boiling. Add eggplant slices and when vinegar reboils, drain. Place slices on cake racks covered with cheesecloth to dry. Arrange slices in layers in sterilized jars with a few basil leaves and a half clove of garlic. Cover with olive oil. Seal and store in a cool, dark, dry place. In order to keep perfectly, eggplant must always remain below surface of oil.

Grape leaves in oil

Ingredients:
2 pounds grape leaves
2 quarts white vinegar
2 teaspoons salt, as needed
Several peppercorns
Olive oil, as needed

Preparation:
Pick vine leaves that are tender and healthy. Wash them to eliminate any traces of fungicide and remove stems. Heat vinegar and salt until boiling. Dip vine leaves into vinegar for thirty seconds. Drain leaves and dry them on a clean cloth. Arrange them cold in sterilized jars. Add a few peppercorns to each jar. Pour oil over them allowing one-half inch head space. Seal. After a few days check the level of the oil and if it has lowered add more oil. Store jars in a cool, dark, dry place.

They can be stuffed with rice, meats, and so on.

Salted grape leaves

Ingredients:
Grape leaves
Salt

Preparation:
Pick, wash and trim leaves as for GRAPE LEAVES IN OIL. Boil a large amount of salted water. Dip grape leaves, a few at a time, and let them boil rapidly for thirty seconds. Drain leaves and spread them out on a cloth to dry. Put them in sterilized jars, pressing lightly. Add some of the salted water filling jar, leaving a one inch head space. Seal jars and sterilize by pressure canner method (see page 9) at ten pounds pressure: Pints one hour and ten minutes; quarts one hour and thirty minutes. Store in a cool, dark, dry place.

These vine leaves are used to wrap various game birds in, such as quail, partridges and other small birds. In Greek, Turkish and Yugoslavian cooking, they are used mostly for wrapping meat stuffings.

Plain leeks

Ingredients:
5 pounds leeks, cleaned and without green leaves
Salt, as needed
10 peppercorns
2 or 3 bay leaves
Olive oil, as needed

Preparation:
Wash leeks in plenty of cold water. Cut them in two inch pieces. If any sand is detected between layers, wash again. Cook leeks in boiling salted water to cover with a couple of peppercorns and some bay leaves. Boil slowly for eight to ten minutes. Drain, reserving cooking water. Discard peppercorns and bay leaves. Pack leeks into sterilized jars, pressing lightly. Pour some of the cooking water, leaving a head space of one inch. Pour in a thin layer of olive oil and seal. Sterilize by pressure canner method (see page 9) at ten pounds pressure: Pints for forty minutes; quarts for fifty minutes. Store in a cool, dark, dry place.

When it is time to use leeks, they should be drained and then cooked according to recipe (in butter, in bechamel, etc.).

Leeks, Indian style

This is an exquisite, appetizing hors d'oeuvre preparation.

Ingredients:
5 pounds leeks
Salt, as needed
Pepper, as needed
1 teaspoon curry powder
½ cup olive oil
Several bay leaves
⅓ cup sultana raisins
2 apples, peeled, cored and sliced
Dry white wine, as needed

Preparation:
Trim, wash and cut leeks as for PLAIN LEEKS. If leeks are very thick, halve them lengthwise for better cooking. Arrange leeks on a large skillet or baking pan side by side in a single layer. Add salt, pepper to taste, curry powder, oil, bay leaves, raisins and apples. Pour in enough dry white wine to cover leeks to one-half their thickness. Lay a piece of wax paper over pan and cover. Heat until wine begins to boil. Simmer until leeks are tender but still firm. With a slotted spoon, carefully remove leeks and arrange in sterilized jars. Press remaining sauce through a food mill and replace in saucepan. Simmer until sauce is of medium thickness. Pour hot sauce over leeks, covering them, leaving a head space of one inch. Seal and sterilize by pressure canner method (see page 9) at the same pressure and time as for PLAIN LEEKS. Store in a cool, dark, dry place.

Preserved lettuce

Ingredients:
Greens (chard, kale, spinach, turnip greens) or lettuce (escarolle, romaine, endive)
Salt
Chopped onion
Peppercorns
Salt pork (or bacon) finely chopped
Juice of 1 lemon

Preparation:
Wash greens or lettuce well, quartering heads through the core. Put greens or lettuce in a pot of boiling salted water. When water reboils drain, reserving cooking water. On the bottom of sterilized jars put some onion, some peppercorns and some salt pork. Put greens or lettuce in jars packing them tightly. Cover with boiling cooking water, leaving a one-inch head space. Add a few drops of lemon juice. Seal and sterilize by pressure canner method (see page 9) at ten pounds pressure: Pints, one hour and ten minutes; quarts, one hour and thirty minutes. Store in a cool, dark, dry place.

Greens or lettuce preserved in this way can be cooked in butter and with meat sauce or served au gratin with grated cheese.

Marinated lettuce

Ingredients:
Lettuce (escarolle or romaine)
Dry white wine
Olive oil
Chopped herbs (composed of parsley, chives, chervil, basil and tarragon)
Lemon juice
Salt
Pepper

Preparation:
Wash, cut, boil and drain lettuce as in PRESERVED LETTUCE. In a pot heat wine, oil, herbs, lemon juice, salt and pepper using one-and one-half cups wine, one-quarter cup oil, the juice of one-half a lemon, one-quarter cup chopped herbs, one-half teaspoon salt and one-eighth teaspoon pepper for every two pounds of lettuce and boil for fifteen minutes. Cool. Put lettuce in sterilized jars, packing it tightly. Divide wine mixture equally between jars, adding reserved cooking liquid until jars are filled to within one inch of top. Seal and sterilize by pressure canner method (see page 9) at the same pressure and time as for PRESERVED LETTUCE. Store in a cool, dark, dry place.

Mint syrup

Ingredients:
3½ pounds clean, perfect green peppermint leaves
Grated rind and juice of 1 lemon
1 pound (2 cups) sugar
½ cup water

Preparation:
Wash peppermint leaves rapidly in cold water and drain well. Press through a food mill or sieve. This operation should be completed within a day without allowing mint or juice to remain long in contact with metal. Collect juice, which will be dark green and thick, in a glass or porcelain bowl. Stir in lemon rind and juice. Cover and set aside for two hours. In a pot combine sugar and water and boil for one minute. Cool to lukewarm and pour it into mint juice before it thickens. Stir well and set aside to cool. Strain syrup through double thickness cheesecloth. Pour into bottles and cap with a bottle capper. Store in a cool, dark, dry place. If after a few days some scum appears on the surface of syrup, skim it off and recap bottles.

Dried mint

Ingredients:
Peppermint, in sprigs or individual leaves

Preparation:
Pick mint for drying during the period when it is most highly perfumed (that is before flowering). Break or cut stems about an inch from ground level. The mint can be dried either by the leaf or by the sprig. In the first case, remove the leaves from the stem, choosing only the greenest, most perfect leaves. Wash them quickly in cold water, then spread them out in a single layer on a clean cloth and place them in the sun, turning them over from time to time. Bring them inside in the evening. It takes a couple of days to dry the mint perfectly. When the leaves are absolutely dry, pack them in dry jars or in boxes lined with wax paper.

If you want to preserve them as sprigs, proceed in the following manner: During the cutting, avoid heaping up the sprigs, otherwise they heat up and the final product will not be up to standard. After removing any spoiled leaves, wash the sprigs in cold water. Shake off excess water gently. Then tie the sprigs one by one on a string and hang up in a dry and airy place or in the sun. When leaves are dry, remove them from the stems and leave them exposed to the sun for a day to complete the drying process. Or, without removing the leaves from the stems, you may wrap the sprigs individually in clean wrapping paper and leave hanging in a cool, dark, dry place.

Piquant button mushrooms in oil

May be served as a vegetable course or as an hors d'oeuvre.

Ingredients:
2 pounds cleaned button mushrooms
Juice of 1 lemon
2 cups olive oil
4 cloves garlic, mashed
3 or 4 dried red peppers
2 tablespoons chopped parsley
1 fresh basil leaf
Salt, as needed

Preparation:
Wash mushrooms in water mixed with lemon juice. Cut very large ones in half and spread them out on a clean cloth to dry; cover with another cloth and press down gently to hasten drying. Pour oil into pyrex or enamelled skillet (but not one of aluminum). Heat oil carefully; it must not smoke. Add garlic and saute until golden. Add mushrooms. Stir and increase heat so that mushrooms cook quickly. Stir frequently and cook for about five minutes until all water has evaporated. Crumble and add peppers, parsley, basil and salt to taste. Pour hot mushrooms into sterilized jars, together with cooking oil. Seal jars and sterilize by pressure canner method (see page 9) at ten pounds pressure: Half-pints and pints for thirty minutes. Do not use quarts. Store in a cool, dark, dry place.

Button mushrooms in salt

Ingredients:
2 pounds very small button mushrooms
2 pounds coarse salt

Preparation:
Wash mushrooms quickly and place in a colander. Place colander into boiling water, covering mushrooms. When water reboils, drain and spread on a cloth to dry for three or four days. Put a layer of salt about a quarter of an inch deep in sterilized jars, then a layer of mushrooms, then another layer of salt. Continue layering, ending with salt. Seal jars and store in a cool, dark, dry place.

When it comes time to use the mushrooms, remove them from the salt and let soak in plenty of cold water for twenty-four hours. Drain and dry them. Fry them in a liberal quantity of hot olive oil, to which a garlic clove has been added. When they are done, sprinkle with a handful of chopped parsley.

Cultivated mushrooms, hunter style

Excellent as an accompaniment to stews, chicken cooked hunter style, etc.

Ingredients:
5 pounds cultivated mushrooms
Juice of 1 lemon
1 cup olive oil
4 garlic cloves, cut into halves
2 onions, chopped
2 bay leaves
2 sage leaves
4 ripe tomatoes, peeled and chopped
½ cup chopped parsley
½ cup white wine
Salt, as needed
Pepper, as needed

Preparation:
Wash mushrooms and place in a bowl of water mixed with lemon juice. Heat oil in two large skillets. Add garlic cloves and mushrooms (dividing them between skillets) and brown them over high heat to avoid their emitting much water. After five minutes, add onions, bay leaves and sage. When mushrooms are fairly dry, add tomatoes, parsley and white wine. Remove and discard garlic. Cook mushrooms for three to four minutes, adding salt and pepper to taste. Put while hot in sterilized jars. Pour a light film of fresh oil on the surface. Seal and sterilize by pressure canner method (see page 9) at the same pressure and time required in PIQUANT BUTTON MUSHROOMS IN OIL. Store in a cool, dark, dry place.

To serve, warm them in a skillet.

Cultivated mushrooms pickled

Ingredients:
5 pounds very firm, small mushrooms
Juice of 2 lemons
1 tablespoon flour
6 cups good quality white wine vinegar
Salt, as needed
3 or 4 whole cloves
Several sticks cinnamon
2 bay leaves
Olive oil, as needed
2 sprigs fresh tarragon
10 peppercorns

Preparation:
Try to get mushrooms all of the same size. Immerse mushrooms in cold water to which has been added juice of 1 lemon and flour for two minutes. Drain and put them in a pot in which three cups water (or white wine vinegar,) one teaspoon salt and remaining lemon juice is boiling. Stir with a wooden spoon and let boil for three to four minutes over very high heat. Drain mushrooms and spread them out to dry on a clean cloth. When mushrooms are dry (several hours should do) arrange them in sterilized jars. Boil vinegar with cloves, cinnamon, and bay leaves, adding salt to taste. Strain and pour while hot over mushrooms in jars. Pour a thin film of olive oil on top, add tarragon and peppercorns. Seal and store in a cool, dark, dry place.

Plain chanterelles

Ingredients:
2 pounds chanterelle mushrooms
Salt, as needed
Several peppercorns
2 whole cloves
2 inch piece of stick cinnamon
2 or 3 fresh basil leaves
1 bay leaf

Preparation:
Trim mushrooms and rinse them quickly in cold water. Cut the largest ones down to the size of the average. Put in a colander. In a pot heat enough salted water to cover mushrooms until boiling. Add mushrooms and remove when water reboils. Drain and dry them in the sun for an hour. Arrange them in sterilized jars, pressing them in gently. Boil one quart water with salt to taste, peppercorns, cloves, cinnamon, basil and bay leaf. Boil for two minutes. Strain and pour over mushrooms, covering them completely. Seal and sterilize by pressure canner method (see page 9) at the same pressure and time as in PIQUANT BUTTON MUSHROOMS IN OIL. Store in a cool, dark, dry place.

When it comes time to use them, drain them from the liquid in which they were preserved and dress them with oil, garlic and chopped parsley or with cream.

Chanterelles in oil

Ingredients:
2 pounds chanterelles (wild mushrooms)
Juice of 1 lemon
Best quality white vinegar, as needed
Salt, as needed
Several peppercorns
Several whole cloves
Several bay leaves
Olive oil, as needed

Preparation:
Select small chanterelles. If necessary, cut large ones in half. Wash them by immersing them quickly in cold water to which has been added lemon juice. Drain immediately. Place chanterelles in a rather large saucepan and cover them with vinegar with salt added to taste. Cover and boil from two to three minutes, drain and put aside on clean towels to dry for two hours. Arrange mushrooms in sterilized jars, pressing down gently. To each jar add several peppercorns, one to two cloves and a crumbled bay leaf. Cover mushrooms with oil. Seal jars and store in a cool, dark, dry place.

Serve them as a vegetable course or in a mixed salad.

Marinated boletus

These are served as hors d'oeuvres.

Ingredients:
5 pounds boletus (or cultivated) mushrooms
Juice of 2 lemons
¼ cup flour
Salt, as needed
2 quarts white vinegar
Several sprigs thyme and bay leaves
Sprig of tarragon
Several peppercorns and whole cloves
2 cloves garlic
Dry white wine, if necessary

Preparation:
If you use cultivated mushrooms for this recipe, select only small firm ones whose gills are not showing.

Wash mushrooms and place in a bowl of cold water mixed with juice of one lemon and flour. Heat a pot of water large enough to cover mushrooms to boiling. Add salt to taste, remaining lemon juice and drained mushrooms. When water reboils, drain mushrooms and let cool on a clean cloth covered with another cloth.

In a large pot combine one quart water, vinegar, thyme, bay leaves, tarragon, peppercorns, cloves and garlic and boil for ten minutes. Strain and cool. Put mushrooms in sterilized jars and pour vinegar mixture over them. If you run short add dry white wine until jar has a head space of one inch. Seal and sterilize by pressure canner method (see page 9) at the same pressure and time for PIQUANT BUTTON MUSHROOMS IN OIL. Store in a cool, dark, dry place.

Dried boletus

After being soaked, dried boletus is used to flavor rice dishes, stews, etc.

Ingredients:
Boletus mushrooms

Preparation:
The best places to dry mushrooms are dry, airy places that can be closed up in case of bad weather or during the night. In addition, the mushrooms must be dried in a shady place and not in the sun.

Trim and clean mushrooms, removing humus. Do not wash them. Slice mushrooms into slices about a sixteenth of an inch thick. Place slices in a single layer on clean paper towels which are placed over racks. Cover with a thin piece of cloth or cheesecloth to keep dust-free. From time to time uncover and turn slices over until drying process is complete. Store in spotlessly clean tins lined with wax paper or in stiff paper bags.

Boletus Piedmont style

Ingredients:
5 pounds boletus (small, firm) mushrooms
1 cup olive oil, about
4 cloves garlic, cut into halves
½ cup chopped parsley
1 bay leaf
¼ cup sultana raisins
¼ cup white wine
1 sprig thyme
Salt, as needed
Pepper, as needed

Preparation:
Wash mushrooms rapidly in cold water. Drain and let dry on a towel. After thirty minutes, cut them into fairly thick slices. Heat oil in a large skillet (not made of aluminum) and saute garlic until golden. Add mushrooms and stir constantly with a wooden spoon. Raise heat and add parsley, bay leaf, raisins, white wine, thyme, and salt and pepper to taste. Mix and cook over heat high enough to evaporate liquid as quickly as possible. Remove garlic. Put mushrooms while hot into sterilized jars. Press mushrooms down lightly. Pour over them a thin film of fresh oil. Seal and sterilize by pressure canner method (see page 9) at the same pressure and time as in PIQUANT BUTTON MUSHROOMS IN OIL. Store in a cool, dark, dry place.

Green olive compote

Ingredients:
7 pounds fresh green olives
Several anchovy fillets
Several fresh basil leaves
A pinch oregano
A small piece dry red pepper
¼ cup capers
Juice of 1 lemon
Salt, as needed
Olive oil, as needed

Preparation:
Pit olives and put them in a ceramic or plastic bowl. Cover with cold water at least five inches above olives. Soak for five or six days, changing water every day. Drain olives and press them lightly between layers of cloth to eliminate as much water as possible. Spread olives out to dry between two dry, clean clothes in an airy place for four hours. Put olives in wide-mouthed jars, in layers, alternating them with anchovy fillets, basil leaves, oregano, a couple of pieces of dried red pepper, capers, lemon juice, one-half teaspoon salt and olive oil. Press down olives with palm of the hand before making another layer. When the jar is filled, press down quite firmly on the olives and cover them completely with oil. Place a disc of wax paper over olives and on top of that a disc of wood or plastic to keep the olives under oil. Store in a cool, dark, dry place.

Olives in brine

Ingredients:
7 pounds sound, not too mature olives
1¼ cups salt
Several whole cloves
Piece of lemon rind
2 teaspoons fennel seeds

Preparation:
Do not pit olives. Soak olives as in GREEN OLIVE COMPOTE. Drain and dry them in a clean towel. Put olives in sterilized jars. Heat three quarts water with salt until boiling. Add cloves, lemon rind and fennel seeds to olives. Pour salted water while hot over olives. Seal jars and store them in a cool, dark, dry place.

Before serving, rinse olives with warm water. Dry them on a cloth and serve dressed with olive oil, adding, if you like, a bit of grated orange or lemon rind or a small bay leaf.

Olives in "vandalusa" sauce

(from the ancient name for Andalusia)

Ingredients:
2 pounds green olives in brine (SEE OLIVES IN BRINE)
4 ounces anchovies, preserved either in salt or oil
4 ounces tuna in oil
1 tablespoon chopped parsley
1 teaspoon dried, chopped chili pepper
4 ounces capers preserved either in salt or in vinegar
1½ cups peeled, chopped fresh tomatoes
Several fresh basil leaves
4 or 5 cloves garlic
Olive oil, as needed

Preparation:
Pit olives with an olive pitter. Slice olives crosswise into rings. Mix remaining ingredients except oil and chop them together finely. Place olive slices and chopped mixture in layers in sterilized jars. Over each layer of olive slices, pour a thin film of olive oil. When jars are filled, cover with olive oil. Seal and sterilize by the pressure canner method (see page 9) at ten pounds pressure: Half-pints and pints for thirty minutes. Do not use quarts. Store in a cool, dark, dry place.

This sauce can be used as an hors d'oeuvre or as a filling for vegetables or as a sauce on rice or pasta, but it must be used with caution, for it is fairly spicy.

Olives in oil, Andalusian style

Ingredients:
2 pounds green, pitted olives in brine (see OLIVES IN BRINE)
4 ounces anchovy fillets, preserved either in oil or salt
4 ounces cleaned chili peppers that have been boiled in vinegar
2 ounces capers, preserved either in salt or in vinegar
4 ounces tuna in oil
1 clove garlic
1 tablespoon each, chopped parsley and basil
1 tablespoon grated Parmesan cheese
Several bay leaves
Olive oil, as needed

Preparation:
Drain largest size olives and pit them with an olive pitter. Spread them out to dry on paper towels. Grind all ingredients except bay leaves and oil. Stuff this mixture into hole in olives. You can use a pastry bag with a small opening. Force the mixture in carefully and as you finish each olive pack tightly in sterilized jars. After each layer, pour in a film of olive oil and add a small piece of bay leaf. On top layer of olives place a disc of wax paper. Cover with oil and seal. Store in a cool, dark, dry place.

These make a very tasty hors d'oeuvre.

Onions, Venetian style

Ingredients:
7 pounds very small, white onions
1 cup olive oil
1 cup sugar
Several whole cloves
2 bay leaves
2 cups peeled, chopped tomatoes
1 ounce (1 square) bitter chocolate, grated
2 cups dry white wine
Salt
Pepper

Preparation:
Bring a pot of water large enough to hold all onions to a boil. Add onions and bring to a boil again as quickly as possible. Drain onions immediately. Cool and peel, leaving them whole. In a large saucepan heat oil and sugar and stir constantly over low heat until sugar is golden. Add dry onions, cloves, bay leaves, tomatoes and chocolate. Pour in wine. Stir and bring to a boil. Simmer covered, stirring occasionally until onions are easily pierced but still hold their shape. Season to taste with salt and pepper.

Remove onions from pan with a slotted spoon and arrange them in sterilized jars. Boil liquid left in pan for five minutes and pour it hot covering the onions. Seal jars and, to be on the safe side, sterilize in a boiling water bath (see page 9) for fifteen minutes. Store in a cool, dark, dry place.

Bittersweet onions

Bittersweet onions are served as an hors d'oeuvre or as a vegetable course with meats.

Ingredients:
7 pounds very small, white onions, as uniform in size as possible
2 tablespoons oil
2 tablespoons butter
1 tablespoon sugar
1 cup peeled, chopped tomatoes
Juice of ½ lemon
¾ cup vinegar
¾ cup white wine
2 whole cloves
1 piece stick cinnamon
1 bay leaf
Salt and pepper
Additional oil

Preparation:
Peel onions as in ONIONS, VENETIAN STYLE.

In a large pot heat oil, butter and sugar until sugar is golden brown. Add onions and let them brown for two minutes. Add remaining ingredients, cover and continue cooking, stirring occasionally. When onions are almost tender, season to taste with salt and pepper. Remove onions with a slotted spoon and place into sterilized jars. Cover with strained hot sauce. Carefully pour a layer of oil on top and seal. Sterilize jars in a boiling water bath (see page 9) for ten to fifteen minutes. Let cool in the same water and store in a cool, dark, dry place.

Onions, Far Eastern style

Onions, Far Eastern style are served as hors d'oeuvres or as a vegetable course with meats.

Ingredients:
5 pounds very small, white onions, peeled
¼ cup sultana grapes
1 tablespoon sugar
1 cup peeled, chopped tomatoes
Grated rind and juice of ½ lemon
¾ cup white vinegar
¾ cup white wine
2 whole cloves
1 cinnamon stick
1 bay leaf
Salt
Pepper

Preparation:
Put onions in a large skillet and add all ingredients. Bring to a boil, stirring constantly. As soon as mixture has come to a boil, lower heat and cover pan. Continue cooking until onions are easily pierced but still hold their shape.

Season to taste with salt and pepper. Add water or wine to keep up level of liquid, if necessary. With a slotted spoon, put onions in sterilized jars. Strain sauce and pour while hot covering onions. Sterilize in a boiling water bath (see page 9) for ten minutes. Store jars in a cool, dark, dry place.

Piquant onions

Ingredients:
7 pounds very small, white onions
1 quart white vinegar
1½ cups sugar
5 whole cloves
10 peppercorns
2 bay leaves
Several basil leaves
1 cinnamon stick
2 cups white wine
Salt, as needed

Preparation:
Peel onions as in ONIONS, VENETIAN STYLE. Dry onions on a cloth for three to four hours.

Boil vinegar with all the ingredients except onions for a minute. Add salt to taste. Put onions in sterilized jars. Strain vinegar and pour while hot over onions. Seal jars and sterilize in a boiling water bath (see page 9) for ten minutes. Store jars in a cool, dark, dry place.

Onions in oil

Ingredients:
5 pounds very small, white onions, peeled
1 quart vinegar
1 cup white wine
5 or 6 whole cloves
1 piece stick cinnamon
¼ cup sugar
2 bay leaves
Salt, as needed
5 or 6 peppercorns
Olive oil, as needed

Preparation:
Peel onions as in ONIONS, VENETIAN STYLE. Put them in a baking pan large enough to hold them all. Add vinegar, white wine, cloves, cinnamon, sugar, bay leaves and salt to taste and bring to a boil for ten minutes or until onions are easily pierced but hold their shape. Drain and place onions on a cloth to dry for two hours. Place onions in sterilized jars. Add peppercorns and cover them with oil. Seal and store in a cool, dark, dry place.

This recipe requires careful preparation. Use onions about three-quarters of an inch in diameter and cook until tender but still firm.

Pickled onions

Ingredients:
5 pounds very small, white onions
1 quart (approximately) white vinegar
½ cup sugar
Some fresh basil leaves
Some bay leaves
Salt, as needed
Several peppercorns

Preparation:
Peel onions as in ONIONS, VENETIAN STYLE. As each onion is peeled, put it on a cloth to dry. After they have all dried, arrange them in sterilized jars, pressing down lightly. Boil vinegar, sugar, basil and bay leaves for one minute, adding salt to taste. Strain and pour while hot over onions. To each jar add a couple of peppercorns and a few basil leaves. Seal jars and store in a cool, dark, dry place.

They are served alone as an hors d'oeuvre or with other pickled vegetables or mixed with canned tuna.

Parsley in oil

Ingredients:
Sprigs of parsley
Olive oil, as needed

Preparation:
Wash parsley and dry on paper towels until completely dry. Cut into small sprigs and pack into small sterilized jars, pressing down lightly. Cover with olive oil and seal. Store in a cool, dark, dry place.

The oil as well as the parsley from this preparation may also be used. The oil has a parsley flavor and is rich in vitamin C. However, its flavor is such that it must not be overdone. It may be tossed with pasta cooked al dente or used in a salad dressing for a mixed salad or added to cooked or fresh sauces.

Dried parsley

Dried parsley may be used alone or mixed with other herbs.

Ingredients:
Sprigs of parsley

Preparation:
Trim stems of parsley and discard any leaves that are not perfect. Dip sprigs in cold water for a moment and shake off excess water. Tie sprigs together in small bouquets with twine. Hang them up in bright sun. Bring bunches inside in the evening or cover them with paper or plastic to protect them from the dew. After three or four days parsley will be perfectly dried. Cut leaves off stems with scissors and fill boxes or jars. Seal and store in a cool, dark, dry place.

Peeled whole tomatoes

Tomato sauce

Beets in vinegar
Pickled cucumbers
Pickled bell peppers
Pickled cauliflower

Italian antipasto

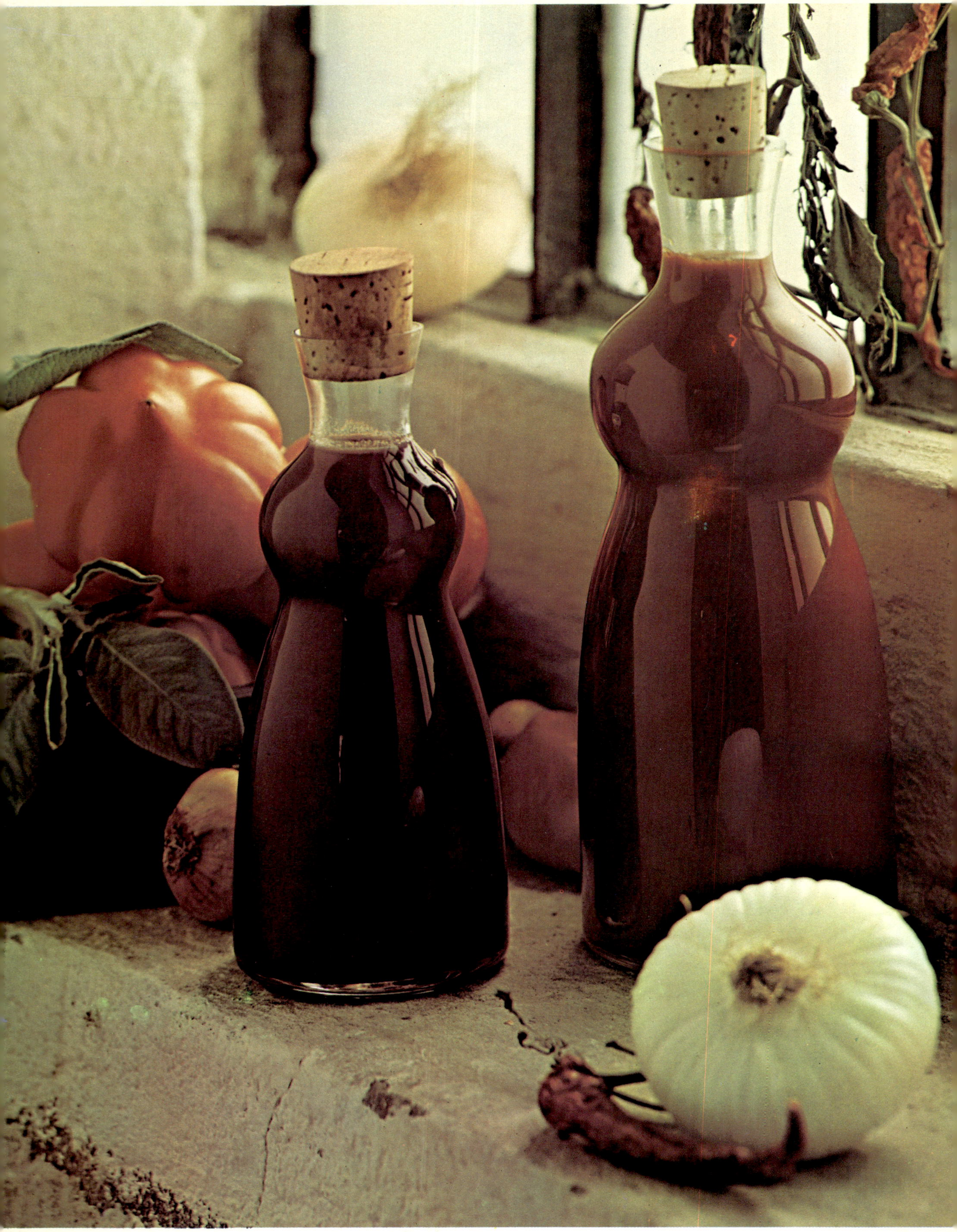

Plain peas

Ingredients:
5 pounds peas
3 tablespoons salt, about
1 tablespoon sugar, about

Preparation:
Shell peas. Boil in lightly salted boiling water to cover in stainless steel or glass pot for three minutes. Drain and dry on paper towels. Put peas in sterilized jars. Mix one quart water with one teaspoon salt and one-and-one-half teaspoons sugar. Bring to a boil and pour while hot over peas, allowing one inch headspace. Prepare more water mixture if necessary. Seal and sterilize by pressure canner method (see page 9) at ten pounds pressure: Pints and quarts for forty minutes. After this operation check to make sure that jars are perfectly airtight, otherwise repeat operation. Store in a cool, dark, dry place.

Gourmet peas

Ingredients:
5 pounds shelled peas
2 onions, sliced
2 tablespoons olive oil
1 pound salad greens (any type) washed and shredded
Salt, as needed
Pepper, as needed

Preparation:
Shell peas, wash and drain. In a large skillet, brown sliced onions in oil. Add salad greens. Cook for a few minutes, then add washed peas, salt and pepper to taste. Add one-half cup water and simmer for ten minutes or until peas are almost cooked. Pour into sterilized jars. There should be just enough liquid to cover peas. If not, just cover with boiling water, leaving a one inch head space. Seal and sterilize by pressure canner method (see page 9) at the same pressure and time as for PLAIN PEAS. Store in a cool, dark, dry place.

To serve, they may be simply warmed plain or added to a couple of slices of diced bacon that have been previously browned in a bit of oil or butter.

Stuffed bell peppers

Ingredients:
7 pounds sound, firm red and yellow bell peppers
2 quarts vinegar
20 to 30 anchovies
Several fresh basil leaves
4 or 5 cloves garlic
Olive oil, as needed

Preparation:
Scorch peppers over an open flame until skin chars slightly. Put in cold water and rub off burned skin with a cloth. Remove stem and seeds and spread them out to dry for about an hour. Heat vinegar to boiling and dip peppers two or three at a time into vinegar for one minute or until soft but still firm. Drain and cut peppers in half and then in crosswise one-half inch wide slices. Place an anchovy fillet on each slice and roll each slice up with the anchovy inside like a jelly roll. Place rolls in sterilized jars, one roll against the other. When you have finished one layer, put in a basil leaf and a piece of garlic and cover with oil. When all the jars are filled, cover with oil and seal. If the level of the oil has fallen after a couple of days, cover with additional oil, seal and store in a cool, dark, dry place.

Red bell peppers, Apulia style

Ingredients:
10 sound, plump red, green or yellow bell peppers
Salt, as needed
White vinegar, as needed
8 ounces salted capers, chopped
11 ounces salted anchovy fillets
4 or 5 cloves garlic
Several sprigs parsley
Several sprigs fresh basil
Olive oil, as needed

Preparation:
Wash peppers well. Remove seeds and stringy portions inside and cut into strips. In a pot, lightly salt enough vinegar to cover peppers and bring to a boil. Boil peppers for about ten minutes. Drain, dry on towels and let cool. The vinegar may be used for other preparations. Place a layer of peppers in sterilized jars. Add a layer of capers, a couple of anchovy fillets, a piece of garlic and several parsley and basil leaves. Repeat layering until jars are filled, then cover with olive oil. Seal and after a day if level of oil has gone down, add more oil so peppers are completely covered. Finally, seal jars and store in a cool, dark, dry place.

Pickled bell peppers

Ingredients:
7 pounds sound, ripe, meaty bell peppers, red, green or yellow
Salt, as needed
Several fresh basil leaves
Several bay leaves
Several sprigs fresh tarragon
Best quality white wine vinegar, as needed

Preparation:
Wash and cut peppers in quarters, discarding seeds and stringy portions. Wash in running water and place them into boiling salted water to cover. Boil only for one minute. Drain and dry them on a rack in the sun for several hours. Put peppers in sterilized jars, adding several basil and bay leaves and several sprigs of tarragon. Cover with vinegar and close jar. Several days later check the level of the vinegar; if it has gone down, add enough vinegar to cover peppers.

There is no hard and fast rule about what herbs to use. For example, between layers whole garlic cloves can be used, or they could be chopped fine with basil leaves.

This preserve is served alone or along with other pickled preserves.

Peppers in brine

Ingredients:
Firm bell peppers, red, green or yellow
White vinegar
Coarse salt
Bay leaves
Whole cloves
Fresh basil leaves

Preparation:
Wash peppers in cold water. Cut them into quarters, discarding seeds and stringy portions. Dry peppers on a cloth in the sun for four hours. Mix one quart water, two cups vinegar, six tablespoons coarse salt, two bay leaves and five or six cloves. Boil for two minutes then cool. Pack peppers tightly in a terracotta jar, adding a few basil leaves and filling to within three inches of the top. Cover peppers with vinegar mixture to two inches above peppers. Close jar with a cork or with heavy wax paper pulled down around lip of jar and tied tightly with string. Store in a cool, dark, dry place. Occasionally check to make sure that peppers are submerged in brine. If not, add more vinegar mixture. Prepare as many batches of the vinegar mixture as necessary for the amount of peppers to be preserved.

Peppers in oil

Ingredients:
5 pounds sound, meaty red, green or yellow peppers
2 cups white vinegar
Salt, as needed
Several peppercorns
Several bay leaves
Several cloves garlic
Several fresh basil leaves
Olive oil, as needed

Preparation:
Wash peppers and cut into lengthwise strips, discarding seeds and stringy inner portions. Set them out in the sunlight for four hours. Put them in a pot and cover them with vinegar. Add salt to taste, peppercorns and bay leaves. Boil for three or four minutes or until peppers are tender but still firm. (Vinegar can be saved for other preparations.) Drain and dry peppers on a rack in the sun for a day. Put peppers in sterilized jars, adding garlic and basil leaves. Cover with oil. After a few days, check to make sure peppers are covered and if not, add additional oil. Seal jars and store in a cool, dark, dry place.

Peppers preserved in this way can be used as an hors d'oeuvre or as a vegetable course with meats.

Pepper relish

Ingredients:
2 pounds sound, meaty red, green or yellow bell peppers
½ cup olive oil
2 onions, chopped
1 clove garlic, chopped
2¼ cups peeled, chopped tomatoes
Salt, as needed
Pepper, as needed
Pinch of sugar
1 bay leaf
Several fresh basil leaves

Preparation:
Remove skin from peppers as in STUFFED BELL PEPPERS. Remove stem and seeds. Cut peppers in half inch strips. In a skillet heat oil and saute onion and garlic until golden. Add peppers, tomatoes and salt and pepper to taste. Add a pinch of sugar and bay leaf. Simmer for five minutes and let cool. Pour pepper relish into sterilized jars and add a few basil leaves. Seal jars and sterilize by pressure canner method (see page 9) at same pressure and time as in PEPPER SAUCE.

To serve, bring pepper relish to a boil in a skillet and serve as a vegetable course with boiled or roasted meats.

Dried chili peppers

Dried chili peppers are crushed and used to flavor sauces, braised meats, etc.

Ingredients:
Chili peppers

Preparation:
Clean peppers thoroughly but lightly with a clean cloth. Thread a large upholstery needle with heavy duty carpet thread and string peppers through stem, keeping peppers about a half an inch apart. Hang thread up in a dry, airy place or in the sun in a sheltered spot where it cannot be exposed to bad weather or the dampness of the night. When peppers are dried, pull them off the thread and keep them in a box lined with wax paper. It should not be airtight. Store box in a cool, dark, dry place.

When peppers are completely dry, stem and core may be removed and pepper ground in a mortar. A very fine strong powder will result, which, after being sifted, can be stored in small jars. However, they can be just as well preserved whole, and when a recipe calls for chili, a piece may be broken off and used to give the dish a spicy flavor.

Chili peppers in syrup

This preparation is served with roast pork and game.

Ingredients:
5 pounds cleaned chili peppers
1 quart white vinegar
Several whole cloves
2 inch piece stick cinnamon
4 cups sugar

Preparation:
Leave half the stem on the peppers. Boil vinegar with peppers, cloves and cinnamon and boil for five to eight minutes. Let peppers cool in vinegar. Drain and let them dry on a clean dish towel. Boil sugar with two cups water for three minutes. It should become about as thick as honey. Put peppers in sterilized jars and cover them with syrup. Seal and store in a cool, dark, dry place. If there was not enough syrup, prepare additional syrup in the above proportions. The syrup should be sufficient to preserve the peppers, but as a precaution they can be sterilized in a boiling water bath (see page 9) for ten minutes.

Pepper sauce

This preserve is especially good to serve with a boiled New England dinner, or as a stuffing for artichokes, eggplants, etc., or as a sauce for pasta.

Ingredients:
5 pounds sound, meaty red, green or yellow bell peppers
5 pounds ripe tomatoes
1 cup olive oil
1 onion, chopped
Several cloves garlic
Several bay leaves
Several fresh basil leaves
Sugar and salt, as needed

Preparation:
Remove skin from pepper as in STUFFED BELL PEPPERS. Cut them into thin strips and spread them out on a cloth to dry. Peel tomatoes by dipping them into boiling water for a few seconds. Core tomatoes and cut into halves. Remove liquid and seeds and set aside to drain. In a large skillet heat oil and saute onion and garlic until golden. Add bay leaves, basil and pepper strips. Saute over high heat for two minutes. Chop tomatoes and add to peppers. Add a pinch of sugar and salt to taste. Boil over a high heat for about ten minutes, stirring with a wooden spoon. The sauce should be on the dry side and fairly thick. Season to taste with salt or sugar. Pour sauce while still hot into sterilized jars leaving a head space of one inch. Seal by pressure canner method (see page 9) at ten pounds pressure: Pints for twenty-five minutes; quarts for thirty minutes. Store in a cool, dark, dry place.

Candied pumpkin

Ingredients:
5 pounds firm pumpkin
1 pound (2 cups) sugar
1½ teaspoons salt
2 cups water
Additional sugar

Preparation:
Peel pumpkin and cut in quarters, removing seeds and filaments. Dice pumpkin. Place pumpkin in a large pot. Cover with water and boil until pumpkin is still firm, but easily pierced. It is difficult to indicate exactly how long pumpkin should be cooked, for it depends upon variety of pumpkin.

In a pot boil sugar, salt and water for five minutes. Drain pumpkin and place it in hot syrup and boil slowly until pumpkin absorbs as much syrup as possible. The pumpkin will be done when it appears almost transparent. Remove from heat and cool to lukewarm. With a slotted spoon, remove pieces of pumpkin from syrup. Replace syrup on heat and boil for two minutes. Remove from heat and replace pieces of pumpkin. Cool pumpkin in syrup, which by now will be quite thick. When syrup is cold, remove pieces of pumpkin and let them dry on a rack set over wax paper in an airy place for one day. Roll pumpkin in sugar. Keep cubes covered in clean dry jars and store in a cool, dark, dry place.

Plain salsify

Ingredients:
5 pounds salsify
Juice of 2 lemons
1 tablespoon all-purpose flour
Salt, as needed

Preparation:
Remove black skin from root with a potato peeler and cut root into two inch lengths. If roots are very thick, halve them lengthwise. As pieces are prepared drop them into a bowl with water to cover. Stir in juice of 1 lemon and flour. Drain and place in a large saucepan. Cover with boiling salted water and simmer for about one hour or until salsify are tender. Drain and arrange pieces in sterilized jars. Add one teaspoon salt and one teaspoon lemon juice to each quart. Cover with boiling water leaving a head space of one inch. Seal jars and sterilize by pressure canner method (see page 9) at ten pounds pressure: Pints for thirty minutes; quarts for forty minutes. Store in a cool, dry, dark place.

When ready to serve, drain off liquid and saute lightly in olive oil in which one or two cloves of garlic have been browned. Or they can be heated for a moment in canning liquid and drained. Mix with oil, lemon, salt and pepper and serve like a salad.

Salsify, Piedmont style

Ingredients:
5 pounds salsify
Juice of 2 lemons
1 tablespoon flour
Salt, as needed
Rind of 1 lemon, in large pieces
3 bay leaves
1 cup dry white wine
1 sprig thyme
⅔ cup olive oil
6 to 8 peppercorns
1 cinnamon stick

Preparation:
Peel, cut and soak salsify as in PLAIN SALSIFY. Heat two quarts salted water to boiling adding remaining lemon juice and rind, bay leaves, wine, thyme, olive oil, peppercorns and cinnamon stick. Add drained salsify and boil slowly for about fifteen minutes, stirring and skimming foam occasionally. Pour salsify and water into a bowl that is not made of metal. Cool. Remove salsify pieces with a slotted spoon and arrange in sterilized jars carefully, packing as tightly as possible, allowing a one inch head space. Strain cooking water and use to cover salsify in jars. If there is not enough liquid, boil more salted water and allow to cool before pouring over salsify. Seal jars and sterilize by pressure canner method (see page 9) at the same pressure and time as for PLAIN SALSIFY. Store in a cool, dark, dry place.

Plain spinach

Plain spinach can be used in making soups, omelettes, croquettes, souffles, etc.

Ingredients:
7 pounds young spinach
Salt, as needed

Preparation:
Remove wilted leaves and heavy stems from spinach. Wash repeatedly in large quantities of cold water. Drain in a colander. Place spinach in a large pot. Cover and cook for five minutes. Drain spinach. Pack while hot into sterilized jars leaving a headspace of one inch. Add one teaspoon salt to each quart. Cover with boiling water. Seal jars and sterilize by pressure canner method (see page 9) at ten pounds pressure: Pints one hour and ten minutes; quarts one hour and thirty minutes. Store in a cool, dark, dry place.

Spinach, Piedmont style

This is a delicious, little-known preserve.

Ingredients:
5 pounds spinach
2 tablespoons sultana raisins
1 cup white wine
1 tablespoon salt, as needed
Pepper, as needed

Preparation:
Trim, wash and drain spinach as for PLAIN SPINACH. Soak raisins in wine for two hours. Put spinach in a large pot with raisins, wine, salt and a pinch of pepper. Bring spinach to a quick boil until leaves are wilted. Spoon spinach and raisins into sterilized jars, adding a little of the water in which they were cooked and leaving a head space of one inch. Seal jars and sterilize by pressure canner method (see page 9) at the same pressure and time as for PLAIN SPINACH. Store in a cool, dark, dry place.

This spinach makes an excellent vegetable course with meats. Heat before serving.

Squash in brine

Ingredients:
5 pounds summer squash, zucchini or chayote squash
Salt, as needed
2 cups white vinegar
1¼ cups sugar
Rind of 1 lemon, in large pieces
Pepper, as needed

Preparation:
Wash squash and cut it into three-quarter inch cubes. Boil cubes for two minutes in salted water to cover. Drain and put into sterilized jars, leaving a head space of one inch. Heat vinegar, sugar, lemon rind, salt and pepper to taste and two cups water and boil for two minutes. Strain and pour while hot over squash. Let squash cool in liquid with jars open. Seal and sterilize by pressure canner method (see page 9) at ten pounds pressure: Pints for thirty minutes; quarts for forty minutes. Store in a cool, dark, dry place.

The squash may be served as an hors d'oeuvre or as a vegetable course with a boiled New England dinner.

Plain tarragon

Ingredients:
Sprigs of tarragon

Preparation:
Use freshly picked sprigs of tarragon, rinse them quickly in cold water and dry them by shaking the sprigs. Pay no attention if a few drops remain. Put the sprigs in very small sterilized jars, as they are more practical. Press them in gently and neatly. When jars are filled, seal and sterilize in a boiling water bath (see page 9) for forty-five minutes, letting them cool in the water. Store in a cool, dark, dry place.

When you open a jar to use some of the tarragon, store what remains in the refrigerator. Tarragon is used for flavoring salads and sauces.

Tarragon in vinegar

Ingredients:
Tarragon sprigs
White wine vinegar
Several peppercorns

Preparation:
Detach sprigs from plant very early in the morning, choosing only those in perfect condition. Wash sprigs by immersing in cold water, removing immediately. Drain on paper towels and dry in ventilated place. When tarragon is dry, place in sterilized jars and fill jars with white wine vinegar; add two or three peppercorns to each jar. Seal jars and store in a cool, dark, dry place.

Use tarragon to flavor sauces, soups, salad dressings; use vinegar as well for it is strongly flavored with tarragon.

Whole tomatoes for sauce

Ingredients:
7 pounds firm, ripe tomatoes (if available, use plum tomatoes)
Salt, as needed
Pepper, as needed
A pinch of sugar
Several fresh basil leaves
Several bay leaves
Olive oil (optional)

Preparation:
Cut off stem end of tomatoes and place them in a colander. Dip into boiling water and remove at once. Cool and peel off skin. Put tomatoes in a large bowl of plastic, crockery or any material other than aluminum and sprinkle with salt, pepper and sugar to taste (which removes some of the acidity of the tomatoes). Add basil and bay leaf. If desired, add one-quarter cup oil to each quart of tomatoes. Put tomatoes in sterilized jars, leaving a half-inch head space. Seal and sterilize by pressure canner method (see page 9) at ten pounds pressure: Pints for thirty-five minutes; quarts for forty-five minutes. Store in a cool, dark, dry place.

Dried tomatoes

Ingredients:
Perfectly ripe plum tomatoes

Preparation:
Wash tomatoes and cut them in half lengthwise. Set them on a clean board with the cut sides up. Put them in sun and dry them slowly, in order to avoid a too sudden loss of juice by evaporation and to keep the skin from shriveling too rapidly and letting the juice run off.

When tomatoes are completely dehydrated, store them in glass jars with lids or simply covered with wax paper. Store in a cool, dark, dry place.

In preparing a sauce or using them to flavor another dish, cook them in a small amount of water until plump.

Peeled whole tomatoes

Ingredients:
Plum tomatoes
Salt
Pepper
Fresh basil leaves

Preparation:
Remove stems and peel tomatoes as in WHOLE TOMATOES FOR SAUCE. Put tomatoes in an enamel or glass bowl. Sprinkle with salt, pepper and add basil leaves and let stand for thirty minutes. Arrange tomatoes in sterilized jars, pressing them in lightly until spaces fill with juice. Seal and sterilize by pressure canner method (see page 9) at the same pressure and time as for WHOLE TOMATOES FOR SAUCE. Store jars in a cool, dark, dry place.

In using tomatoes to make tomato sauce for pasta, heat oil and brown garlic and sliced onion in a skillet. Add several tomatoes, together with a pinch of sugar to eliminate the acidity of the tomatoes and simmer until sauce is thick.

Tomato sauce

Ingredients:
11 pounds tomatoes
2 onions, sliced
½ cup olive oil
Salt, as needed
Pepper, as needed
Several fresh basil leaves
¼ cup sugar

Preparation:
Wash tomatoes and drain. Cut off stem and squeeze tomatoes to remove seeds and juice. Grind unpeeled tomatoes through a coarse blade in a grinder. In a saucepan not made of aluminum, brown onions in oil. Add tomatoes, salt and pepper to taste. Cook for about ten minutes, stirring and skimming foam. Add basil leaves and sugar. Pour hot sauce into sterilized jars. Seal and sterilize by pressure canner method (see page 9) at the same pressure and time as for WHOLE TOMATOES FOR SAUCE. Store in a cool, dark, dry place.

This is an excellent sauce for pizza.

Tomato puree

Ingredients:
11 pounds ripe tomatoes
Several bay leaves
1 pinch salt
1 teaspoon pepper
¼ cup sugar
Olive oil, as needed

Preparation:
Cut stems off tomatoes and squeeze out the seeds and juice. Put tomatoes in a large pot (not of aluminum) adding a couple of bay leaves, salt, pepper and sugar (to remove the acidity). Boil slowly, stirring with a wooden spoon and skimming foam. Let tomatoes boil for about fifteen minutes. Press tomatoes through a sieve or food mill. Replace in saucepan. Heat, stirring constantly to prevent sticking. Simmer until a thick paste. Season to taste with salt. Pour hot into sterilized jars. Pour a thin layer of olive oil on surface. Seal and sterilize by pressure canner method (see page 9) at the same pressure and times as for WHOLE TOMATOES FOR SAUCE. Store in a cool, dark, dry place.

Tomato concentrate

Ingredients:
11 pounds tomatoes
2 onions, chopped
2 stalks celery, chopped
2 carrots, chopped
½ cup olive oil
Several bay leaves
3 cloves garlic, cut into halves
1 sprig fresh thyme
Several fresh basil leaves
2 tablespoons sugar
Salt, as needed
Pepper, as needed

Preparation:
Cut tomatoes in half and squeeze them to remove juice. Drain for thirty minutes. Meanwhile, in a large saucepan brown onions, celery and carrots in oil until golden. Add herbs and tomatoes. Simmer until sauce becomes very thick. The thicker the sauce, the better. Add sugar, salt and pepper to taste. Press the sauce through a sieve or food mill. Pour puree obtained into sterilized jars, leaving a head space of one-half inch. Seal and sterilize by pressure canner method (see page 9) at the same pressure and time as for WHOLE TOMATOES FOR SAUCE. Store in a cool, dark, dry place.

Tomato sauce with herbs

Ingredients:
11 pounds tomatoes, peeled and chopped
A small handful of fresh basil leaves, chopped
½ cup chopped parsley
Several fresh sage leaves, chopped
A sprig of fresh rosemary
1 teaspoon oregano
2 or 3 cloves garlic

Preparation:
Peel tomatoes as for WHOLE TOMATOES FOR SAUCE. Coarsely chop tomatoes and put them in a colander to drain. Mince basil, parsley, sage leaves, rosemary, oregano and garlic. Pour chopped tomatoes in a pot that is not aluminum. Add herbs and boil slowly stirring and skimming foam for five minutes. Pour hot into sterilized jars. Seal jars and sterilize by pressure canner method (see page 9) at the same pressure and time as for WHOLE TOMATOES FOR SAUCE. Store in a cool, dry, dark place.

This is an excellent sauce for pasta. Add a little olive oil and heat. Also excellent added to stews or to chicken in casserole.

Plain tomato juice

Ingredients:
Sound, ripe tomatoes

Preparation:
Pick only sound, ripe tomatoes. Wash them quickly and press them through a sieve or food mill that will hold back seeds and skins. Pour juice in dark glass bottles (green or brown) that are sterilized. Cap with a bottle capper and sterilize by pressure canner method (see page 9) at the same pressure and time as for WHOLE TOMATOES FOR SAUCE. Store in a cool, dark, dry place.

Tomato juice must be prepared on the same day that tomatoes are picked and juice must be bottled and sterilized immediately after having been sieved to prevent fermentation.

According to one's taste, brandy, lemon juice or sugar may be added to the tomato juice according to the following proportions: For each quart of tomato juice, add one-third cup brandy or the juice of two lemons with two tablespoons sugar; or if sugar alone is used, two-thirds cup. Prepared in this way, the tomato juice may be served as an appetizer without added seasoning.

Plain truffles

Ingredients:
Truffles
Coarse salt
Peppercorns
Lemon

Preparation:
Clean truffles thoroughly by brushing them lightly to get rid of any humus. Do not wash. Heat enough water to cover truffles adding three tablespoons coarse salt and one or two peppercorns to each quart of water. Boil water for two minutes, remove from heat and stir in juice of one-half a lemon to each quart of water. Cool. Put cleaned truffles in sterilized jars (use very small jars) and pour water over them slowly, allowing a headspace of one inch. Seal and sterilize by pressure canner method (see page 9) at ten pounds pressure: Half-pints or smaller for thirty minutes.

Store in a cool, dark, dry place.

Liver and truffles

This is one of those recipes which, when successful, gives a great sense of satisfaction.

Ingredients:
2 pounds fresh liver (goose, chicken or calves liver)
Salt and white pepper, as needed
4 ounces pork
5 ounces fresh pork fat
2 ounces white Alba truffles
½ to ⅔ cup best quality brandy

Preparation:
Cut calves liver into one-half inch thick slices. Clean and trim liver carefully, removing veins, fat, etc., and especially gall bladder. Put liver in a bowl and wash in repeated changes of cold water for four hours. Remove from water and spread out on a cloth to dry. After ten minutes liver should be dry. Sprinkle with salt and pepper, place in a glass bowl and let stand for a day in a cool place.

Grind pork and pork fat by running it through the smallest blade of a meat chopper several times, until a homogeneous, almost creamy mixture. Dry liver pieces and with the point of a sharp knife cut a slit in each piece. Brush truffles and cut into slivers. Stuff a sliver of truffle in each piece of liver.

In a skillet fry pork and pork fat. Prepare jars (use small sterilized ones). Pour a thin film of pork and pork fat (a quarter of an inch or less) on the bottoms of the jars. Lay down a layer of liver, tightly packed, sprinkle with brandy, and pour another layer of pork fat. The pork fat is used to fill the spaces between one piece of liver and the next, therefore, not much is needed. Fill jars leaving a one-half inch head space. Cover last layer with wax paper. Seal jars and sterilize by pressure canner method (see page 9) at ten pounds pressure: Pints for one hour and fifteen minutes; quarts for one hour and thirty minutes. Store in a cool, dark, dry place.

This preparation can be used as an hors d'oeuvre, for stuffing roast meats, or as a spread.

Truffle sauce

Ingredients:
8 ounces white truffles
2 cups good dry Marsala
1 tablespoon minced shallots
2 bay leaves
1 sprig thyme
15 peppercorns
½ cup tomato pulp
½ cup meat gravy
1 pinch sugar
Juice of ½ lemon

Preparation:
Mince truffles. Combine remaining ingredients except lemon juice, in a pot and boil for about ten minutes, skimming foam. Press mixture through a sieve, pressing the herbs and spices as well as pulp. Replace in pot and add truffles. Boil for four or five minutes or until sauce is thick. Stir in lemon juice and pour hot sauce into small sterilized jars. Seal and sterilize in a boiling water bath (see page 9) for fifteen to twenty minutes. Store in a cool, dark, dry place.

To use, pour sauce into a small skillet or saucepan and bring to a boil. Stir in pat of butter.

Marinated zucchini

This is an excellent summer hors d'oeuvre, stimulating to the appetite.

Ingredients:
5 pounds small zucchini
Salt, as needed
Pepper, as needed
Olive oil, as needed
White vinegar, as needed
Peppercorns
Several juniper berries
2 bay leaves
1 sprig fresh basil leaves

Preparation:
Wash zucchini and cut them lengthwise into slices, all about the same length and about a quarter of an inch thick. Sprinkle slices with salt and pepper. Mix well and put zucchini in a colander and drain two hours. Fry slices in hot oil one-quarter inch deep until golden on both sides. Drain and spread out on a cloth to dry. Boil equal parts of olive oil and vinegar with peppercorns, juniper berries, bay leaves and salt to taste for one minute. Cool. Put zucchini in sterilized jars with a few basil leaves in each jar. Cover with oil and vinegar mixture and seal jar. After a few days, check level of oil and vinegar and if they do not cover the zucchini, add more. Seal jars and serve after a week.

Store in the refrigerator.

Marinated zucchini, Rumanian style

This is served as an hors d'oeuvre.

Ingredients:
7 pounds firm zucchini
1½ cups olive oil
6 lemons, sliced
5 onions, chopped
1 teaspoon peppercorns
1 pinch thyme
Several bay leaves
Several fresh basil leaves
1 clove garlic, chopped
Salt, as needed

Preparation:
Cut tips off zucchini and clean with a damp cloth. Cut in crosswise slices about half an inch thick. In a pot mix remaining ingredients with six cups water. Bring to a boil. Place zucchini into a colander and dip into boiling mixture for one minute. Reserve cooking liquid. Spread slices on a cloth to dry in a single layer. Place slices in sterilized jars loosely, leaving a head space of one inch. Do not press down firmly. Bring cooking liquid to a boil again. Strain and pour it hot over zucchini. Seal and sterilize by pressure canner method (see page 9) at the same pressure and time as for SQUASH IN BRINE. Store in a cool, dark, dry place.

Garlic herb vinegar

For flavoring salads, sauces, etc.

Ingredients:
1 quart white vinegar
Several fresh basil leaves, chopped
2 scallions, chopped
2 cloves garlic, chopped
6 or 7 peppercorns, crushed
2 whole cloves

Preparation:
Mix vinegar and herbs and spices. Let stand for one day, then strain into sterilized bottle through several layers of cheesecloth. Seal and store in a cool, dark, dry place.

Tarragon vinegar

Ingredients:
1 quart white wine vinegar
1 or 2 sprigs fresh tarragon

Preparation:
Pour vinegar into a sterilized bottle. Wash tarragon in water, shake off excess and add to vinegar. Seal and store in a cool, dark, dry place. After a week, vinegar can be used to flavor salads or mayonnaise and other cold dressings.

Aromatic vinegar

Ingredients:
1 quart vinegar
2 cloves garlic, chopped
1 shallot, chopped
1 pinch thyme
1 cup chopped parsley
1 sprig fresh rosemary
Several fresh sage leaves
5 peppercorns
1 whole clove
1 bay leaf

Preparation:
Combine all ingredients and boil for five minutes. Cool and then strain through a double thickness cheesecloth. Pour into sterilized bottles. Seal and store in a cool, dark, dry place.

Rosewater vinegar

Rosewater vinegar is used to flavor potato salads, cucumbers, etc.

Ingredients:
1 quart white wine vinegar
3 ounces fragrant rose petals

Preparation:
Pour vinegar in a glass bowl. Pick roses early in the morning. Wash petals, removing the yellow point at the base of the petal and add them to vinegar. Let stand covered at room temperature for ten days. Strain vinegar through double thickness cheesecloth. Pour into sterilized bottles. Seal and store in a cool, dark, dry place.

Raspberry flavored vinegar

This preparation is of venerable age and is still used among the peasants in various regions of Italy and France as a thirst-quencher during dry, hot weather. They add a few drops of the vinegar to a glass of cold spring water. It is also excellent for dressing salads.

Ingredients:
1 quart red wine vinegar
2 cups raspberries
Rind of ½ lemon, in large pieces
Juice of 1 lemon

Preparation:
Pour vinegar into a two-quart sterilized bottle. Pick raspberries when they are ripe. Put them into bottle. Add lemon rind and juice. Seal bottle and shake it slightly and put it in a cool, dark, dry place for two to three weeks. After this period of time, strain vinegar through double thickness cheesecloth, squeezing the raspberries. Replace in bottle and store in a cool, dark, dry place.

Miscellaneous preserves

Salted vegetables for minestrone

Ingredients:
5 pounds mixed vegetables (celery, carrots, leeks, zucchini, cabbage, etc.)
½ cup coarse salt

Preparation:
Peel, trim, wash and dry vegetables. Cut into bite-size pieces. Mix in a large bowl with salt. Put vegetables into a clean crock, press down pieces and keep them pressed down with a plastic disc. Cover top of vegetables with a layer of salt. Cover with a very clean cloth, seal and store in a cool, dark, dry place.

When it is time to use the vegetables for the minestrone, let them soak for a day, changing the water several times if necessary to remove excess salt. Or, the vegetables can be cooked in unsalted water or stock.

Vegetables can be used for other recipes.

Minestrone

If you use freshly picked vegetables, resultant soup is particularly fragrant and delicious.

Ingredients:
Mixed vegetables (carrots, celery, potatoes, leeks, peas, zucchini, parsley and a few peeled tomatoes)
Stock
Salt

Preparation:
Use only freshest and best vegetables. Pick over, peel or trim and wash. Drain and cut vegetables to whatever shapes and sizes you prefer. Cook in boiling water for three minutes. Drain. Put vegetables in sterilized jars. Cover vegetables with cold stock or add one teaspoon salt to each quart and fill with boiled cooled water. Seal jar and sterilize by pressure canner method (see page 9) at the same pressure and time as for VEGETABLE MACEDOINE.

To serve, merely pour contents of jar into a pot and bring to a boil, adding only some grated cheese or, if only water was used as the preserving liquid, a bit of olive oil. Rice, small forms of pasta, or croutons may be added.

Garden medley

Ingredients:
2 pounds carrots
2 pounds celery
2 pounds cauliflower
2 pounds onions
1 pound white turnips
1 cucumber
⅔ cup coarse salt, about
3 quarts white vinegar
10 peppercorns
2 cloves garlic
3 or 4 bay leaves

Preparation:
Peel or trim vegetables. Wash in cold water and then cut into bite-size pieces. If desired, use a knife with a wavy blade to cut patterns in carrots and turnips. Heat a large amount of salted water to boiling. Add each vegetable separately and cook until vegetable is half cooked. Remove with a slotted spoon and spread them out on a cloth to dry. Be careful to cook each of the vegetables to the same consistency. Arrange vegetables in layers in sterilized jars leaving a one-inch head space. In a large pot add three quarts water to vinegar. Add remaining coarse salt, peppercorns, garlic and bay leaves. Boil for three minutes, then cool. Strain liquid and pour into jars, covering vegetables. Seal and store in a cool, dark, dry place.

Vegetable macedoine

Ingredients:
5 pounds of a variety of vegetables (carrots, potatoes, celery, green beans, peas, etc.)
Salt, as needed

Preparation:
Clean, prepare and wash vegetables. Use comparatively little celery as its marked flavor is apt to overwhelm the flavor of the other vegetables. Dice vegetables and put into small sterilized jars leaving a one-inch head space. Tap bottoms of jars down on a cloth to pack vegetables in tightly. Add one teaspoon salt to each quart jar. Boil enough water to cover vegetables in the jars. Let cool, then pour over vegetables, leaving at least half an inch of space between water and the top of the jar. Seal jars and sterilize by pressure canner method (see page 9) at ten pounds pressure: Pints for thirty-five minutes; quarts for forty minutes.

Store in a cool, dark, dry place.

To use the macedoine, drain off the water and dress the vegetables with mayonnaise, which gives the classic Russian salad. Or, heat the vegetables in butter together with a peeled, chopped tomato and serve as a vegetable course.

Italian antipasto

This hors d' oeuvre of mixed vegetables can be eaten either cold or hot.

Ingredients:
7 pounds firm bell peppers
7 pounds small eggplants
Several pinches salt
Several pinches ground pepper
3 quarts white vinegar
Several whole cloves
Several peppercorns
5½ ounces anchovy fillets
10 ounces green olives, pitted and sliced
Several fresh basil leaves
1 tablespoon chopped parsley
Olive oil, as needed

Preparation:
Wash peppers and cut into quarters, removing seeds. Wash eggplant, but do not peel. Cut in crosswise quarter-inch slices. Sprinkle the slices with salt and pepper and drain in a colander for several hours. Bring vinegar to a boil, add cloves and peppercorns. Add peppers and boil for one minute. Remove peppers with slotted spoon and spread them out to dry on a cloth. Boil eggplant slices in the same way. Drain and spread on a cloth to dry. Arrange eggplant, peppers, anchovy fillets and olives in layers in sterilized jars. On each layer put two basil leaves, a pinch of chopped parsley and pour over some olive oil. Fill jars leaving a one-inch head space. Cover all with olive oil and seal. Sterilize jars by pressure canner method (see page 9) at ten pounds pressure: Pints for thirty minutes; quarts for forty minutes. Store in a cool, dark, dry place.

Marinade for fried fish

This is a very tasty marinade for preserving various small fresh or salt water fish.

Ingredients:
(Sufficient for 4½ pounds of fried fish)
1¾ cups olive oil
10 or 12 cloves garlic, chopped fine
2 tablespoons chopped parsley
1 quart white vinegar
3 bay leaves
6 or 7 peppercorns, ground

Preparation:
Heat oil in a large pot and just before it begins to smoke, add garlic, parsley and vinegar. Bring to a boil and add bay leaves and pepper. Let boil for one minute and then cool to lukewarm. Fry portion size pieces of fish according to your favorite recipe (do not use breading). Drain on absorbent paper and cool. Place pieces in large crocks or glass containers. Pour marinade over fried fish. The fish must be completely covered by the marinade in order to be preserved for a long time (about a month in a cool place). A plate may be used to keep fish submerged in marinade. It is ready to eat after a week and makes an excellent hors d'oeuvre.

Ketchup

This is served with boiled meats, to color mayonnaise or for dressing grilled beef.

Ingredients:
2 oinions, chopped
2 carrots, chopped
2 stalks celery, chopped
1 clove garlic, chopped
½ cup olive oil
3 pounds ripe tomatoes
1 cup sugar
2 cups white vinegar
5 red bell peppers, seeded and chopped
1 bay leaf
1 pinch thyme
1 pinch ground cinnamon
1 teaspoon English mustard
1 teaspoon cornstarch
2 whole cloves
Salt, as needed
Pepper, as needed

Preparation:
Saute onions, carrots, celery and garlic in oil in a heavy stainless-steel or enamel pot until golden. Add tomatoes and let boil for about ten minutes, skimming foam every five minutes. Add remaining ingredients and simmer sauce slowly until it becomes somewhat thick as applesauce. Stir occasionally to prevent sticking. Press sauce twice through a sieve or food mill. Boil another two minutes. Salt and pepper to taste. Pour sauce hot into sterilized jars or bottles. Seal. If you wish to keep it for a couple of years, sterilize in a boiling water bath (see page 9) for about ten minutes. Store in a cool, dark, dry place.

Italian mustard

Ingredients:
1¼ cups dry mustard
2 cups white vinegar
¼ cup sugar
2 shallots, minced
1 stalk celery, chopped
8 whole cloves
1 pinch ground cinnamon
1 sprig thyme
2 bay leaves
10 anchovy fillets
1 cup olive oil
Salt, as needed
Pepper, as needed

Preparation:
Mix mustard with vinegar and let stand for several hours. Combine remaining ingredients in a pot and pour vinegar and mustard over them. Boil slowly until sauce is thick and vegetables are tender. Remove cloves and press mixture through a fine sieve twice. Season to taste with salt and pepper.

To give your mustard a special flavor, add one-third cup brandy or whiskey. Replace sauce in pot and boil again, stirring constantly to prevent sticking. When it reaches the consistency of marmalade, pour hot into small sterilized jars.

This mustard can also be flavored with herbs like mint, anise, fennel, etc. Add them before mixture is passed through sieve.

Dried herb mixtures

Ingredients:
Sage
Rosemary
Thyme
Marjoram
Tarragon
Basil
Parsley
Mint
Fennel
Dill
Oregano

Preparation:
A number of mixture of dried herbs can be made that are especially useful in flavoring various dishes. Here are a few.

OREGANO, SAGE, ROSEMARY and THYME: Chop herbs very fine. Spread them out on a surface covered with wax paper in a shady but clean and airy spot. From time to time toss chopped herbs, keeping them as spread out as possible so that drying takes place in as short a time as possible. When herbs are perfectly dry, which you can test by crumbling them between the fingers, put them in clean dry jars and store them in a cool, dark, dry place.

These four herbs give a particularly fine flavor in preparing chicken in casserole, squabs, etc. Half a teaspoon is enough to flavor a chicken of three and one-half pounds.

MARJORAM, SAGE, TARRAGON and ROSEMARY: Prepare and preserve as above. This mixture is used to flavor roasted or braised beef.

ROSEMARY, PARSLEY, BASIL and MARJORAM: Prepare and preserve as above. Used principally for flavoring fillings for vegetables (artichokes, eggplant, zucchini, etc.)

SAGE, THYME, TARRAGON and MINT: Prepare as above. Used to flavor vinegar and sauces.

DILL, FENNEL, SAGE and TARRAGON: Prepare as above. Used to flavor baked or grilled fish.

After a year, with the arrival of the new season and fresh herbs, it is advisable to renew one's stock of herbs, discarding any that may be left over, since much of their perfume has been lost after so many months.

Curry sauce

This sauce is served with various roast meats, game or chicken or to give flavor to other sauces. It is very spicy and should be used sparingly.

Ingredients:
1½ pounds apples, peeled, cored and diced
1 cup sugar
½ cup white vinegar
2 tablespoons curry powder
1 cup chopped red and yellow bell peppers
2 cloves garlic, chopped
1 cup sultana raisins
Pinch of ginger
1 bay leaf
Juice of 2 lemons
1¼ cups dry white wine
Salt, as needed

Preparation:
Combine ingredients in a large pot, stir and let stand, covered, for several hours, stirring ingredients occasionally. Bring slowly to a boil, stirring occasionally. Let cook slowly until apples and peppers are very tender. Press entire mixture through a sieve or food mill twice to obtain a smooth, well-blended sauce. Replace sauce in pot. Season to taste with salt. If sauce is too liquid, thicken it with a small amount of cornstarch mixed with white wine. Bring to a boil and boil for two minutes. Pour hot sauce into small sterilized bottles and cap them immediately with a bottle capper. Store in a cool, dark, dry place.

Devil's sauce

Generally served with grilled red meats.

Ingredients:
½ cup sugar
½ cup white wine
3 to 4 shallots, chopped
1 teaspoon peppercorns, crushed
3 cloves garlic, chopped
Several fresh sage leaves
A sprig of fresh tarragon
2 bay leaves
A pinch thyme
1 cup red wine vinegar
4 ounces salted anchovies
Juice of 1 lemon
4 to 5 dry chili peppers
1 tablespoon chopped dried mushrooms
1 teaspoon dry mustard
Salt, as needed

Preparation:
Heat sugar in a small skillet without stirring until golden brown. Pour in white wine slowly to avoid spattering and stir over low heat until sugar is dissolved. In a saucepan, combine shallots, peppercorns, garlic, herbs and vinegar. Boil until liquid is reduced by one quarter. Stir in caramelized sugar mixture and remaining ingredients. Boil for about five minutes, stirring and skimming foam. Add salt to taste. Press sauce while hot through a fine sieve or food mill. Add salt, if necessary. Cool and then pour into small sterilized bottles. Seal and store in a cool, dark, dry place.

Bagnet-ross sauce

Ingredients:
7 pounds tomatoes, chopped
2 pounds red, yellow or green bell peppers, chopped
1 pound onions, chopped
2 cups dry white wine
½ cup sugar
Spices to taste (cinnamon, cloves, nutmeg and a little pepper)
Coarse salt to taste

Preparation:
Combine all ingredients, adding spices and salt to taste, in a large pot that is not made of aluminum. Boil gently, stirring occasionally, until a rather thick sauce. This will take about three hours. Press sauce through a fine sieve or food mill. Replace in pot and boil for another five minutes. Pour sauce into sterilized jars. Seal and sterilize in a boiling water bath (see page 9) for thirty minutes.

This is a very tasty sauce that makes a fine accompaniment to various boiled dishes or a sauce for pasta, just heat and add olive oil or butter.

Springtime sauce

Ingredients:
8 ounces carrots, chopped
8 ounces celery, chopped
1 onion, chopped
2 cloves garlic, chopped
1 bunch parsley, chopped
1 sprig rosemary
½ cup olive oil
1 pound tomatoes, peeled and chopped
2 whole cloves
1 bay leaf
1 pinch sugar
Salt, as needed
Pepper, as needed

Preparation:
Grind carrots, celery, onion, garlic, parsley and rosemary through the coarse blades of a meat grinder. Pour into a pot and add oil, tomatoes, cloves, bay leaf and sugar. Bring to a boil and simmer for about thirty minutes, stirring occasionally. The sauce should become rather thick. Season to taste with salt and pepper. Pour hot sauce into sterilized jars of medium size. Seal and sterilize in a boiling water bath (see page 9) for fifteen to twenty minutes. Store in a cool, dark, dry place.

When using sauce, pour it into a small skillet and heat. It is a very tasty sauce for all kinds of pasta and for rice.

Garlic in oil

Ingredients:
30 cloves garlic
Olive oil, as needed

Preparation:
Peel and mince garlic. Put paste obtained in a small, sterilized jar. Cover with oil to an inch above garlic. Stir with a wooden spoon, close jar and keep in a cool, dark, dry place.

If you use only the oil, replace the amount used with fresh oil so garlic is always well covered. This very simple preparation has two advantages, using an oil that is pleasantly and delicately perfumed with garlic, and of using, if a more marked flavoring is desired, minced garlic.

Garlic in oil may be used in two ways; as a flavored oil or as a preserved oil.

Eggplant rolls

Ingredients:
7 pounds small eggplants
Salt, as needed
Pepper, as needed
Olive oil, as needed
4 to 5 tomatoes, chopped
5 to 6 cloves garlic
4 to 5 chili peppers, coarsely chopped
Several fresh basil leaves
8 to 10 anchovy fillets

Preparation:
Wash and dry eggplant and cut into quarter-inch slices lengthwise. Sprinkle slices with salt and pepper and place in a colander. Put a weight on them and drain for four hours. Fry slices in one-half inch oil. One by one, as slices are done, spread them out to drain on a cloth or paper towels. Add more oil, if necessary. Roll up each eggplant slice like a jelly roll and place them in sterilized jars. Cook tomatoes until mushy and thick. Press through a sieve and season sauce to taste with salt and pepper. Each layer of eggplant rolls should be alternated with a few slices of garlic, small pieces of chili pepper, a basil leaf, some of the tomato sauce and half an anchovy fillet. Fill jars leaving one inch head space. Pour olive oil into jars until eggplant is covered, and cover with a disc of wax paper. Seal jars and sterilize by pressure canner method (see page 9) at ten pounds pressure: Pints for thirty minutes; quarts for forty minutes. Store in a cool, dark, dry place.

Stuffed grape (vine) leaves, Venetian style

Ingredients:
8 ounces zucchini
½ cup olive oil
30 to 40 large, tender vine leaves
½ cup white vinegar
8 ounces raw rice, cooked and drained
12 ounces ground lean pork
8 ounces tomatoes, peeled and chopped
2 tablespoons chopped sultana raisins
1 pinch saffron
1 teaspoon chopped fresh basil
Salt and pepper, as needed
1 cup dry white wine

Preparation:
Wash zucchini and chop finely. Saute in two tablespoons of the oil until tender. Wash and drain vine leaves. Drop into boiling water to cover with vinegar added. Drain leaves and spread out on a cloth to dry. Mix sauteed zucchini, rice, pork, tomatoes, raisins, saffron and basil. Stir in one teaspoon salt and one-quarter teaspoon pepper until well blended. Spoon small amount of filling on a vine leaf. Fold over the left and right sides of the leaf, then roll up from the bottom. The stuffed vine leaf should resemble a sausage. Continue stuffing leaves and as each one is completed place it in sterilized jars. Pack well. As each layer is completed, pour a thin film of remaining olive oil and a sprinkling of wine over rolls. When jar is filled to about three-quarters of an inch of the top, cover with a disc of wax paper. Seal and sterilize by pressure canner method (see page 9) at ten pounds pressure: Pints for one hour and fifteen minutes; quarts one hour and thirty minutes.

Chicken in gelatin

Ingredients:
1 "barnyard" chicken (i.e., not a commercially raised one)
1 cup dry white wine
a bouquet composed of carrot, celery and onion
Salt and pepper, as needed
Some thyme, sage and rosemary leaves

Preparation:
Pluck, singe, draw, wash and dry chicken. Cut it into quarters, separating it at the joints so that no bone splinters get into flesh. Bone breast and thighs. Mix two quarts water with tips of wings, feet and breast and thigh bones. Add white wine, carrot, celery and onion bouquet. Boil broth until it is reduced by half. Strain, season to taste with salt and pepper and cool. Spread pieces of chicken out on a cloth and sprinkle with salt, pepper and half of the chopped thyme, sage and rosemary leaves. Let drain in a colander for one hour. Put pieces of chicken in sterilized jars, packing them in neatly and adding the remaining herbs. Pour in cold broth to cover. Seal and sterilize by pressure canner method (see page 9) at the same pressure and times as for DUCK, FRIULI STYLE. Store in a cool, dark, dry place.

Preserved loin of pork

Ingredients:
7 pounds loin of pork (or other rather fatty cut)
1 sprig fresh rosemary
2 sprigs thyme
Several fresh sage leaves
3 to 4 cloves garlic
1½ cups white wine
Salt and freshly ground pepper, as needed

Preparation:
Cut loin of pork into pieces that will fit into jars. Place pieces on a flat surface. Sprinkle with salt and pepper. Rub salt and pepper well into pork. Let stand thirty minutes. Arrange pieces of pork in sterilized jars, leaving a three-quarter inch head space. Add rosemary, sage, thyme, slices of garlic and wine. If pork is very lean, add olive oil in the proportion of one-and-one-half cups oil to pork. Fresh, sweet rendered pork fat may be used. Seal jars and sterilize by pressure canner method (see page 9) at the same pressure and time as for STUFFED GRAPE LEAVES, VENETIAN STYLE. Store in a cool, dark, dry place, checking jars frequently for first two weeks. If fat completely covers pork it will keep for over a year, otherwise only a few months.

Cut into slices, the loin of pork may be served cold, or it may be heated in a small quantity of the fat in which it was preserved.

Duck, Friuli style

This is a very old preparation still used in the country regions of Friuli; if obtainable prepare with ducks raised and fed in the old-fashioned way. This recipe can be prepared using commercial ducks.

Ingredients:
7 pounds duck
Salt and pepper, as needed

Preparation:
Clean ducks by rubbing with a clean cloth. Cut them in half and bone them, leaving the fat on the flesh. Reserve bones. Sprinkle pieces of duck with salt and freshly ground pepper and lay them in a single layer on an inclined drainboard to drain for one day. Cut halves of ducks into pieces and put them into sterilized jars leaving a head space of one inch. Cover bones with water adding salt and simmer for one hour. Strain broth, adding salt to taste. Cool. Pour broth over ducks. Seal and sterilize by pressure canner method (see page 9) at ten pounds pressure: Pints for one hour and fifteen minutes; quarts one hour and thirty minutes.

Quail in oil

This is an appetizing preparation that makes it possible to have something unusual on hand for any eventuality. The recipe is still very popular in mountain villages.

Ingredients:
15 freshly killed quail
3 cups dry white wine
2 cups white wine vinegar
4 to 5 whole cloves
3 to 5 juniper berries
2 bay leaves
1 sprig thyme
Several peppercorns
Salt, as needed
Olive oil, as needed

Preparation:
Pluck quail, singe and clean. Split them open down the back. In a pot large enough to hold all quail, combine wine, vinegar and remaining ingredients except olive oil, adding salt to taste. When liquid boils, add quails and cook slowly for about fifteen minutes or until half cooked. Remove with a slotted spoon and place them on a cloth to dry in an airy place. Arrange them in sterilized jars adding two peppercorns and a thin film of olive oil to every layer. When jar is filled, leaving a one-inch head space, cover quails with oil. Seal jars and allow quails to absorb oil. If necessary add more oil to cover. Store in a cool, dark, dry place.

If this form of preserving should leave you uneasy, sterilize jars by pressure canner method (see page 9) at ten pounds pressure: Pints one hour and five minutes; quarts one hour and fifteen minutes.

Chicken and vegetables alla certosina

This preparation is served cold whether as an hors d'oeuvre or as a main dish.

Ingredients:
2 pounds carrots
1 pound potatoes
10 ounces celery
10 ounces zucchini
10 ounces fresh peas
8 ounces peeled, chopped tomato pulp
1 chicken, about 6 pounds
Salt, as needed and several peppercorns
1 onion, quartered
1 bay leaf and 1 sprig tarragon or thyme
8 envelopes unflavored gelatin

Preparation:
Peel or trim vegetables thoroughly. Quarter chicken and cook in three quarts salted water with peppercorns, onion, one of the carrots, bay leaf and tarragon or thyme.

Dice remaining carrots, potatoes, celery and zucchini. When chicken is tender, drain and cool. Reserve cooking liquid. Remove skin and bones and cut chicken into cubes as vegetables. Put chicken and vegetables in large bowl. Mix thoroughly before putting in jars, leaving head space of one inch.

Stir gelatin into one and one-half cups of the cold broth. Stir over low heat until gelatin is dissolved. Stir this mixture into remaining broth. Strain broth and season to taste with salt. Pour broth into jars, covering chicken and vegetables. Seal jars and sterilize by pressure canner method (see page 9) at ten pounds pressure: Pints for one hour and five minutes; quarts for one hour and fifteen minutes. Store in a cool, dark, dry place. It will take about a day for gelatin to set.

Marinated eel

Ingredients:
7 pounds medium-sized eels
Rind of 1 lemon, in large pieces
Juice of 1 lemon
2 cups dry white wine
Salt, as needed
Several peppercorns
1 sprig thyme
4 to 5 bay leaves
1 onion, sliced
1 carrot
1 stalk celery, sliced
2 to 3 whole cloves
⅔ cup olive oil

Preparation:
Cut heads off eels; skin, wash, dry and cut them into two inch lengths. Heat five to six quarts water in a large pot with lemon rind and juice, half of the white wine, salt to taste, peppercorns, thyme, bay leaf, onion, carrot, celery and cloves until boiling. Add eel and bring to a boil again. Lower heat and cook slowly for five minutes. Let eel cool in cooking water. Remove pieces with a slotted spoon and place directly in sterilized jars, arranging pieces neatly. Strain cooking liquid. Add olive oil and a little more than one quart of the cooking liquid to remaining white wine. Boil for one minute, adding salt to taste. Cool. Pour liquid into jars, covering eels and leaving a one-half inch head space. Seal and sterilize by pressure canner method (see page 9) at ten pounds pressure: Pints for one hour and forty minutes. Store in a cool, dark, dry place.

Sardines in oil

Ingredients:
5 pounds very fresh sardines
Salt, as needed
2 to 3 bay leaves
Several peppercorns
Olive oil, as needed

Preparation:
Clean sardines. Remove head, gills, fins, guts and scales. Wash sardines with cold water. Sprinkle with salt and freshly ground pepper. Place a clean towel or cloth on an inclined drainboard and place sardines in a single layer to drain for two to three hours. Dry them carefully with paper towels. Arrange in sterilized jars, packed neatly and closely together, leaving a one-inch head space. Place a piece of bay leaf, several peppercorns and a film of oil on each layer. Cover sardines with oil, wait for five minutes and add more if it is absorbed. Seal jars and sterilize by pressure canner method (see page 9) at ten pounds pressure: Pints for one hour and forty minutes. Store in a cool, dark, dry place.

Weights and measures

Cup measures

1 American cup holds 8 fluid oz. or ½ American pint

Spoon measures

1 American Teaspoon holds approx. $^1/_6$ fluid oz.
1 American Tablespoon holds 3 tsps. or ½ fluid oz.

Avoirdupois/metric weights

1 oz. = 28.35 grams
4 oz. = 113.4 grams
8 oz. = 226.8 grams
1 lb. 453.6 grams

Metric/avoirdupois weights

1 gram = 0.035 oz.
100 grams = 3½ oz. (approx.)
250 grams = 9 oz. (approx.)
1 kilogram (kg.) = 1,000 grams (2.20 lb. approx. 2¼ lb.)

Liquid measures

1 gill = 4 fluid oz. (½ cup) = $^5/_6$ Imperial gill
1 pint = 16 fluid oz. (2 cups) = $^5/_6$ Imperial pint
1 quart = 2 pints = $^5/_6$ Imperial quart
1 gallon = 4 quarts = $^5/_6$ Imperial gallon
1 litre = 35.2 fluid oz.

Temperatures

	Electric	Gas
Very cool	250°F. (121°C.)	¼
	275°F. (135°C.)	½
Cool	300°F. (149°C.)	1,2
Warm	325°F. (163°C.)	3
Moderate	350°F. (177°C)	4
Fairly hot	375°F. (191°C.)	5
	400°F. (204°C.)	6
Hot	425°F. (218°C.)	7
Very hot	450°F. (232°C.)	8
	475°F. (246°C.)	9

To convert Centigrade to Fahrenheit, multiply by 9, divide by 5 and add 32. To convert Fahrenheit to Centigrade, subtract 32, multiply by 5 and divide by 9.